"As someone who has followed the *Ambitious Kitchen* blog for a long time, I have been craving a book by Monique for years. Quite frankly, she's exceeded my expectations in her debut book. The recipes are bold yet approachable and are sure to ignite your culinary passion. From comforting family favorites like her Weeknight Chicken Picadillo to adventurous twists like her Chipotle Gouda Pumpkin Turkey Enchiladas, Monique effortlessly combines creativity with approachability, ensuring each dish is a success. This book is an instant classic for me!"

—ALEX SNODGRASS, *New York Times* bestselling author and creator of *The Defined Dish*

"To say I'm excited for the world to see Monique's first cookbook is an understatement! Monique's zest for feeding herself and her family nourishing, colorful, and delicious meals shines through on every single page. From the Comforting Portobello, Poblano & Pepper Jack Cheese Enchilada Skillet to the Mini Pesto Turkey Meatballs, these are recipes that you can incorporate into your everyday life! Nothing is overly complicated or fussy, just delightful, beautiful, healthy-ish food! It's exactly how I want to eat every single day!

—GABY DALKIN, *New York Times* bestselling author and creator of *What's Gaby Cooking*

"*The Ambitious Kitchen Cookbook* is an invitation to make your meals more nutritious, more flavorful, and . . . more fun! In addition to 125 mouthwatering recipes (Coffee Lover's Baked Oatmeal! Caramelized Corn Brown Butter Pasta!), Monique shares tips (like how to freeze anything) and substitutions to help you fit healthy, delicious home cooking into your everyday life."

—JEANINE DONOFRIO, author of *Love & Lemons Simple Feel Good Food*

"Monique's e_____ you to cook _____ book. Her recipes are boldly flavored and prove that healthy food can be anything but boring. There's plenty for everyone in *The Ambitious Kitchen Cookbook,* and I'm particularly excited about the vegetarian mains chapter. Every recipe features a vibrant photo, and the book is beautifully designed—you'll want to display it on your coffee table when it's not in your kitchen!"

—KATHRYNE TAYLOR, author of *Love Real Food* and *Creator of Cookie and Kate*

"Monique's heart and soul shines through these pages and jumps out in the form of easy weeknight meals, cookies for your family, and smoothies for busy mornings (just to name a few). Monique shows us that ambitious food isn't about unnecessarily complicated food; instead it's about food that brings comfort, warmth, and ease."

—ADRIANNA ADARME, creator of *A Cozy Kitchen* and author of *The Year of Cozy*

"Monique's recipes have long been a staple in my kitchen, and her cookbook somehow takes it to another level. These are the types of recipes that will get you excited about cooking—novel, flavor-packed, nutrient-forward, and easy enough to fit into our busy lives. An instant classic!"

—LIZ MOODY, author of *100 Ways to Change Your Life* and host of *The Liz Moody Podcast*

125 ridiculously good for you,
sometimes indulgent, and
absolutely never boring recipes
for every meal of the day

THE
ambitious
kitchen
COOKBOOK

monique volz

PHOTOGRAPHS BY KRISTIN TEIG

CLARKSON POTTER/PUBLISHERS
New York

TO SIDNEY, VIGGO, AND LACHLAN
It is such an honor to be your mama.
I love you forever.

contents

intro- duction

It took me years to realize how much food has the power to create a positive change in all of our lives, whether that means connecting with others over a homemade meal made from the heart, baking to soothe your soul when you're in need of comfort, or taking time to nourish your body with better-for-you ingredients. I wrote this cookbook to help you do the same: to help you discover boldness, unique flavors, creativity, health, and, above all, the unique happiness that food can bring to your life. Maybe you're seeking the perfect dish to bring to a gathering. Maybe you're looking for a show-stopping recipe to become a tradition in your home. Maybe you need to put a nutrient-packed meal on the table for picky kids or toddlers, as I do regularly for my husband and three little boys. Maybe you, like me, are learning to nourish yourself after years of disordered eating. The best recipes rise to all of these occasions. I've created this cookbook to be your guide, your foundation, for meeting these challenges with joy and experimentation. My years of kitchen trial and error will help you customize most of these recipes to make them your own, whether you want to add a little extra nutrition or a little extra heat, or you're looking to make them gluten-free or dairy-free. And my years of rediscovering food as a source of joy will help you, as well, to become your healthiest, most satisfied, most authentic self—no matter where you are in your journey to discover your own Ambitious Kitchen.

your meaning of ambition

In one of my most vivid memories, my mother crouches over a tiny charcoal Weber grill parked outside the front door of our tiny duplex in Minneapolis, peering at our dinner. As a single mom, she worked around the clock at several different jobs to support my teenage brother and nine-year-old me, but when the sun went down on humid summer evenings, we knew we'd have her full attention—and the full extent of her ambition.

On her way home, she'd swing by a fish market and pick up whatever was fresh, often halibut, salmon, or mahi mahi. Tonight, swordfish. She opened up our *Encyclopaedia Britannica* and we all peered at the fish's long, pointy bill. We brainstormed how she should season the fish, perhaps with a bit of sazón, the seasoning mix beloved in her Puerto Rican family. Then my mother cut a fresh lemon into thin wheels, tucked them into foil with the fish, and laid it over the coals next to baby red potatoes and long, thin spears of asparagus. When everything was done, we perched on the steps, plates on our laps, enjoying the moist, flaky fish, the potatoes that my mother had lavished with butter, and, most of all, the warmth of talking to each other for the first time all day.

It wasn't until much later in life that I realized that food was my mother's way of connecting with us. It was a place for her passion and creativity to shine through. It was a refuge from her hectic life, where she could find happiness, joy, comfort, and nourishment, all in one. It was her way of proudly making her food her own and flexing her creativity. It was her own Ambitious Kitchen.

food was my mother's way of connecting, a place for her passion and creativity to shine

a complicated relationship with food

I would spend the next decade in upheaval, trying to reclaim the kitchen as my refuge. My highest highs and lowest lows were spent with my father, a man who lit up every room with his roaring laugh, his warm, outgoing personality, and his striking bright blue eyes, but a man who also struggled with alcoholism and drug addiction. He would spend hours with me in the kitchen baking our favorite ultra-fluffy yellow cake coated with rich chocolate buttercream and infused with Dad's secret splash of coffee, or creating the world's most indulgent au gratin potatoes to serve with our weekly special Sunday night dinner. Dad always encouraged me to go after my dreams, to seek out my creativity and experiment with doing the things I loved the most. When we were together, he inspired me to be the best version of myself and I thought of him as my very best friend; we were two peas in a pod who could giggle for hours upon hours. But my father also had a dark side that controlled him. He often abruptly left me alone in his house for hours or even days, a terrifying experience for a little girl. He would return with no explanation and the smell of alcohol on his breath.

Dad's beautiful smile was somehow able to mask his pain; he knew how to hide his addictions and function well in society. He was a man who wanted to show up fully for his daughter when needed but just never could arrive. When I was eighteen, on a late-summer evening just a few days before my first day of college, he died suddenly from a drug overdose.

For the next two years, I was inconsolable. I would cry at the mere mention of his name. I gained a little weight, just enough to be self-conscious and to start working out heavily. I ate little during the day and binged at night. I tried to control my life by starving myself, and then at night I stuffed down feelings of panic, anxiety,

and grief. Eventually I lost so much weight that I couldn't find any jeans that fit me. I ignored my mom's pleas for me to stop losing weight because, secretly, the perfectionist in me loved losing weight. This unhealthy cycle, combined with my internalized grief, led to a diagnosis of anorexia—an eating disorder that had spiraled out of control. When my heartbeat slowed to thirty-two beats per minute and my doctors were so concerned that they sent me to the hospital, it was clear that I needed to address my grief, my emotional health, and my relationship with food.

But how could I do this after regarding food as the enemy for so long? How could I find the comfort and joy that I had once experienced in front of the little grill outside our duplex? How could I find both pleasure and nourishment in food without the food controlling me?

It was in that dark space, full of confusion and longing, that I sat on my unmade bed and created a blog called *Ambitious Kitchen*.

redefining ambition, reclaiming the kitchen

My website had nothing to do with making money or building a career. It was about rediscovering the parts of my life where food had led to joy, comfort, warmth, and security. It was about giving myself permission and grace to grieve my father's death by celebrating and recapturing our wonderful memories made through food, like when we piled a lemon pie high with meringue because he knew it would delight his mother. It was about a teenage me cooking for my mom, knowing that having a piping hot chicken pot pie on the table after a long day at work would make her so thankful. It was about returning to the excitement of cooking in the kitchen with my Puerto Rican grandma Gloria, aka G. She was an avid salsa dancer who clicked around her kitchen in high heels often cooking brunch for twenty of her family and friends. Her true joy in life was spending two straight days cooking everyone's favorites, anticipating their hugs upon arrival and smiles of delight with each bite of her incredible breakfast potatoes (seasoned with sazón, of course) and my grandfather's favorite banana muffins. It was about infusing the bold flavors, like those of G's heritage, into my own cooking.

I had regarded so many foods as off-limits for years. But as I looked to reclaim joy in food, I thought about how I could find my own version of what it meant to be healthy and still true to my authentic self. I re-created the lip-smacking good chicken enchiladas with creamy refried beans that my mom used to make for me, complete with fresh avocado-tomato salsa and made-from-scratch enchilada sauce. I began to feel the same comfort and excitement that I had felt those nights around the grill, and I found that this happiness radiated to other parts of my life. Instead of avoiding barbecues and parties because I was afraid I wouldn't be able to eat the food, I started accepting invitations and eating the food. Instead of denying myself gelato on vacation, I saved room for some and enjoyed it!

Instead of focusing on what I shouldn't eat, or mentally subtracting ingredients from dishes, I began to focus on what I could add: more healthy fats, more fresh fruits and vegetables, and more herbs, making my food more delicious and helping me feel my best.

What's more, I found that experimenting with food helped me process the grief, pain, and sorrow of the trauma I had experienced.

I cooked from the heart, with passion and vulnerability and love, and it brought me the peace and connection I very much needed. I created grain-free chocolate cakes with a splash of coffee that reminded me of Dad and how he used to add coffee to all of his chocolate-based desserts. I remembered him as I made a more nutritious version of his famous fried chicken, then I piled it high with a tangy cabbage slaw and creamy avocado slices to make my body feel nourished and satisfied. I tried making his cucumber salad with Greek yogurt, which not only increased the protein but also tasted better. I made the food my own, and it didn't feel like all-or-nothing. I was getting to a place where my own waves were steady. I was also finding my passion for inspiring others in the kitchen by making recipes more nutritious or creative than any store-bought or restaurant version.

I cooked from the heart & it brought me peace & connection

finding your ambition

The more I shared with readers, the more I realized how different everyone's version of better-for-you really was. As more and more readers found my site, the questions piled up:

Can I make this dairy-free? Can I make this gluten-free? If I don't have ripe bananas, can I substitute something else? Can I make this with instant oats instead of rolled oats? How can I make this less sweet? More spicy?

I welcomed every single one of these questions, because I firmly believe that Ambitious Kitchen is for everyone. Finding your own Ambitious Kitchen means finding a safe space to experiment, exercise your creativity, and discover what you really want from your cooking.

As you turn the pages, please consider yourself a guest at my table. Maybe we'll make my mom's rice and beans or my nana's chicken stew. We'll prepare chicken meatloaves topped with my nana's whipped potatoes mixed with carrots, which add just the right amount of earthy sweetness while lightening up the dish. We'll even make a gigantic Pop-Tart to impress everyone (including yourself)! Writing this cookbook brought me the same joy that G found cooking a big brunch on the weekends, and the same thrill that my mother once found at the fish store. I hope it helps you discover that happiness, too.

Together, let's find your Ambitious Kitchen.

how to use this book

you do you

That's right, you do YOU. Being ambitious means getting creative and experimenting, being flexible, and finding what works best for you. This book isn't meant to show you that there's only one way to make a recipe. Sometimes it's about using what you have on hand, substituting when it works best for you, *but also* encouraging you to try something new.

Throughout this book, you will find two helpful notes after many of the recipes:

make it your way

These tips are your starting point for making a swap in recipes. I know from years of experience that making a recipe exactly as written isn't always possible (due to dietary restrictions, personal preference, or because you just don't have some ingredients on hand!). Dairy-free or gluten-free? Whenever possible, I'll share what you can swap to make the recipe just as good. Want to switch up the ingredients but not mess up the flavors? If it can be modified, you will find how to do so here. As always, feel free to experiment as you get more comfortable in the kitchen!

make it nutrient-dense

When you want to add *more* nutrition to my recipes, look to these suggestions for throwing in extra protein, veggies, nuts, and other nutrient-packed ingredients. Most of the recipes in this cookbook include the most vibrant fruits and vegetables to amplify both nutrition and flavor, but if there's a way to increase the nutrition factor further, I'll suggest it here.

all about substitutions

I always suggest sticking as close to the recipe as possible to ensure that it works, but if that's not possible for you, use this as your guide. Just remember that you are substituting at your own risk! These are general guidelines: see Make It Your Way following a recipe for specifics.

sweeteners

There's room (and necessity!) for all sweeteners in life, but in case you want or need to sub, here's your guide.

BROWN SUGAR AND COCONUT SUGAR
I state my strong preference in each recipe, even though most of the time, these are interchangeable. The two aren't that different nutritionally, and I find myself reaching for brown sugar more often, as it boosts the flavor depth and moisture content of your baked goodies. I always have coconut sugar in my pantry for when I want a recipe to be refined sugar–free. Dark brown sugar (my personal fav!) has slightly more molasses and moisture and gives more caramel flavor in baked goods. Light brown sugar will work just fine, too. No sweat!

LIQUID SWEETENERS
Most of the time, honey, pure maple syrup, and date syrup can be used interchangeably. The important thing to remember is that each of these has a unique flavor profile, so sometimes substituting one for the other changes the flavor, especially in baked goods. Date syrup is the most nutritious, but I also find it the most bland and the least sweet.

eggs

I don't recommend substituting eggs in most of my recipes. The exception: baked goods. Flax eggs are generally your best bet if you want to swap in baking. You only need one ingredient: flaxseed meal! While a flax egg won't provide structure, it does help bind everything together nicely. I recommend using them in cookies, muffins, quick breads, and brownies or bars. You can try them in cakes, but sometimes they make baked goods bake up a little flatter and denser, so sub at your own risk!

How To Make a Flax Egg:
In a small bowl, stir together 1 tablespoon flaxseed meal + 3 tablespoons of water. Allow the mixture to sit at room temperature for 5 to 10 minutes until gelatinous.

dairy (and lack thereof)

Dairy is the easiest thing you can swap out in recipes. There are so many fantastic options on the market that make it possible!

MILK

Most of my recipes already use a dairy-free milk of choice. When one uses whole milk, it's typically for flavor: the milk adds fat and creaminess, such as in slurries or sauces, or where the texture and richness might be affected by using a dairy-free milk (like a creamy pasta). That said, you can still make a swap and use your favorite; the end result might just be a little different.

DAIRY-FREE MILK

In baking recipes, feel free to use your preference. I keep unsweetened almond milk on hand the most because I can use it in both cooking and baking. Some dairy-free milks are sweetened: I always recommend purchasing unsweetened, so you can control the end product.

In cooking sauces or pastas, I recommend using a neutral dairy-free milk, such as unsweetened almond milk (my preference) or cashew milk. I've found that cashew milk is the most neutral in flavor, but it can also be the hardest to find.

WHEN *NOT* TO SUBSTITUTE MILK

Some of my recipes, such as curries, call for canned coconut milk. In general, these instances are strictly for flavor and are critical to the recipe. Sometimes I do like to use light coconut milk in cooking (and smoothies!) because it doesn't feel as rich on the tongue, but if you prefer full-fat coconut milk, please be my guest!

YOGURT

Several of my recipes use plain whole-milk Greek yogurt (or skyr; my go-to is Siggi's plain whole-milk). It adds protein and moisture and has a wonderfully creamy consistency. All of these recipes were tested with Siggi's, but going another route for Greek yogurt shouldn't be a problem. I do not recommend swapping low-fat or fat-free yogurt in my recipes; we need fat and creaminess to make them work!

Sour cream is a great swap for both sweet and savory dishes. If you're dairy-free, try coconut milk–based yogurts; I love Siggi's plant-based and Culina.

CHEESE

Ah, beloved cheese! There are plenty of dairy-free cheeses on the market that can be substituted, but unless you find one you personally enjoy, I don't suggest them because they can change the texture of the final product. If you are lactose-free, know that most cheeses sold by Cabot don't have lactose!

flour: all the possibilities!

I keep a wide selection of flours in my pantry because I love to bake everything from cinnamon rolls (which require bread flour!) to muffins (white whole wheat) and even my favorite grain-free cakes (almond and coconut flours!). Sometimes I use these flours to achieve the proper texture, but sometimes it's because I want to keep a recipe gluten-free or nutrient-dense. Should you decide to swap, let this guide you:

BREAD FLOUR

This high-protein flour is amazing in yeast breads, rolls, and even pizza. I generally do not recommend swapping anything for bread flour because it will change the texture: yeast breads will be less fluffy and cinnamon rolls less chewy.

WHITE WHOLE-WHEAT FLOUR

This is more nutrient-dense than all-purpose flour, and I love the nutty texture and flavor it lends to recipes. My best advice is to start by swapping half of the all-purpose flour with white whole-wheat flour and see how you like the results. Feel free to use white whole-wheat flour and whole-wheat pastry flour interchangeably. I do not recommend using regular whole-wheat flour in my recipes as it can make baked goods too dense.

ALMOND FLOUR

I love using fine blanched almond flour in my recipes for many reasons. It's such a nutrient powerhouse (hello healthy fats, protein, and fiber), and it adds tremendous flavor and a subtle sweetness to baked goods that can't be beat. I do not recommend using almond meal (which is made from raw almonds) or subbing any other flour for almond flour because the texture and flavor will change too much. Almond flour works best in most baking recipes when combined with another flour, such as all-purpose, white whole-wheat, oat, or coconut flour. My favorite is Bob's Red Mill Super-Fine.

COCONUT FLOUR

I adore this, but you really only need it for a handful of things. It's a very absorbent flour that soaks up lots of liquid and increases the density of baked goods. I love using coconut flour in grain-free baked goods to add a little structure. A small amount goes a long way, which is why I do not recommend swapping it unless the recipe indicates otherwise.

OAT FLOUR

Say hello to one of my absolute favorite flours ever! You can easily make it at home (see below) and it happens to be gluten-free, as long as you use certified gluten-free oats. It's cheap, it's nutritious, and it is absolutely incredible in baked goods thanks to its texture and ability to hold moisture.

In baked goods, sometimes oat flour can be substituted for all-purpose flour and white whole-wheat flour: use 1⅓ cups (approximately 120 grams) of oat flour for every 1 cup of all-purpose or white whole-wheat. I love using it in pancakes, waffles, cookies, and cakes in combination with other flours to add nutrition. Experiment by swapping a little oat flour at a time and increase as you feel more comfortable. I do NOT recommend swapping all of the flour for oat flour in most recipes, as it may change the texture too much.

Do not under any circumstances use oat flour as a substitute in recipes that use yeast. Oat flour also doesn't work well in recipes that do not have eggs to provide structure. I also do not recommend using oat flour in cooking.

> **Make Your Own Oat Flour:**
> Place oats into a blender or food processor and blend or pulse, scraping down the sides as necessary, until the mixture resembles a fine flour. Before using in recipes, be sure to measure out the desired amount of oat flour. As a reminder, oat flour is best measured by weight, not volume. Store in an airtight container for up to 3 months.

gluten (and lack thereof)

Gluten is sneaky! If it's a concern, always buy ingredients that are certified gluten-free. Here are some swaps for common items in this cookbook.

FLOUR
When trying to make a recipe gluten-free, it's best to use a 1:1 gluten-free all-purpose flour in place of all-purpose flour. This also works well in flour-based sauces. I recommend King Arthur's Gluten-Free Measure-For-Measure Flour. I do not recommend using gluten-free flour when a recipe uses yeast.

BREAD CRUMBS
My favorite is Aleia's gluten-free panko.

SOY SAUCE
Easy gluten-free swaps include tamari or coconut aminos. Tamari is a little saltier, and I personally prefer the taste of coconut aminos.

FISH SAUCE
I suggest purchasing Red Boat, which is gluten-free. Other brands sometimes contain gluten.

GOCHUJANG & SAMBAL OELEK
These spicy pastes are both unique in their own right. They're sometimes gluten-free and sometimes not, depending on the brand. Most of the time sambal oelek is gluten-free, while gochujang is not. Check labels if it's a concern!

PASTA
An easy swap! Brown rice pasta (I like Jovial) is your best bet, as it still adds the starchiness you'll need in your reserved pasta water. I'm also a huge fan of DeLallo's gluten-free orzo. If a recipe calls for pearl couscous, a gluten-free short pasta, such as orzo can be a great substitution.

butter and oil

My recipes *need* fat and flavor from butter or oil: they can never simply be omitted. However, they can be swapped.

If a cooked dish calls for butter, you can easily use vegan butter or oil instead. My favorite brand of vegan butter is Miyoko's. Unfortunately, you cannot brown vegan butter; you won't get the same flavor. Melt it instead.

In general, I prefer using avocado oil when cooking over high heat, extra-virgin olive oil when cooking over medium heat, and coconut oil for flavor (only use unrefined virgin coconut oil that's solid at room temp). I love toasted sesame oil for a flavor boost in some recipes. You'll also need a good-quality nonstick cooking spray that only contains oil, no additives.

For baking, most of the time you can use virgin coconut oil or vegan butter as a replacement for butter. In frostings, it's always best to use softened vegan butter.

nut and seed butters

I like to keep peanut butter, almond butter, cashew butter, and tahini on hand. Most of the time nut and seed butters are interchangeable, but using something other than what the recipe calls for can change the flavor. Please use all-natural nut and seed butters with only the nut/seed + salt as the ingredients (remember, salt adds more flavor!). My preferred brands are Smucker's or Trader Joe's (nut butters) and Soom (tahini). If you're looking to make something nut-free, sunflower seed butter or a nut-free granola butter (I like Oat Haus) are great options.

---

two seasoning obsessions

Homemade Sazón: This essential Puerto Rican spice mixture is used in many of my recipes. Goya's version uses MSG, so I prefer to make my own (it's in the Flavor Bible, page 237).

Adobo Forever: I use *a lot* of all-purpose adobo seasoning, which is common in Latin American cooking and is delicious, versatile, and inexpensive. I recommend the Goya brand with pepper. Do not skip it, as it adds both flavor and additional salt!

how to freeze (almost) everything

A stocked freezer has been a huge time-saver for me, especially since becoming a mom. It allows me to enjoy my own cooking and baking as long as possible. Here's how I do it.

NOTE: I store almost everything in an airtight container or reusable silicone bag, unless noted otherwise.

breakfast

BREADS
Wrap the bread loaf or individual slices tightly in foil, then place in a container or bag for up to 3 months. Thaw at room temperature.

MUFFINS
Cool completely, then freeze for up to 3 months. Thaw at room temperature, or microwave in 30-second intervals until warm.

BAKED OATMEAL & OATMEAL CUPS
Cool completely, then freeze for up to 3 months. To reheat cups or individual slices, microwave from frozen in 30-second intervals for 1 to 2 minutes, or until warm. To reheat the entire baked oatmeal, cover the pan with foil and reheat from frozen in the oven at 350°F for 20 to 25 minutes.

PANCAKES & WAFFLES
Place on a parchment-lined baking sheet in a single layer so the pancakes or waffles aren't touching and freeze for 30 minutes, then place in containers or bags and freeze for up to 3 months. To reheat pancakes, microwave for 30 to 60 seconds or bake at 350°F for 10 minutes. Use a toaster to reheat and crisp up waffles directly from the freezer.

CINNAMON ROLLS
• To freeze unbaked: After the first rise, and once they are rolled, sliced, and placed in the pan, cover the pan with plastic wrap and foil, then freeze. Once ready to bake, thaw in the fridge overnight, then place in a warm spot until the rolls have doubled in size, 60 to 90 minutes. Bake as directed.
• To freeze after baking: Leave the icing off the cinnamon rolls. Cool the cinnamon rolls to room temperature, then double-wrap the pan with plastic wrap and foil and freeze, or freeze individual cinnamon rolls in a container or bag for up to 3 months. Defrost at room temperature, warm in the oven at 350°F for 10 to 15 minutes or in the microwave for 20 to 30 seconds, then frost. The icing is also freezer-friendly!

SCONES
Freeze after shaping the dough, then bake directly from frozen, adding 5 to 10 minutes to the baking time.

QUICHES
Cool completely, then freeze individual slices in containers for up to 3 months. You can also freeze the entire quiche at once if you have a large enough freezer-safe bag or container. Microwave frozen or thawed slices until warm. Reheat an entire frozen quiche in the oven at 350°F until warm in the middle, 30 to 35 minutes.

lunch & dinner

SOUPS, STEWS, CURRIES & CHILIS
Cool completely. Leave a little space in the container, as the liquid will expand, and freeze for up to 3 months. Thaw in the fridge before reheating on the stovetop or in the microwave. Freeze without noodles or rice, as those will expand and begin to disintegrate when frozen.

BURGERS
Freeze before or after cooking for up to 3 months. If you're stacking them, layer with wax or parchment paper to prevent sticking. Thaw raw burgers in the fridge before cooking or cook directly from frozen, adding to the cooking time, as necessary. Thaw frozen cooked burgers in the fridge, then microwave or reheat on the stove for a few minutes on each side.

MEATBALLS
Freeze cooked meatballs with or without their sauce for up to 3 months. Thaw in the fridge, then heat in a pan on the stove until warm. Or, freeze raw meatballs by placing formed meatballs on a parchment-lined baking sheet and freeze for 2 hours, then transfer to a container or bag and freeze for up to 3 months. Thaw in the fridge, then cook as directed.

MEATLOAVES
• **To freeze unbaked:** Shape the meatloaf, double wrap it well in plastic wrap and foil, and freeze for up to 3 months. Thaw in the fridge, then bake as directed.
• **To freeze baked:** Cool completely, wrap well in foil before placing in a container or bag, and freeze for up to 3 months. Thaw in the fridge, remove the foil, and bake at 350°F until heated through, 30 to 45 minutes.

CASSEROLES (SUCH AS LASAGNAS, ENCHILADAS & NOODLE-BASED CASSEROLES)
• **To freeze unbaked:** Assemble, leaving off any bread crumb toppings, then double wrap with foil and freeze. Thaw overnight in the fridge before baking as directed.
• **To freeze a baked casserole:** Cool to room temperature, wrap the pan in foil or slice into servings before transferring to a container, and freeze for up to 3 months. Thaw overnight in the fridge, then bake, covered, at 350°F until heated through, 30 to 45 minutes.

STIR-FRIES & SHEET PAN MEALS
Cook as directed, then cool to room temperature Freeze protein, veggies, and sauce for up to 3 months. Thaw in the fridge, then heat in a pan on the stove until warm.

PIZZA DOUGH
Allow dough to go through the first rise in the recipe, then lightly coat the pizza dough with oil to prevent sticking, transfer to a large airtight container, seal, and freeze for up to 3 months. When ready to bake, thaw dough in the fridge overnight, then bring to room temperature 90 minutes before rolling it out and baking as directed.

STUFFED PEPPERS
• **To freeze after baking:** Cool the baked stuffed peppers to room temperature and place in an airtight container, or wrap peppers individually in plastic wrap and foil, and freeze for up to 3 months. To reheat, let the peppers thaw in the fridge before baking them at 350°F for 45 to 50 minutes.
• **To freeze unbaked:** Assemble the stuffed peppers in the pan, then double wrap the pan with foil and freeze for up to 3 months. Once ready to bake, thaw the peppers in the fridge, then bake as directed.

desserts

COOKIE DOUGH
Roll into balls, place on a parchment-lined baking sheet, freeze for 30 minutes, then transfer to a container or bag and freeze for up to 3 months. Bake from frozen, adding a few extra minutes of baking time, or bring to room temperature and bake as directed.

BAKED COOKIES
Cool completely, then transfer to a baking sheet in a single layer and freeze the cookies for 1 hour. Once cookies are frozen, place them in a bag or container in layers separated by wax or parchment paper. Freeze for up to 3 months.

FROSTED CAKES
Freeze for at least 2 hours to set the frosting, then double wrap in foil before placing in a container or bag and freeze for up to 2 months. Defrost in the fridge.

UNFROSTED CAKES
Freeze in individual layers, each wrapped in plastic wrap and foil, and placed in a container or bag. Thaw in the fridge overnight, then bring to room temperature before frosting and serving.

BROWNIES & BARS
Cool completely, then wrap the entire pan in foil and freeze, or cut into individual slices or bars, place in containers or bags, and freeze for up to 3 months. Thaw at room temperature.

CRISPS & CRUMBLES
Assemble, but do not bake. Cover with plastic wrap, then foil, and freeze for up to 3 months. Bake the frozen crisp at 350°F until golden and bubbly, about 1 hour.

PIE DOUGH
• **To freeze before rolling:** Make the pie dough and assemble into discs as directed, then wrap in plastic wrap, place in a bag, and freeze for up to 3 months. Once ready to bake, thaw in the fridge overnight then roll it out and bake as directed.
• **Freeze after rolling out:** Freeze and shape the pie dough in the pan then wrap well in plastic wrap and place in a bag.

5 rules
for your ambitious kitchen

1 always be saltin'

Salt makes everything magical and more flavorful! I always use Diamond Crystal Kosher Salt. Do not substitute another kosher salt; your food will be more salty. If you use table salt or sea salt, you'll likely need less. I love flaky sea salt for finishing! And don't forget to heavily salt your pasta water: I typically use 1 tablespoon of kosher salt for every pound of pasta.

2 always be brownin' (that butter)

Brown butter adds a nutty, caramel-like flavor that just can't be beat. I always use salted butter for browning because it adds more oomph! If all you have is unsalted, feel free to add ¼ teaspoon kosher salt for every 8 tablespoons (1 stick) of butter.

3 always be toastin'

Whenever possible, toast your nuts for added crunch and flavor:

IN THE OVEN: Preheat the oven to 350°F. Spread nuts out in an even layer on a sheet pan. For softer nuts, such as pecans, pistachios, and walnuts, bake for 5 to 8 minutes. For harder nuts, such as almonds, hazelnuts, and macadamia nuts, bake for 8 to 10 minutes. Nuts are done when slightly golden and fragrant. Once done, transfer to parchment paper or a plate to cool.

ON THE STOVE: Add nuts to a cold, dry skillet or pan over medium heat. Toast, stirring frequently, until browned in spots and fragrant, 5 to 10 minutes.

4 always be weighin' . . . well, if you can

When it comes to baked goods, technically you'll get the best outcome when you weigh your ingredients with a scale. If you don't have a scale, that's okay! When measuring, use a spoon to fluff up your flour to generate a lot of air, then gently spoon into a measuring cup until full. Level it off by sweeping the top with the flat side of a butter knife. Never shake the measuring cup or pack down your flour!

5 always use instant yeast

This is also known as quick-rise, and it's faster and easier. If you only have active yeast, proof it first: Dissolve the yeast in the warm liquid called for in the recipe (about 115°F) with 1 teaspoon sugar and wait until it begins to bubble or foam, which means the yeast is activated, about 5 minutes. The dough may take slightly longer to double.

change your morning, change your life

I grew up never eating breakfast: My mom was always darting about, frazzled, trying to herd us out to catch a 6:00 a.m. city bus to school for me, work for her. That rushed feeling became my norm into adulthood. What I didn't realize was not only was I missing out on fuel for my body, but I was also missing out on the joys that come from breakfast time: The little moments with my kids, making something to delight and surprise my husband, or lingering over a leisurely, nourishing weekend brunch. I created these recipes with the hope that they will help bring happiness to your morning, and that it will spill into the rest of your day.

it's
smoothie
time,
baby

We all love smoothies, but you know mine are just a little bit extra. I pack a ton of nutrition in there, plus they're so full of natural sweetness and flavor that you don't even taste the nutrient boosters, such as flaxseed, hemp, or spinach. They're a breeze to whip up, you can give them to kids to sip during busy mornings or any time you need a nourishing snack, *and* you can make them in every color of the rainbow! All of these are gluten-free and can easily be made dairy-free, vegan, or vegetarian.

1. For each smoothie, place all the ingredients in a high-powered blender *in the order they are listed*—this will make blending much easier. Blend until smooth, periodically stopping the machine to stir and scrape down the sides, if necessary, about 1 minute. Add more milk to thin to your desired consistency, if necessary.

2. Pour the smoothie into a glass or a bowl and top with any of the optional toppings you like—you do you. Serve immediately.

OPTIONAL TOPPINGS

Granola

Nut butter

Hemp hearts

Chia seeds

Shredded coconut

Chocolate chips or cacao nibs

Crunchy cereal

make it nutrient-dense

FOR A BOOST OF PROTEIN:
Add 1 scoop of your favorite protein powder to any of these smoothies before blending.

FOR A BOOST OF VEGGIES:
Add 1 to 2 cups of fresh spinach to any of these smoothies before blending.

i dream of strawberries and cream

Protein and healthy fats provide the creamy, dreamy texture.

¾ cup unsweetened almond milk or canned light coconut milk, plus more as needed

⅓ cup plain whole-milk Greek yogurt (or sub dairy-free yogurt)

1½ cups frozen strawberries

¼ cup raw cashews

2 large pitted Medjool dates

1 teaspoon vanilla extract

½ teaspoon almond extract

glowing skin vitamin A smoothie

Filled with vitamins A and C—both wonderful for your skin.

½ cup fresh orange juice or canned light coconut milk, plus more as needed

1 medium orange, peeled and segmented, membrane removed

1 cup frozen mango chunks

1 large carrot, peeled and cut into 2-inch chunks

1 (½-inch) slice fresh ginger, peeled

anti-inflammatory tummy soothing smoothie

Stomach upset? Hungover? Sip on this one. It's packed with digestive-friendly ingredients.

½ cup plain whole-milk Greek yogurt (or sub dairy-free yogurt)

½ cup canned light coconut milk, plus more as needed

1 small clementine or orange, peeled and segmented, membrane removed

1 cup frozen pineapple chunks

½ frozen ripe banana

1 (½-inch) slice fresh ginger, peeled

1 teaspoon chia seeds

¼ teaspoon ground turmeric

wonder woman's essential smoothie

Vitamins and minerals with a refreshing, tropical vibe.

¾ to 1 cup canned light coconut milk, as needed

Zest of 1 lime

2 tablespoons fresh lime juice

2 cups fresh spinach

1 frozen ripe banana

½ cup frozen mango or pineapple chunks

2 tablespoons hemp hearts

omega-3 wild blueberry tahini smoothie

Fiber and antioxidants never tasted so good.

¾ to 1 cup dairy-free milk of choice, as needed

1 cup frozen wild blueberries (regular will also work)

1 frozen ripe banana

2 tablespoons tahini (or sub natural creamy peanut, almond, or cashew butter)

1 teaspoon vanilla extract

1 teaspoon hemp hearts

2 teaspoons chia seeds

Zest of 1 lemon (optional)

wake me up brazil nut cacao coffee smoothie

Double energy from coffee and nutrient-rich nuts—and a sneaky dose of cauliflower, too.

½ cup cold brew or cooled leftover coffee

¼ to ½ cup canned light coconut milk, as needed

1 cup frozen cooked cauliflower (or sub ice)

3 large pitted Medjool dates

3 large Brazil nuts (or sub ¼ cup raw cashews or 2 tablespoons natural creamy peanut butter)

2 tablespoons cacao or unsweetened cocoa powder

1 teaspoon vanilla extract

1 scoop protein powder of choice (plant-based, if desired)

VEGETARIAN

sweet breakfast
scones
2 WAYS

MAKES 8 ■ **PREP TIME: 15 MINUTES, PLUS 20 MINUTES CHILLING TIME**
■ **COOK TIME: 25 MINUTES**

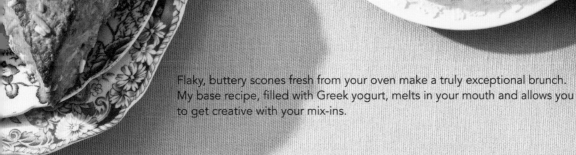

Flaky, buttery scones fresh from your oven make a truly exceptional brunch. My base recipe, filled with Greek yogurt, melts in your mouth and allows you to get creative with your mix-ins.

BASE SWEET SCONE DOUGH

2 cups (240 grams) all-purpose flour

⅓ cup (67 grams) granulated sugar

1 tablespoon baking powder

¼ teaspoon kosher salt

6 tablespoons (85 grams) VERY COLD salted butter, diced into ½-inch cubes

¾ cup (169 grams) plain or vanilla whole-milk Greek yogurt

¼ cup (60 grams) milk of choice, plus 2 tablespoons for brushing

1 teaspoon vanilla extract

½ teaspoon almond extract

1. Line a baking sheet with parchment paper and set aside.

2. **Make the base dough:** In a large bowl, whisk the flour, sugar, baking powder, and salt. Use a pastry cutter or your fingers to squeeze the butter into the flour mixture until it resembles pea-size clumps.

3. In a medium bowl, whisk the Greek yogurt, milk, and the vanilla and almond extracts. Make a well in the center of the dry ingredients, then add the wet ingredients and stir until the mixture comes together into a moist, somewhat sticky dough.

4. **Add the mix-ins:** Stir just until evenly distributed.

5. Lightly flour a surface. Turn the dough out and knead it a few times with your hands, until the dough just begins to come together. Transfer the dough to the prepared baking sheet and gently pat and press the dough into an 8-inch circle, about ¾-inch thick. Cover with plastic wrap and place in the freezer for 20 minutes.

6. Preheat the oven to 400°F.

7. Cut the dough into 8 wedges and place back onto the prepared baking sheet at least 2 inches apart. Brush the tops of the scones with 2 tablespoons of milk.

8. **Bake the scones:** Bake until the tops are golden brown, 21 to 26 minutes. Allow the scones to cool on the baking sheet for 5 minutes before serving.

BIRTHDAY CAKE SCONES

You deserve sprinkles, even if it's not your birthday.

MIX-INS

¼ cup (40 grams) artificial dye-free rainbow sprinkles

GLAZE AND TOPPING

½ cup (57 grams) powdered sugar

2 teaspoons milk of choice, plus more as needed

¼ teaspoon almond extract

2 tablespoons artificial dye-free rainbow sprinkles

Make the glaze: While the scones cool, in a small bowl, whisk the powdered sugar, milk, and almond extract until smooth. If necessary, add more milk, 1 teaspoon at a time, until the glaze is pourable. Drizzle over cooled scones and top with 2 tablespoons sprinkles. Serve right away, or wait until glaze sets, about 5 minutes.

WHITE CHOCOLATE BLUEBERRY SCONES

Like blueberry muffins, but even better.

MIX-INS

1 cup (150 grams) fresh blueberries

½ cup (90 grams) white chocolate chips

TOPPING

1 tablespoon coarse sugar

Add the topping: Sprinkle the scones with the coarse sugar after brushing with milk and before baking.

make it your way

LEMON BLUEBERRY SCONES: Skip the white chocolate chips and instead fold in zest of 1 large lemon. Drizzle the scones with the lemon glaze from the Iced Lemon Oatmeal Cookies on page 251.

savory breakfast
scones
2 WAYS

MAKES 8   PREP TIME: 15 MINUTES, PLUS 20 MINUTES CHILLING TIME
COOK TIME: 25 MINUTES

Forget bagels, try these warm, savory scones instead.

BASE SAVORY SCONE DOUGH

2 cups (240 grams) all-purpose flour

1 tablespoon baking powder

½ teaspoon kosher salt

6 tablespoons (85 grams) VERY COLD salted butter, diced into ½-inch cubes

¾ cup (169 grams) plain whole-milk Greek yogurt

4 to 6 (60 to 90 grams) tablespoons milk of choice, as needed, plus 2 tablespoons for brushing

1. Line a baking sheet with parchment paper and set aside.

2. **Make the base dough:** In a large bowl, whisk the flour, baking powder, and salt. Use a pastry cutter or your fingers to squeeze the butter into the flour mixture until it resembles pea-size clumps.

3. In a medium bowl, whisk the Greek yogurt and 4 tablespoons (60 grams) of the milk. Make a well in the center of the dry ingredients, then add the wet ingredients and stir until the mixture comes together into a moist, somewhat sticky dough. If it is too wet, add another 1 or 2 tablespoons of flour.

4. **Add the mix-ins:** Stir just until evenly distributed.

5. Lightly flour a surface. Turn the dough out and knead it a few times with your hands, until the dough just begins to come together. Transfer the dough to the prepared baking sheet and gently pat and press the dough into an 8-inch circle, about ¾-inch thick. Cover with plastic wrap and place in the freezer for 20 minutes.

6. Preheat the oven to 400°F.

7. Cut the dough into 8 wedges and place back onto the prepared baking sheet at least 2 inches apart. Brush the tops of the slices with 2 tablespoons of milk. Add any toppings now.

8. **Bake the scones:** Bake until the tops are golden brown, 21 to 26 minutes. Allow the scones to cool on the baking sheet for 5 minutes before serving.

BACON, DATE & GOAT CHEESE SCONES

Salty, sweet, tangy, all in one.

MIX-INS

8 ounces (226 grams) bacon, cooked and chopped (½ cup)

¾ cup (130 grams) large pitted Medjool dates, chopped

6 ounces (170 grams) goat cheese (or feta), crumbled

GARNISH

Flaky sea salt (I like Maldon)

VEGETARIAN

SCALLION JALAPEÑO CHEDDAR SCONES

A classic combination that's now for breakfast.

MIX-INS

3 scallions, chopped

2 jalapeños, diced (remove seeds if you are sensitive to heat)

4 ounces (113 grams) shredded sharp Cheddar cheese (1 cup)

TOPPINGS

2 ounces (57 grams) shredded sharp Cheddar cheese (½ cup)

1 jalapeño, sliced

Add the toppings: Cover the scones with the cheese and jalapeño slices after brushing the dough with milk and before baking.

make it your way

Drizzle these with honey or Quick Hot Honey (page 231) for an outrageously good sweet-and-spicy scone.

dreamy coffee lover's baked oatmeal

SERVES 6 ■ PREP TIME: 10 MINUTES ■ COOK TIME: 25 MINUTES

Nonstick cooking spray

WET INGREDIENTS

1 cup (236 grams) canned light coconut milk (or sub dairy-free milk of choice)

¾ cup (170 grams) fresh brewed coffee or cold brew, at room temperature

⅓ cup (104 grams) pure maple syrup

2 large eggs

2 teaspoons vanilla extract

DRY INGREDIENTS

2 cups (190 grams) rolled oats (gluten-free, if desired)

2 teaspoons espresso powder

1 teaspoon baking powder

¼ teaspoon kosher salt

MIX-INS AND TOPPING

⅓ cup (60 grams) chocolate chips plus 2 tablespoons for topping

½ teaspoon virgin coconut oil

Flaky sea salt (I like Maldon)

Greek yogurt or milk of choice, for serving (optional)

Dear beloved coffee lovers: This one's for you! Somehow it ends up tasting just like an oat milk latte when it's served warm with milk that soaks up the coffee and chocolate flavors. This chic oatmeal for grown-ups only was inspired by my mom, who always adds a splash of her favorite flavored creamer and a little coffee to her bowl of oatmeal. So I thought, why not add coconut milk (for a little richness, sweetness, and a hint of coconut flavor) and coffee here, too? And hey, chocolate chips never hurt anyone.

1. Preheat the oven to 350°F. Grease an 8-inch square pan with cooking spray.

2. **Mix the wet ingredients:** In a large bowl, whisk the coconut milk, coffee, maple syrup, eggs, and vanilla until smooth and combined.

3. **Add the dry ingredients:** Add the oats, espresso powder, baking powder, and salt to the wet ingredients and mix with a wooden spoon until well combined.

4. **Add the mix-ins:** Fold in ⅓ cup (60 grams) of the chocolate chips. Pour the mixture into the prepared baking dish and smooth the top.

5. **Bake the oatmeal:** Bake until the oatmeal is set and slightly golden on the edges, and a knife comes out mostly clean with just a few crumbs attached when inserted, 25 to 30 minutes. Cool for 5 to 10 minutes before drizzling with chocolate.

6. **Make the topping:** Place 2 tablespoons of the chocolate chips and the coconut oil in a small microwave-safe bowl. Microwave in 30-second intervals, stirring in between, until melted and smooth. Generously drizzle over the oatmeal then sprinkle with flaky sea salt. Slice into 6 pieces and serve warm in bowls, with a bit of milk poured over, if desired.

7. **To store:** Cool completely then cover the pan with foil before transferring to the fridge. The oatmeal will keep well for up to 4 days, and you can reheat individual slices in the microwave for 30 to 60 seconds. You can also store individual slices in airtight containers or reusable silicone bags for quick, on-the-go breakfasts. For freezing instructions, see page 20.

make it your way

TO MAKE DAIRY-FREE: Use dairy-free chocolate chips.

make it nutrient-dense

For a fiber and protein boost, stir in 2 tablespoons of hemp hearts with the oats.

famous blender banana oatmeal pancakes

MAKES 10 ▪ PREP TIME: 15 MINUTES ▪ COOK TIME: 10 MINUTES

If there's one pancake recipe I find myself coming back to again and again, it's this one, which so many of my readers have declared their favorite, too. Maybe it's because the batter is MADE IN THE BLENDER (so easy!). Or because they're packed with protein, hearty oats, and absolutely no flour. Or because I can make fluffy mini pancakes that my kids love but also big versions topped with mini chocolate chips *plus* a drizzle of peanut butter *and* a sprinkle of flaky sea salt, because I'm extra like that. Any way you choose, they're SENSATIONAL!

1. Preheat the oven to 200°F if you'd like to keep your pancakes warm between batches.

2. **Make the batter:** Place the ingredients in a blender in this order: the bananas, eggs, milk, vanilla, oats, baking powder, cinnamon, and salt. Blend on high speed until completely smooth, 30 seconds to 1 minute. Let the batter sit in the blender to thicken for 5 minutes while you heat up your pan.

3. **Cook the pancakes:** Place a large nonstick griddle or skillet over medium heat and lightly coat with coconut oil. Once the oil has melted, add approximately ¼ cup of the batter for each pancake (use 1 tablespoon for mini pancakes), leaving room for the batter to spread and, if necessary, use the back of a spoon to spread about ½ inch thick; cook until the pancakes slightly puff up and you see a few bubbles along the edges, 2 to 4 minutes.

4. To check if the pancakes are ready to be flipped, lift a corner of the pancake with a flexible spatula turner; if they are golden brown on the bottom, this usually indicates that it's time to flip.

5. Gently flip the cakes and cook until golden brown on the underside, about 2 minutes more. If you find the pancakes are browning too quickly, or if the griddle or pan starts smoking at any point, reduce the heat to medium-low. Transfer the finished pancakes to a baking sheet and place in the oven to keep warm.

6. Wipe the skillet clean and repeat with more oil as needed and the remaining batter.

7. **Add toppings:** Transfer the pancakes to a plate, choose one or several toppings, and serve warm.

8. **To store:** Keep any leftover pancakes in the fridge in an airtight container or reusable silicone bag for up to 5 days. Reheat in the microwave until warm, about 30 seconds. For freezing instructions, see page 20.

PANCAKES

2 medium extra-ripe spotty bananas

2 large eggs

½ cup (120 grams) milk of choice

1 teaspoon vanilla extract

1½ cups (143 grams) rolled oats (gluten-free, if desired)

2 teaspoons baking powder

½ teaspoon ground cinnamon

½ teaspoon kosher salt

Virgin coconut oil or vegan butter, for greasing the skillet

OPTIONAL TOPPINGS

Fresh berries

Nut butter

Pure maple syrup

Mini chocolate chips

make it your way

CHOCOLATE CHIP OATMEAL PANCAKES: Fold in ⅓ cup (60 grams) mini chocolate chips after blending the batter.

make it nutrient dense

For a superfood boost, stir 1 tablespoon of any of the following into the batter: flaxseed meal, chia seeds, or hemp hearts. When adding chia or flax, you may need to add an extra 1 to 2 tablespoons of milk, as they have a tendency to soak up a good amount of liquid.

blissful blueberry high-protein pancakes (or waffles!)

SERVES 4 TO 6; MAKES 12 ∎ **PREP TIME: 10 MINUTES** ∎ **COOK TIME: 20 MINUTES**

WET INGREDIENTS

1 cup (225 grams) vanilla whole-milk Greek yogurt

1 cup (240 grams) milk of choice, plus more as needed

2 large eggs

2 tablespoons coconut sugar (optional, if you like sweeter pancakes or waffles)

1 teaspoon vanilla extract

1 teaspoon almond extract

DRY INGREDIENTS

2½ cups (230 grams) oat flour (gluten-free, if desired)

1 tablespoon baking powder

¼ teaspoon kosher salt

COOKING AND MIX-INS

Salted butter, for greasing

1¼ cups (188 grams) fresh or frozen blueberries

4 tablespoons (57 grams) salted butter, melted (for waffles)

OPTIONAL TOPPINGS

Extra blueberries

Plain or vanilla whole-milk Greek yogurt

Nut butter

Pure maple syrup

Blueberry compote or jam

Granola

These high-protein pancakes and waffles are SO FLUFFY, you won't even believe it, PLUS they are made entirely with fiber-rich oat flour (which is easy to make on your own; see page 18) AND they taste just like cake (thanks to almond extract). Anyone who wants more protein can enjoy these after a workout. Kids will gobble them up! They are always in our freezer, waiting to be heated up when anyone needs a filling breakfast and a smile on their face.

1. Preheat the oven to 200°F if you'd like to keep your pancakes or waffles warm between batches.

2. **Mix the wet ingredients:** In a large bowl, whisk the Greek yogurt, milk, eggs, coconut sugar (if using), vanilla, and almond extract until well combined and smooth.

3. **Mix in the dry ingredients:** Add the oat flour, baking powder, and salt, and mix until just combined. Allow the batter to sit for 5 to 10 minutes while you heat up your pan; it will thicken up but remain pourable.

4. **If making pancakes:** Place a large nonstick griddle or skillet over medium heat and lightly coat with butter. Once the butter is melted, add approximately ¼ cup of the batter to the griddle for each pancake, leaving room for the batter to spread; if necessary, use the back of a spoon to spread about ½ inch thick. Immediately drop 8 blueberries onto each pancake and cook until the pancakes slightly puff up and you see a few bubbles along the edges, 2 to 4 minutes. Lift a corner of the pancake with a flexible spatula turner; if they are golden brown on the bottom, this usually indicates that it's time to flip.

5. Gently flip the cakes and cook until golden brown on the underside, about 2 minutes. If you find that the pancakes are browning too quickly, or if the skillet starts smoking at any point, reduce the heat to medium-low. Wipe the skillet clean and repeat with more butter and the remaining batter. Transfer the finished pancakes to a baking sheet and place in the oven to keep warm.

6. **If making waffles:** Stir the melted butter directly into the batter until well combined, then fold in the blueberries. Preheat the waffle iron and lightly coat with butter. Once the waffle iron is hot, pour just enough batter onto the waffle iron to cover most of the surface area and close the lid. Cook according to the manufacturer's directions; once the waffle is crisp and golden, transfer to a wire rack in a single layer. Repeat with the remaining batter.

7. **Add toppings:** Serve warm with one or several toppings, if desired.

8. **To store:** Keep any leftover pancakes or waffles in an airtight container or reusable silicone bag in the fridge for up to 5 days. Reheat pancakes in the microwave until warm, about 30 seconds; toast waffles until they're crispy to your liking. For freezing instructions, see page 20.

make it your way

CHOCOLATE CHIP PANCAKES OR WAFFLES: Instead of blueberries, stir ¾ cup (135 grams) of dark or semisweet chocolate chips into the batter before cooking.

no-knead pumpkin cranberry walnut harvest bread

MAKES 1 LOAF ▪ **PREP TIME: 15 MINUTES, PLUS 3 HOURS RISING TIME** ▪ **COOK TIME: 35 MINUTES**

DRY INGREDIENTS

3 cups (360 grams) bread flour, plus more for dusting

⅔ cup (80 grams) dried cranberries or dried cherries

Heaping ½ cup (56 grams) chopped walnuts or pecans

½ cup (57 grams) white whole-wheat flour (or sub more bread flour)

½ cup (48 grams) rolled oats, plus 1 tablespoon for topping

1 tablespoon whole flaxseed

2¼ teaspoons (one ¼-ounce package) instant yeast

1½ teaspoons kosher salt

1 teaspoon ground cinnamon or pumpkin pie spice (optional)

WET INGREDIENTS

1 cup (240 grams) water, plus more for topping

1 cup (244 grams) pumpkin puree

⅓ cup (112 grams) honey (or sub pure maple syrup)

1 tablespoon extra-virgin olive oil

SERVING

Salted Honey Butter (page 235; optional)

Flaky sea salt (I like Maldon)

This hearty bread is easy to make, will fill your home with a cozy aroma, and is packed with nutrients. The key to the deliciousness is to make sure you get a slice nice and toasted before serving so that the edges are super crunchy. I'm also a huge fan of using it to make grilled cheese or turkey sandwiches after Thanksgiving. This bread is the perfect weekend project to do with your family or friends, or to bake for someone you care about. Because after all, baking = love.

1. **Prepare the dry ingredients:** In a large bowl, whisk the bread flour, cranberries, walnuts, white whole-wheat flour, oats, flaxseed, yeast, salt, and cinnamon (if using) until well combined. Set aside.

2. **Prepare the wet ingredients:** In a large microwave-safe bowl, stir together the water and the pumpkin puree until well combined. Microwave in 30-second intervals until slightly warmer than bath water, or approximately 115°F, 1 to 2 minutes. Stir in the honey and olive oil. Add the pumpkin mixture to the dry ingredients and mix with a wooden spoon until just incorporated and the dough is slightly sticky and shaggy. Cover the bowl with plastic wrap and a towel and let stand at room temperature until doubled in size, about 2 hours.

3. **Form the dough:** Generously flour a surface. Turn out the dough and sprinkle with a little flour. Using floured hands, grab one corner of the dough, stretch it upward, and fold it over to the opposite side of the ball. Grab the next corner, stretch it upward, and fold it over. Repeat with the remaining two corners. Then repeat the full set again, for a total of 8 folds. Flip the dough over and shape into a ball.

4. Line a large bowl with parchment paper. Place the dough in the bowl and cover with plastic wrap and a towel. Allow the dough to rest again until fully proofed and you can poke your finger about an inch into the dough without the indentation bouncing back immediately, 1 hour.

5. About 15 minutes into the second proof, place a 4- to 6-quart Dutch oven or oven-safe pot with a lid in the cold oven on the middle rack. Preheat the oven to 425°F with the pot in the oven for 30 minutes. Fill a small bowl with water and place it next to the oven.

6. **Bake the bread:** Remove the pot from the oven and, taking care not to burn yourself, immediately add the parchment paper with the dough into the pot. Brush the dough with a little water, then sprinkle 1 tablespoon of oats over the top. Cover with the lid and bake for 25 minutes.

7. Remove the lid from the pot and continue baking until the bread is golden and makes a light hollow sound when tapped, 8 to 12 minutes. Carefully grab on to the parchment paper and immediately remove bread from the pot and transfer to a wire rack. Allow the bread to cool completely, at least 2 hours, before cutting into 12 slices.

8. **To serve:** Toast the slices until nice and golden brown on the edges. Serve with optional Salted Honey Butter and a little flaky sea salt.

9. **To store:** Place bread in a reusable silicone bag for up to 2 days, then transfer to the fridge. To freeze the baked bread, allow it to cool to room temperature, then cover the baked loaf tightly in plastic wrap then wrap in foil or place in a reusable silicone bag. Freeze for up to 3 months. You can also slice your bread before freezing it, so you can take out individual slices for toasting and serving.

better-for-you banana muffins

MAKES 10 ■ PREP TIME: 10 MINUTES ■ COOK TIME: 25 MINUTES

In my opinion, everyone needs a go-to banana muffin. You know, the one you want to tell everyone about. The one you bake for yourself, your kids, your family. The one you keep in the freezer when you need a sweet midmorning snack or even a quick on-the-go breakfast. The best part though? These banana muffins aren't just delicious—they're nutritious and naturally gluten-free, thanks to a combo of gluten-free oat flour (see how to easily make your own on page 18), almond flour, and flaxseed meal!

WET INGREDIENTS

3 medium extra-ripe spotty bananas, mashed

¼ cup (78 grams) pure maple syrup (or sub honey)

¼ cup (56 grams) virgin coconut oil, melted and cooled

2 large eggs, at room temperature

3 tablespoons milk of choice

1 teaspoon vanilla extract

DRY INGREDIENTS

1 cup (92 grams) oat flour (gluten-free, if desired)

1 cup (112 grams) fine blanched almond flour

2 tablespoons flaxseed meal

1 teaspoon ground cinnamon

1 teaspoon baking powder

½ teaspoon baking soda

¼ teaspoon kosher salt

MIX-INS AND TOPPINGS

½ cup (90 grams) dark chocolate chips, plus 2 tablespoons for topping

⅓ cup (37 grams) chopped walnuts, plus 2 tablespoons for topping (optional)

Flaky sea salt, for topping (I like Maldon; optional)

1. Preheat the oven to 350°F. Line a 12-cup muffin tin with 10 muffin liners.

2. **Mix the wet ingredients:** In a large bowl, whisk the mashed bananas, maple syrup, coconut oil, eggs, milk, and vanilla until well combined.

3. **Add the dry ingredients:** Add the oat flour, almond flour, flaxseed meal, cinnamon, baking powder, baking soda, and salt. Mix with a wooden spoon until well combined and smooth.

4. **Add the mix-ins and toppings:** Gently fold in ½ cup (90 grams) of the chocolate chips and ⅓ cup (37 grams) of the walnuts (if using). Divide the batter evenly between the prepared liners and sprinkle the remaining 2 tablespoons of chocolate chips and 2 tablespoons of walnuts (if using) evenly over the muffins.

5. **Bake the muffins:** Bake until a tester inserted into the middle comes out clean, 23 to 28 minutes. Let cool in the muffin tin for 5 minutes, sprinkle with sea salt, if desired, then remove and transfer to a wire rack to cool completely.

6. **To store:** Keep muffins in an airtight container or reusable silicone bag at room temperature for 1 day, then store in the fridge for up to 4 days. I recommend warming them up in the microwave for 15 to 30 seconds before eating. For freezing instructions, see page 20.

make it your way

TO MAKE DAIRY-FREE: Use dairy-free chocolate chips and dairy-free milk of choice.

make it nutrient-dense

To add a fiber and protein boost, stir 2 tablespoons of hemp hearts or 1 scoop of protein powder into the batter before baking.

diy sweet & salty protein bars

MAKES 8 TO 10 ▪ **PREP TIME: 15 MINUTES, PLUS 2 HOURS CHILLING TIME** ▪
COOK TIME: NO COOKING REQUIRED!

Years ago, when I was learning how to refuel my body, I would grab whatever store-bought protein bar was available for a quick snack. I remember gobbling down bars with fake fiber and ingredients I couldn't even pronounce. Once I realized that I could make a satisfying, DIY, nutrient-dense protein bar at home full of superfoods and real ingredients, I never went back. These sweet-salty nutrient-powerhouse bars promise to keep you both satisfied and nourished and my kids delightfully think they taste like candy bars.

1. Line an 8 × 4-inch loaf pan with parchment paper.

2. **Mix the bar ingredients:** In a medium bowl, mix together the nut butter, honey, vanilla, cinnamon, and salt until smooth. Stir in the protein powder, flaxseed meal, oats, coconut, chia, and hemp hearts (if using) until well combined. You may need to use your hands to help the mixture come together. Fold in the dried cherries (if using).

3. Transfer the mixture to the prepared pan and spread out evenly. Use the bottom of a measuring cup to press the mixture down firmly.

4. **Make the topping:** Place the chocolate chips and coconut oil in a small microwave-safe bowl. Microwave in 30-second intervals, stirring in between, until melted. Drizzle the melted chocolate back and forth over the bars.

5. **Chill:** Refrigerate until completely hardened, about 2 hours. Sprinkle with sea salt, lift it out of the pan, transfer to a cutting board, and cut into 8 to 10 squares or bars.

6. **To store:** Cover the bars and store in the fridge for up to 1 week, or individually wrap them in plastic wrap, then place in an airtight container or reusable silicone bag and freeze for up to 3 months. Thaw individual bars in the fridge or at room temperature before enjoying.

make it your way

TO MAKE DAIRY-FREE: Use dairy-free chocolate chips and dairy-free protein powder.

TO MAKE VEGAN: Use pure maple syrup or date syrup, dairy-free chocolate chips, and plant-based protein powder.

TO MAKE VEGETARIAN: Use a plant-based protein powder.

BARS

¾ cup (192 grams) natural creamy peanut butter, almond butter, or cashew butter

⅓ cup (112 grams) honey (or sub pure maple syrup or date syrup)

1 teaspoon vanilla extract

½ teaspoon ground cinnamon

¼ teaspoon kosher salt

½ cup (40 grams) unflavored or vanilla protein powder of choice (I like collagen peptides)

⅓ cup (40 grams) flaxseed meal

¼ cup (24 grams) rolled oats (gluten-free if desired)

¼ cup (21 grams) unsweetened shredded coconut

1 teaspoon chia seeds

2 tablespoons hemp hearts (optional)

¼ cup (30 grams) dried cherries (optional)

TOPPING

2 tablespoons dark or semisweet chocolate chips

½ teaspoon virgin coconut oil

Flaky sea salt (I like Maldon)

morning glory zucchini carrot muffins

MAKES 10 ▪ PREP TIME: 20 MINUTES ▪ COOK TIME: 25 MINUTES

Nonstick cooking spray

WET INGREDIENTS

1 medium zucchini

1 cup (100 grams) shredded carrots (from 2 medium carrots)

½ cup (156 grams) pure maple syrup

⅓ cup (83 grams) unsweetened applesauce

⅓ cup (75 grams) virgin coconut oil, melted and cooled

2 large eggs, at room temperature

1 teaspoon vanilla extract

DRY INGREDIENTS

1 cup (92 grams) oat flour (gluten-free, if desired)

¾ cup (85 grams) white whole-wheat flour

½ cup (43 grams) unsweetened shredded coconut

1 teaspoon baking soda

1 teaspoon ground cinnamon

¼ teaspoon ground nutmeg

¼ teaspoon kosher salt

MIX-INS

⅓ cup (37 grams) chopped walnuts or pecans

⅓ cup (53 grams) raisins or chopped Medjool dates

TOPPINGS

2 tablespoons rolled oats (gluten-free, if desired)

1 tablespoon coconut sugar (optional)

People call me the Muffin Queen for a reason. And that's because I am known to whip up some damn good healthy muffins. These fluffy babes taste like a cross between carrot cake and zucchini bread and pair absolutely perfectly with a cup of coffee. I've also found that my kids LOVE them, which is great because they are packed with both fruits and veggies and naturally sweetened with maple syrup. The coconut, raisins (or dates!), and nuts give them a little something extra, too.

1. Preheat the oven to 350°F. Line a muffin tin with 10 muffin liners and grease the inside of the liners with cooking spray to prevent sticking.

2. **Prepare the wet ingredients:** Shred the zucchini, then place the shredded zucchini in a paper towel or a clean dish towel and squeeze out excess moisture. Measure out 1 heaping cup of zucchini and transfer to a large bowl (save any extra for smoothies or stir-fries). Add the carrots, maple syrup, applesauce, coconut oil, eggs, and vanilla. Whisk until well combined.

3. **Prepare the dry ingredients:** In a second large bowl, whisk the oat flour, white whole-wheat flour, coconut, baking soda, cinnamon, nutmeg, and salt.

4. Add the dry ingredients to the wet ingredients and mix with a wooden spoon until just combined.

5. **Add the mix-ins:** Gently fold in the walnuts and raisins.

6. **Bake the muffins:** Evenly divide the batter among the muffin liners. Sprinkle the tops with oats and coconut sugar (if using). Bake until a tester inserted into one of the muffins comes out clean or with just a few crumbs attached, 23 to 28 minutes. Allow the muffins to cool in the pan for 5 minutes, then remove and transfer to a wire rack to finish cooling completely.

7. **To store:** Keep muffins in an airtight container or reusable silicone bag at room temperature for 1 day, then store in the fridge for up to 3 days. I recommend warming them up in the microwave for 15 to 30 seconds before eating. For freezing instructions, see page 20.

make it your way

TO MAKE GLUTEN-FREE: Use 1:1 gluten-free all-purpose flour instead of white whole-wheat flour.

Instead of applesauce, use 1 ripe mashed banana.

Instead of coconut oil, use melted butter or vegan butter.

make it your way

TO MAKE DAIRY-FREE: Use vegan butter and dairy-free yogurt.

TO MAKE GLUTEN-FREE: Use 1:1 gluten-free all-purpose flour.

LEMON BLUEBERRY POPPY SEED COFFEE CAKE: Stir 2 tablespoons of poppy seeds into the dry ingredients.

lovely lemon blueberry coffee cake

SERVES 12 ▪ **PREP TIME: 15 MINUTES** ▪ **COOK TIME: 45 MINUTES**

Coffee cake is basically just an excuse to eat a slice of cake for breakfast and I am here for it. So is my husband, who is at his happiest and most adorable while drinking hot coffee out of his usual red mug in one hand and eating coffee cake straight out of the pan with the other. I created this just-sweet-enough beauty for him and for my wonderful readers, who always fall in love with any of my recipes involving lemon. And because I cannot stand coffee cake that is dry as hell, this one is made with high-protein Greek yogurt to keep it moist. I never regret making the lemon yogurt glaze, and you won't either.

1. Preheat the oven to 350°F. Generously coat a 9-inch round springform pan with cooking spray, or line a 9-inch round cake pan or an 8-inch square pan with parchment paper and spray with cooking spray.

2. **Make the streusel topping:** In a medium bowl, mix the flour, brown sugar, and lemon zest. Add the melted butter and stir together with a fork until it resembles clumps of wet sand. You may need to use your hands/fingers to form into nice thick clumps. Cover the bowl with plastic wrap and place in the fridge for later.

3. **Mix the wet ingredients:** In a large bowl, whisk the Greek yogurt, maple syrup, eggs, lemon zest, lemon juice, and almond extract until well combined, smooth, and creamy. Whisk in the melted butter until emulsified, about 1 minute.

4. **Prepare the dry ingredients and mix-ins:** In a medium bowl, whisk 1¾ cups (210 grams) of the flour, the baking powder, baking soda, and salt. Add the dry ingredients to the wet ingredients and use a wooden spoon to mix until combined; do not overmix.

5. In a small bowl, toss the blueberries with the remaining 2 tablespoons of flour until evenly coated. Using a rubber spatula, fold the blueberries into the batter. Transfer the batter to the prepared pan and, using a spatula, spread into an even layer. Sprinkle with the streusel topping.

6. **Bake the cake:** Bake until a tester inserted into the middle comes out clean with just a few crumbs attached, 45 to 50 minutes. Allow the cake to cool in the pan for 30 minutes before glazing.

7. **Make the glaze:** In a small bowl, mix together the Greek yogurt, powdered sugar, lemon zest, and lemon juice until well combined and smooth. If necessary, add more lemon juice, 1 teaspoon at a time, to thin out the glaze so that you can easily drizzle it over the cake. Drizzle the glaze back and forth over the cake. Cut into 12 slices and serve.

8. **To store:** Keep coffee cake in an airtight container for 1 to 2 days, then transfer to the fridge for up to 5 days.

Nonstick cooking spray

STREUSEL TOPPING

1 cup (120 grams) all-purpose flour

½ cup (107 grams) packed dark brown sugar

Zest of 1 lemon

5 tablespoons (71 grams) salted butter, melted

WET INGREDIENTS

½ cup (113 grams) plain or vanilla whole-milk Greek yogurt

½ cup (156 grams) pure maple syrup

2 large eggs, at room temperature

Zest of 1 large lemon

¼ cup (50 grams) fresh lemon juice (from 1 large lemon)

½ teaspoon almond extract

8 tablespoons (113 grams) salted butter, melted and cooled

DRY INGREDIENTS AND MIX-INS

1¾ cups (210 grams) all-purpose flour, plus 2 tablespoons

1 teaspoon baking powder

½ teaspoon baking soda

¼ teaspoon kosher salt

1½ cups (225 grams) fresh blueberries

LEMON GLAZE

¼ cup (56 grams) plain whole-milk Greek yogurt

2 tablespoons powdered sugar

1 teaspoon lemon zest

2 teaspoons fresh lemon juice, plus more as needed

the best cinnamon rolls you'll ever eat
(PAGE 54)

the best cinnamon rolls you'll ever eat

MAKES 9 ■ PREP TIME: 40 MINUTES, PLUS 2 HOURS RISING TIME ■ COOK TIME: 20 MINUTES

DOUGH

¾ cup (180 grams) milk (whole milk or 2% preferred)

2¼ teaspoons (one ¼-ounce package) quick-rise (instant) or active dry yeast

¼ cup (50 grams) granulated sugar

4 tablespoons (57 grams) salted butter, melted and cooled

1 large egg plus 1 large egg yolk, at room temperature

3 cups (360 grams) bread flour, plus more as needed

¾ teaspoon kosher salt

Extra-virgin olive oil, for greasing the bowl

FILLING

4 tablespoons (57 grams) salted butter, softened

⅔ cup (142 grams) packed dark brown sugar

1½ tablespoons ground cinnamon

CREAM CHEESE FROSTING

4 ounces (112 grams) cream cheese, softened

¾ cup (85 grams) powdered sugar

3 tablespoons salted butter, softened

½ teaspoon vanilla extract

With a whopping 28 million views and counting on the blog post, these BIG, fluffy cinnamon rolls are the most popular recipe on my site. Yes, they can look rather intimidating at first, but trust me, they are a labor of love guaranteed to impress anyone. I first made these for my now-husband and his friends, and since then, they've transformed into both an Easter and Christmas brunch tradition that absolutely cannot be missed! When *TODAY* anchor Dylan Dreyer made them on the show to help reveal her pregnancy, I was stunned by the number of web views the recipe got in one week. I was most gratified that Dylan made them with her then-four-year-old son, using my recipe to connect the two of them and share such happy news with viewers. I hope you find just as much comfort, love, and joy in making and eating these as I do. You'll notice that the recipe calls for bread flour, which is worth seeking out because it helps create the most chewy, fluffy, soft cinnamon rolls you'll ever eat!

1. **Prepare the dough:** In a small microwave-safe bowl, warm the milk by microwaving it for 45 seconds to 1 minute, until it registers 115°F on a thermometer and feels like warm bath water.

2. Place the warmed milk in the bowl of a stand mixer fitted with the paddle attachment and sprinkle the yeast on top. (If using active dry yeast, add the sugar now and let the yeast sit with the sugar until foamy, about 5 minutes.) If you haven't already, add the sugar, then the melted butter, egg, and egg yolk. Mix on medium speed until well combined, 30 seconds. (Alternatively, mix with a wooden spoon until well combined.) Remove the bowl from the mixer and use a wooden spoon to stir in the flour and salt until a dough begins to form (this will prevent flour from flying everywhere!).

3. **Knead the dough:** Place the dough hook on the stand mixer and return the bowl to the mixer. Mix the dough on medium speed until it comes together and feels soft and slightly sticky, 8 to 10 minutes. If it's too sticky—meaning it's sticking to the bottom of the mixer— add another 1 to 3 tablespoons bread flour, 1 tablespoon at a time. (Alternatively, you can use your hands to knead the dough for 8 to 10 minutes on a well-floured surface.) Meanwhile, place a clean dish towel in your dryer to warm.

4. Lightly grease a large bowl with olive oil. Transfer the dough ball to the bowl, then cover with plastic wrap and the warm towel. Allow the dough to rise until doubled in size, 1 to 1½ hours. (This may be more or less time depending on the time of year, the humidity, and the temperature in your home.) You will know the dough has risen enough when you poke your finger into the dough about an inch without the indentation bouncing back immediately.

BANANA NUT CINNAMON ROLLS:
Add 2 sliced ripe bananas and
½ cup (56 grams) of chopped
walnuts on top of the cinnamon
sugar mixture just before rolling.

ORANGE CINNAMON ROLLS:
Add the zest of 1 large orange to
the cinnamon sugar mixture. Add
1 teaspoon grated orange zest
and 1 to 2 tablespoons of fresh
orange juice to the cream cheese
frosting.

OVERNIGHT CINNAMON ROLLS:
Follow steps 1 through 8, then
place the cut rolls into the
parchment paper–lined pan,
cover the pan with plastic wrap,
and refrigerate overnight or up
to 16 hours. In the morning, let
the rolls rise on the counter until
doubled in size and puffy, 60 to
90 minutes, then bake as directed.

5. Generously dust a surface with flour. Turn out the dough and use a rolling pin to roll the dough into an 10 × 14-inch rectangle.

6. **Prepare the filling:** Spread the softened butter over the dough, leaving a ¼-inch margin at the far short side of the rectangle. In a small bowl, mix together the brown sugar and cinnamon. Use your hands to sprinkle the mixture over the butter, then gently rub the brown sugar mixture into the butter.

7. Starting from the short side without the margin, very tightly roll up the dough. Seal the far edge of the dough as best you can by pinching the dough together just slightly, then make sure the dough log is seam-side down. Cut a ½ inch off the ends of the dough, as the ends won't have enough filling; feel free to discard (or bake separately as yummy extras). Use your hands to give the dough log a gentle push inwards on both ends so that it compacts slightly, as it may have stretched out a bit during the rolling process.

8. Using unflavored dental floss or a serrated knife, cut the dough into nine 1-inch slices.

9. Line a round or square 9-inch pan with parchment paper. Place the rolls in the prepared baking pan. Cover with plastic wrap and a towel and let rise again until the rolls have puffed up, are doubled in size, and touching each other in the pan, 45 minutes to 1 hour.

10. Meanwhile, preheat the oven to 350°F.

11. **Bake the cinnamon rolls:** Once the rolls have risen, remove the plastic wrap and towel and bake until golden brown on the edges, 20 to 25 minutes. Not overbaking the rolls ensures that they will stay soft in the middle. Cool for 10 minutes.

12. **Prepare the cream cheese frosting:** In the bowl of a stand mixer fitted with the whisk attachment, combine the cream cheese, powdered sugar, butter, and vanilla. Beat on low speed for 30 seconds, then increase to medium-high speed until smooth and fluffy, 1 to 2 minutes. (Alternatively, whisk the frosting by hand.) Spread the frosting over the warm rolls and serve.

13. **To store:** Cover the whole pan with plastic wrap and foil or place individual cinnamon rolls in airtight containers or silicone bags and store in the fridge for up to 5 days. Reheat the cinnamon rolls individually in the microwave in 15 second intervals until warm. For freezing instructions, see page 20.

bacon, goat cheese & caramelized onion quiche with sweet potato crust

SERVES 6 ■ PREP TIME: 20 MINUTES ■ COOK TIME: 1 HOUR 20 MINUTES

Nonstick cooking spray

CRUST AND BACON

1 large sweet potato, cut into ⅛-inch-thick slices

4 to 6 slices thick-cut bacon, depending on how much you love bacon

CARAMELIZED ONIONS

1 tablespoon extra-virgin olive oil

2 medium yellow onions, thinly sliced

¼ teaspoon kosher salt

3 cups fresh spinach, roughly chopped

1 garlic clove, minced

FILLING AND GARNISH

6 large eggs

⅓ cup whole milk or unsweetened almond milk

¼ teaspoon kosher salt

Freshly ground black pepper

4 ounces goat cheese, crumbled

1 to 2 tablespoons chopped chives

While quiche is perfect for brunch and entertaining, I find myself always down to eat a slice no matter the time of day. I love having a quiche on hand for busy weeks when I know I'm not going to have a ton of time to cook, but still want to nosh on something nutritious and flavorful. This one has it all: caramelized onions give it a slight sweetness, bacon adds that salty element every quiche needs, and goat cheese brings a perfect creamy tang. Oh, and we can't forget about the sweet potato crust that holds it all together and keeps it FUN. This is truly the most flexible recipe for mixing and matching based on what you have in your fridge, so don't be afraid to get a little, dare I say . . . ambitious.

1. Preheat the oven to 375°F. Grease a 9-inch pie pan with cooking spray.

2. **Bake the crust:** Working in a circular motion, place the sweet potato slices all around the bottom and sides of the pie pan in a single layer, cutting some in half so they fit with as few gaps as possible. It's okay if they touch or slightly overlap. The potatoes will shrink when baked. Use more cooking spray to coat the entire layer of potatoes. Bake until the sweet potatoes are fork-tender, about 20 to 25 minutes. Set aside to cool.

3. **Bake the bacon:** While the crust begins to cook, line a large baking sheet with parchment paper. Place the bacon on the baking sheet in a single layer, add to the oven with the sweet potatoes, and bake until the bacon has reached your desired level of crispiness, 20 to 30 minutes. Use tongs to transfer the bacon to a cutting board, blot with a paper towel to absorb excess grease, then chop the bacon into bite-sized pieces. Set aside.

4. **Caramelize the onions:** While the bacon and sweet potatoes cook, warm the oil in a large skillet over medium heat. Once the oil is hot, add the onions and salt and cook, stirring occasionally, until tender, soft, and a rich, dark, caramel color, about 35 minutes. If the onions are getting too dark or sticking too much, add a few teaspoons of water to deglaze the pan. Once the onions are caramelized, reduce the heat to low, stir in the spinach and garlic, and cook, stirring frequently, until the spinach wilts, about 2 minutes. Remove from the heat and evenly distribute the mixture over the baked sweet potato crust.

5. **Prepare the filling:** In a medium bowl, whisk the eggs, milk, salt, and a few grinds of pepper until pale, yellow, and fluffy, about 1 minute. Pour over the veggies and sprinkle goat cheese crumbles and bacon pieces evenly on top.

6. **Bake the quiche:** Bake until set, puffed, and golden on the edges of the egg, 30 to 35 minutes. Garnish with chopped chives. Allow to cool for at least 10 minutes before cutting into 6 slices. Store covered in the fridge for up to 5 days.

tip

Caramelize the onions up to 2 days ahead of time and store in the fridge until ready to use. Use on top of pizza, stir into pasta, or use in quesadillas or grilled sandwiches.

make it your way

TO MAKE VEGETARIAN: Leave out the bacon.

Swap out the bacon for 2 cooked, chopped breakfast chicken sausage links.

Swap Yukon Gold potatoes for sweet potatoes.

Swap feta cheese, sharp Cheddar cheese, or even a spicy Gouda for the goat cheese.

the breakfast burritos that should always be in your feezer (PAGE 60)

the breakfast burritos that should always be in your freezer

MAKES 10 TO 12 ■ PREP TIME: 30 MINUTES ■ COOK TIME: 30 MINUTES, PLUS 15 MINUTES ASSEMBLY TIME

ONION AND PEPPER MIXTURE

1 tablespoon extra-virgin olive oil

½ cup very finely diced yellow onion

½ cup very finely diced green bell pepper

½ cup very finely diced red bell pepper

½ cup very finely chopped fresh cilantro

1 jalapeño, seeded and very finely diced

1 (4-ounce) can diced green chiles

3 garlic cloves, minced

POTATOES

2 tablespoons extra-virgin olive oil

1½ pounds Yukon Gold potatoes, cut into ½-inch cubes

½ teaspoon adobo seasoning

½ teaspoon kosher salt

¼ teaspoon ground cumin

¼ teaspoon ground coriander

¼ teaspoon garlic powder

¼ teaspoon sweet paprika

Freshly ground black pepper

EGGS

10 large eggs

2 tablespoons milk of choice (or sub water)

½ teaspoon kosher salt

Freshly ground black pepper

1 tablespoon salted butter

Roughly one hour of prep work gets you ten wildly flavorful freezer-friendly burritos chock-full of protein and veggies that really fill you up with just a few minutes of reheating. And let's be honest, we enjoy them no matter the time of day it is (my kids love 'em for dinner). In fact, I practically lived off of my freezer stash after my babies were born. What really sets these apart is the addition of a fragrant Puerto Rican–inspired cooking base of peppers and spices, plus the addition of well-seasoned potatoes. Once you've tried these, you'll never go back to basic burritos again.

1. **Make the onion and pepper mixture:** In a large nonstick skillet or pot, warm the olive oil over medium heat. Once the oil is hot, add the onion, green and red bell peppers, cilantro, jalapeño, green chiles, and garlic. Sauté, stirring occasionally, until the onion and peppers are tender, about 5 minutes. Transfer the mixture to a large bowl and set aside.

2. **Make the potatoes:** In the same skillet over medium heat, add the olive oil, potatoes, adobo, salt, cumin, coriander, garlic powder, paprika, and pepper to taste. Cook, stirring occasionally, until the potatoes are browned and tender, 10 to 12 minutes. (If the potatoes are burning at all, cover the pan and/or add a tablespoon of water.) Stir the potatoes into the bowl of peppers and onions and set aside.

3. **Scramble the eggs:** In a large bowl, whisk the eggs with the milk, salt, and a few grinds of pepper. Wipe the same skillet clean, then place over medium-low heat and warm the butter, swirling to evenly distribute it around the surface of the pan as it melts. Pour in the eggs and cook undisturbed for 1 minute, then use a spatula to make figure eights throughout the eggs, folding over until the eggs are fluffy but still slightly wet, 2 to 4 minutes. Remove from the heat and set aside.

4. **Assemble:** Warm the tortillas in the microwave, in batches if necessary, for 30 seconds to make them easier to roll. Lay out the warm tortillas on a large surface. (I find it saves time to assemble all the burritos at once versus just a few at a time.) Evenly distribute the eggs in a line in the middle of each tortilla, about 2 to 3 tablespoons per burrito. Add 2 to 3 tablespoons of the potato mixture in a line next to the eggs, then add 2 to 3 tablespoons of pinto beans on the other side of the eggs. Top with 2 to 3 tablespoons of cheese, a few shakes of hot sauce, and a sprinkle of cilantro. Tuck the ends of each burrito in, then roll them up. You can either serve them immediately, refrigerate in an airtight container for 2 to 3 days, or wrap each burrito individually in plastic wrap, then in foil, and place in the freezer for up to 3 months. (Enjoy any leftover filling in extra burritos or with scrambled eggs.)

ASSEMBLY

10 to 12 medium-size soft flour or whole-wheat tortillas

1 (15-ounce) can pinto beans, drained and rinsed

6 ounces shredded sharp Cheddar cheese (1½ cups)

Your favorite hot sauce

½ cup chopped fresh cilantro

SERVING

1 tablespoon extra-virgin olive oil, for pan-frying (optional)

Plain whole-milk Greek yogurt or Spicy Cilantro Yogurt Sauce (page 236)

Avocado slices

Hot sauce or salsa

5. **To serve immediately:** If you like them a little crispy on the outside like I do, in a skillet, warm 1 tablespoon olive oil over medium heat. Once the oil is hot, place a burrito (or several) seam-side down and cook until golden brown, 3 to 4 minutes, then flip and cook until the other side is golden brown, another 3 to 4 minutes. Serve warm with Greek yogurt, avocado, and hot sauce.

6. **To serve from the fridge:** Preheat the oven to 350°F. Place the burritos on a baking sheet in the oven and bake until hot throughout, 5 to 10 minutes. Or you can microwave them until hot, 1 to 2 minutes. If you like them a little crispy on the outside, follow the directions in step 5.

7. **To serve from the freezer:** Remove each burrito from the foil and plastic wrap and microwave until warmed through, 2 to 3 minutes. For a crispier burrito, after microwaving, brush with a little olive oil, then transfer to a toaster oven and bake at 350°F for 10 minutes, or follow the skillet instructions in step 5.

cheddar, bacon & scallion grilled cheese breakfast naan

MAKES 2 SANDWICHES ■ PREP TIME: 10 MINUTES ■ COOK TIME: 30 MINUTES

BACON AND EGGS

4 slices thick-cut bacon

4 large eggs

1 tablespoon milk of choice (or sub water)

½ teaspoon kosher salt

Freshly ground black pepper

1 tablespoon salted butter

2 scallions, green parts only, thinly sliced

GRILLED CHEESE NAAN

1 tablespoon salted butter, at room temperature

2 pieces naan (I like Stonefire)

4 ounces shredded sharp Cheddar cheese (1 cup)

10 to 12 pickled jalapeño slices, to taste

1 to 2 cups arugula (optional)

1 tablespoon honey (optional)

Flaky sea salt (I like Maldon; optional)

the best bacon ever

My cold-oven method is one of the best ways to make bacon because it cooks at a lower temperature at first and renders the bacon fat beautifully, so that the bacon is perfectly cooked, golden brown and crispy.

On lazy weekend mornings, I started making these breakfast sandwiches, kicked up a notch with scallions and pickled jalapeños. (They also happen to be perfectly acceptable for dinner.) My husband, Tony, loves naan, the Indian flatbread, and I have become a fan of stuffing it with anything and everything. It's an easy way to create a flatbread sandwich that's crispy on the outside and soft on the inside—truly the best of both worlds and so freaking delicious. This sandwich can be a little messy with the drizzle of honey as a finish, but in my opinion, it's 100 percent worth adding a sweet element to really bring it to the next level.

1. **Cook the bacon:** Line a baking sheet with parchment paper. Place the bacon in a single layer on the prepared baking sheet and transfer to the middle rack of a cold oven. (This helps the bacon render more evenly and yields flat and crispy bacon.) Turn the oven to 425°F and bake until crisp, 15 to 25 minutes. Use tongs to transfer the bacon to a cutting board, blot with a paper towel to absorb excess grease, then tear the bacon slices in half and set aside.

2. **Cook the eggs:** In a large bowl, whisk the eggs with the milk, salt, and a few grinds of pepper. Place a medium nonstick pan over medium-low heat and melt the butter, swirling to evenly distribute it around the surface of the pan. Once the butter is melted, pour in the egg mixture and cook undisturbed for 1 minute, then use a spatula to make figure eights, folding the eggs over themselves to gently scramble. Cook until the eggs are fluffy but still slightly wet, 2 to 4 minutes. Remove from the heat, then gently stir in the scallions and transfer to a plate.

3. **Make the grilled cheese:** Spread ½ tablespoon of butter on one side of each piece of naan. Flip each naan over so that the buttered side is on the bottom. Top one half of each piece of naan with ¼ cup of cheese, half of the scrambled eggs, 4 bacon half slices, and 5 or 6 pickled jalapeños. Top each with the remaining ¼ cup of cheese, then fold the empty side over the stuffed side.

4. Wipe the same skillet clean, then warm over medium heat. When the pan is hot, add the sandwiches and cook until the cheese is melted and the naan is golden brown, 3 to 5 minutes per side. (If your sandwiches are coming unfolded, it helps to place a heavy-bottomed skillet, like a cast-iron, on top to keep them closed and achieve maximum contact with the hot pan. This helps get an extra-crispy crust!) Transfer the sandwiches to a cutting board. If using arugula, gently open each sandwich and stuff with half the arugula, then close. Drizzle each sandwich with ½ tablespoon of honey and sprinkle with flaky sea salt, then cut in half and enjoy immediately. (If you're worried about honey getting on your hands, you can always skip it and the salt.)

gotta love big salads

I'm a huge fan of salads, which is why I knew I had to have an entire chapter in my cookbook devoted to them. And I'm here to prove that salads aren't just supposed to be served on the side (though that's completely welcomed, too!). I *love* making these recipes for friends who assume that all salads are soggy and boring. They gasp at the array of colors, marvel at the crunch, and walk away happy and satisfied. I intentionally loaded up these salads with flavors, textures, and easy-to-whip-up dressings that demand attention. For the price of one restaurant salad, you can make an even better salad that you can meal prep for the week or feed your whole family for the night. I hope these recipes show your family and friends how salads can be a true source of both flavor and pleasure.

AK HOUSE SALADS

DAIRY-FREE (IF MODIFIED), **GLUTEN-FREE**,
VEGAN (IF MODIFIED), VEGETARIAN

SERVES 4 TO 6 AS A MAIN DISH, 6 TO 8 AS A SIDE SALAD
■ **PREP TIME: 15 MINUTES**
■ **COOK TIME: 10 TO 25 MINUTES**

There are two seasonal salads I love serving guests when they come over
during the summer and winter months. Everyone adores the flavors and
they're a breeze to whip up! They include simple homemade dressings that
can be made ahead of time, with fresh, unique ingredients, and a crunchy
element that makes them feel a little bit fancy. These are BIG salads for
serving, but feel free to halve the recipe for fewer people or add a protein
to make them a main meal. They're best enjoyed the day you serve them;
the colorful ingredients will be most delicious when gobbled up quickly.

1. Make the ingredients as directed in each recipe.

2. **Assemble the salad:** In a large bowl or on a serving platter, toss the
   greens with half of the dressing. Top with the remaining ingredients.
   Drizzle with the rest of the dressing or pass it at the table. Serve
   immediately.

make it your way

TO MAKE DAIRY-FREE AND
VEGAN: Leave out the cheese in
each recipe or use dairy-free feta.

PISTACHIO ALMOND CRUNCH

½ cup shelled pistachios

¼ cup sliced almonds

1 tablespoon pure maple syrup

¼ teaspoon kosher salt

ASSEMBLY

10 ounces (8 to 10 cups) spring mix, fresh baby spinach, or spinach

Basic But Worthy Balsamic Dressing (page 234)

2 cups halved strawberries or 2 just-ripe peaches, pitted and sliced or diced

¾ cup fresh corn kernels (from 1 ear)

1 avocado, sliced or diced

½ cup sliced red onion

4 ounces feta cheese, crumbled

Ripe, juicy fruit meets cool, crunchy greens.

Make the pistachio almond crunch: Line a plate with parchment paper. In a medium skillet, toast the pistachios and almonds over medium heat, stirring frequently, until lightly golden brown and fragrant, 7 to 10 minutes. Remove from the heat and immediately add the maple syrup and salt. Stir for about 30 seconds to coat the nuts, then transfer to the parchment paper to cool and harden before assembling the salad.

AK SUMMER HOUSE SALAD

Sweater weather deserves
color on the table.

SWEET POTATOES

2 medium sweet potatoes, cut into
½-inch cubes

2 tablespoons extra-virgin olive oil

1 tablespoon pure maple syrup

½ teaspoon kosher salt

½ teaspoon garlic powder

½ teaspoon chili powder

¼ teaspoon ground cinnamon

¼ teaspoon cayenne pepper
(optional, for a kick of heat)

SWEET AND SALTY PECANS

⅔ cup pecans (or sub walnuts)

1 tablespoon pure maple syrup

¼ teaspoon kosher salt

ASSEMBLY

10 ounces (8 to 10 cups) baby
spinach, arugula, or a mix

Maple–Apple Cider Dressing
(page 231)

2 ripe Bartlett pears or 1 large
Honeycrisp apple, cored and
thinly sliced

⅔ cup pomegranate seeds or
dried cranberries

¼ cup sliced red onion

4 ounces goat cheese or
Gorgonzola cheese,
crumbled

1. Preheat the oven to 375°F. Line a large baking sheet
   with parchment paper.

2. **Roast the sweet potatoes:** Place the sweet potato
   cubes on the prepared pan and drizzle with the
   olive oil and maple syrup, then sprinkle with the salt,
   garlic powder, chili powder, cinnamon, and cayenne
   (if using). Toss well to coat, then spread out in a
   single layer. Roast until the sweet potatoes are fork-
   tender, tossing halfway through, 25 to 30 minutes.
   Cool for 10 minutes.

3. **Make the sweet and salty pecans:** While the
   sweet potatoes roast, line a plate with parchment
   paper. In a medium skillet, toast the pecans over
   medium heat, stirring frequently, until fragrant,
   5 to 8 minutes. Remove from the heat and
   immediately add the maple syrup and salt. Stir for
   about 30 seconds to coat the nuts, then transfer
   to the parchment paper to cool and harden before
   assembling the salad.

superfood broccoli salad with grains, nuts & seeds

SERVES 4 AS A MAIN DISH, 6 AS A SIDE SALAD ■ PREP TIME: 20 MINUTES ■ COOK TIME: 15 MINUTES

FARRO

2 cups vegetable broth or water

1 cup pearled farro, rinsed and drained

½ teaspoon kosher salt

SALAD

1 large head of broccoli, florets only, or 5 cups broccoli florets, very finely chopped

1 (15-ounce) can chickpeas, drained and rinsed

1 cup shredded carrots (from 2 medium carrots)

¾ cup large finely chopped pitted Medjool dates (or dried cranberries or cherries)

½ cup chopped fresh parsley

½ cup chopped fresh cilantro

⅓ cup finely diced red onion

Lemon Vinaigrette (page 235) or Sunshine Dressing (page 230)

Freshly ground black pepper

MIX-INS

⅓ cup roasted salted pepitas

⅓ cup roasted shelled pistachios

⅓ cup toasted sliced almonds

4 ounces feta cheese, crumbled

Kosher salt

Every time I eat this salad, I feel like my skin is glowing thanks to all of the nutrients and vitamins in the veggies, herbs, and nuts! It boasts a beautiful array of colors, flavors, and textures and reminds me of a protein-rich, nutritious reinvention of the classic midwestern mayo-loaded broccoli salad that was a staple of my childhood. It's also great for make-ahead lunches—I love to scoop this up with pita crackers, or just serve them on the side for extra crunch.

1. **Make the farro:** In a medium pot, combine the broth, farro, and salt and place over medium-high heat. Bring to a boil, then cover, reduce the heat to low, and cook until tender, about 15 minutes. Remove from the heat and drain any excess water, then set aside to cool for 10 minutes.

2. **Toss the salad:** In a large bowl, combine the farro, broccoli, chickpeas, carrots, dates, parsley, cilantro, and red onion. Pour the dressing all over and use tongs to toss until well combined. Season to taste with freshly ground black pepper (I like lots!).

3. **Add the mix-ins:** Toss in the pepitas, pistachios, almonds, and feta. Taste and add additional salt, as necessary. Serve immediately.

4. **To store:** Keep any leftover salad in an airtight container and store in the fridge for up to 3 days.

tip

Save time by cooking the farro beforehand and storing in the fridge for up to 2 days until ready to use in this salad.

make it your way

TO MAKE DAIRY-FREE AND VEGAN: Leave out the feta or use dairy-free feta.

TO MAKE GLUTEN-FREE: Use 1 cup cooked and cooled quinoa instead of farro.

herby greek olive chickpea couscous salad

SERVES 4 AS A MAIN DISH, 6 AS A SIDE SALAD ▪ PREP TIME: 20 MINUTES ▪ COOK TIME: 10 MINUTES

Can a hearty vegetarian salad really be the life of the party? YES, and you'll believe it once you taste this unbelievably colorful creation that gets beauty from mini sweet peppers and fresh herbs, texture from pearl couscous, and heartiness from chickpeas. Trust me, it's going to be hard to stop spooning it into your mouth. It can be a side dish or a main, and you can store it for a few days in the fridge! This is a salad everyone will love.

1. **Cook the couscous:** In a medium pot, combine the water, couscous, and salt and place over medium-high heat. Bring to a boil, then cover, reduce the heat to low, and cook until tender, about 10 minutes. Drain the excess water, rinse with cold water, drain again, and transfer to a large bowl.

2. **Make the salad:** In the large bowl with the couscous, add the chickpeas, tomatoes, mini sweet peppers, cucumbers, Kalamata and Castelvetrano olives, pepperoncini, basil, parsley, and red onion and toss. Pour the dressing over everything and use a large spoon or tongs to toss until well combined. Add the feta cheese over the top and gently toss again to combine. Serve immediately.

3. **To store:** Keep any leftover salad in an airtight container and store in the fridge for up to 3 days.

COUSCOUS

2 cups water

1½ cups (8 ounces) pearl couscous

½ teaspoon kosher salt

SALAD

1 (15-ounce) can chickpeas, drained and rinsed

1½ cups cherry tomatoes, halved

8 mini sweet peppers (mix of orange, yellow, and red), stems removed and sliced

2 Persian cucumbers, quartered lengthwise and sliced (or sub 1 English cucumber, quartered lengthwise and sliced)

½ cup pitted, chopped Kalamata olives

½ cup pitted, chopped Castelvetrano green olives

½ cup sliced pepperoncini

½ cup chopped fresh basil

½ cup chopped fresh parsley

¼ cup halved and thinly sliced red onion

Greek-Inspired Lemon Vinaigrette (page 235)

4 ounces feta cheese, crumbled

make it your way

TO MAKE DAIRY-FREE OR VEGAN: Leave out the feta or use dairy-free feta.

TO MAKE GLUTEN-FREE: Sub a small gluten-free pasta of choice for the couscous.

Sub in any small pasta for the couscous, such as 8 ounces of ditalini or orzo. Pearled barley or farro are also excellent options.

southwestern brussels sprouts salad with cilantro lime vinaigrette

SERVES 4 AS A MAIN DISH, 6 AS A SIDE SALAD ■ PREP TIME: 25 MINUTES
■ COOK TIME: NO COOKING REQUIRED!

1 pound Brussels sprouts, ends trimmed and outer leaves removed

Heaping 1 cup shredded red cabbage

Cilantro Lime Vinaigrette (page 231)

1½ cups fresh corn kernels (from 2 ears)

1 (15-ounce) can black beans, drained and rinsed

1½ cups cherry tomatoes, halved

1 cup chopped fresh cilantro

½ cup sliced scallions

1 jalapeño, seeded and diced

4 ounces cotija cheese, crumbled (or sub feta cheese or goat cheese)

Kosher salt and freshly ground black pepper

TOPPINGS

2 avocados, sliced or diced

½ cup roasted and salted pepitas

Tortilla chips, crushed for topping or left whole for scooping

Did you know that shredded raw Brussels sprouts can create the most fabulous, stays-good-for-days, crunchy salad base? I love tossing them into this bright, herby salad with my favorite Cilantro Lime Vinaigrette. Its tart-sweet flavor sneaks into every nook and cranny of the sprouts, and everything stays crunchy in the fridge, just waiting to be scooped up with chips one day and enjoyed on its own the next. This will be the MVP of your next summer barbecue, and on a sweltering day, it's even better than nachos.

1. **Shred the Brussels:** In a food processor fitted with the slicing attachment, shred the Brussels sprouts. You can also thinly slice them with a sharp knife or carefully shred them using a mandoline.

2. **Prepare the salad:** In a large bowl, combine the shredded Brussels sprouts and red cabbage and pour the dressing all over, using tongs to toss everything together, then marinate at room temperature for about 15 minutes to add flavor to the Brussels sprouts and help break down the cruciferous veggies.

3. Add the corn, beans, tomatoes, cilantro, scallions, jalapeño, and cotija. Toss well to combine. Add kosher salt and freshly ground black pepper to taste.

4. **Top and serve:** Transfer to a large serving platter, if desired, or leave in the bowl. If serving immediately, garnish with avocado and pepitas. Top with crushed tortilla chips, or serve with whole chips to scoop up the salad. If preparing the salad ahead of time, wait to add the toppings until ready to serve.

5. **To store:** Keep any leftover salad in an airtight container and store in the fridge for up to 3 days.

make it your way

TO MAKE DAIRY-FREE OR VEGAN: Leave out the cheese or use dairy-free feta.

make it nutrient-dense

BOOST THE PROTEIN: Add in 2 cups of cooked and chopped or shredded chicken breast or cooked shrimp. I suggest doubling up on the Cilantro Lime Vinaigrette (page 231) and using it as a marinade for the chicken or shrimp. This is also amazing with my Hot-Honey Glazed Salmon That Goes with Everything (page 193).

avocado grape kale salad with peanut-tahini dressing

**SERVES 4 AS A MAIN DISH, 6 AS A SIDE SALAD ▦ PREP TIME: 30 MINUTES
▦ COOK TIME: NO COOKING REQUIRED!**

Humble brag: I started eating kale way before kale was cool to eat, and it's still one of my favorite bases for hearty salads. You absolutely must massage it with dressing and let it sit, which helps to break down its bitterness and texture and infuses every bite with flavor. This ingenious combination of juicy, sweet grapes, creamy avocado, and crunchy roasted peanuts—plus a savory Peanut-Tahini Dressing—was inspired by one that used to be on the menu at Crosby's Kitchen, one of my go-to Chicago restaurants. Do not forget the fresh mint and cilantro—they are musts for this show-stopping salad!

1. **Make the salad:** In a large bowl, combine the kale and dressing, reserving 1 to 2 tablespoons of dressing for later. Use your hands to massage the kale with the dressing for about 5 minutes or so; you want to get it mixed really well to help break down the bitterness of the kale. Let it sit and marinate at room temperature for 10 minutes.

2. Using tongs, toss the cabbage, cilantro, and mint with the kale.

3. **Add the toppings:** If preparing the salad ahead of time, wait to add the toppings until ready to serve. If serving immediately, transfer the salad to a serving platter, if desired, then top with the grapes, avocado slices, scallions, and peanuts. Drizzle the salad with the extra reserved dressing. Season with salt and pepper to taste.

4. **To store:** Keep any leftover salad in an airtight container and store in the fridge for up to 4 days.

SALAD

8 cups stemmed and finely chopped Tuscan or Lacinato kale

Peanut-Tahini Dressing (page 233)

1 to 2 cups shredded green or red cabbage

½ cup chopped fresh cilantro

2 tablespoons chopped fresh mint

TOPPINGS

1 cup halved seedless red grapes

1 avocado, sliced

⅓ cup sliced scallions

⅓ cup finely chopped roasted peanuts

Kosher salt and freshly ground black pepper

make it nutrient-dense

ADD PROTEIN OF CHOICE: Toss in ¾ cup of roasted chickpeas and/or ½ cup of cooked quinoa. This salad is also excellent with 1 to 2 cups of shredded rotisserie chicken.

farmers' market arugula peach pasta salad

SERVES 6 AS A MAIN DISH, 8 TO 10 AS A SIDE DISH ■ PREP TIME: 20 MINUTES
■ COOK TIME: 10 MINUTES

SALAD

Kosher salt

8 ounces fusilli or bowtie pasta

Lemon Basil Vinaigrette (page 235)

4 ounces feta cheese or goat cheese, crumbled

5 ounces (4 to 6 cups) arugula

1½ cups cherry tomatoes, halved

1½ cups fresh corn kernels (from 2 ears)

2 large slightly ripe but still firm peaches (or sub nectarines), pitted and sliced

2 Persian cucumbers, sliced

½ cup Pickled Red Onions (page 237)

Freshly ground black pepper

GARNISH

1 avocado, sliced

2 ounces feta cheese or goat cheese, crumbled

⅓ cup roasted shelled pistachios, roughly chopped

6 to 8 large fresh basil leaves, torn

Pasta salad just got a major upgrade, and in my family, it's not summer until this pretty salad has landed at a barbecue or two! This one includes all of my favorite summer produce and is essential for the early days of stone fruit season, when sun-kissed peaches and nectarines start appearing at farmers' markets. Grab them along with sweet corn, cherry tomatoes, and cucumbers and toss 'em with a sweet, tart, and herby vinaigrette.

1. **Make the salad:** Bring a large pot of generously salted water to a boil over high heat. Stir in the pasta and cook according to package directions until al dente. Reserve ¼ cup of pasta water, then drain the pasta and transfer to a large bowl.

2. Pour the dressing over the warm pasta and add a little of the reserved pasta water to moisten. Immediately add the feta and gently toss. Cover and refrigerate for at least 1 hour or up to 2 days if you want to serve this as a cold pasta salad. Otherwise, to serve slightly warm, proceed with the recipe and serve immediately.

3. Add the arugula, cherry tomatoes, corn, peaches, cucumbers, and Pickled Red Onions to the pasta. Toss to combine. Taste and add salt and a few grinds of pepper. The pasta salad will keep well in an airtight container in the fridge for up to 3 days.

4. **Garnish:** When you're ready to serve, top with avocado slices, extra feta, pistachios, and basil.

make it your way

TO MAKE GLUTEN-FREE: Use gluten-free pasta.

FARMERS' MARKET ARUGULA PEACH PASTA SALAD WITH SALAMI (OR BACON): Make this even heartier and more flavorful by adding in a few ounces of sliced, chopped salami or chopped bacon.

spicy buffalo ranch chicken chop chop salad

SERVES 4 AS A MAIN DISH, 6 AS A SIDE SALAD ▪ PREP TIME: 30 MINUTES ▪ COOK TIME: 20 MINUTES

CHICKEN

¼ cup buffalo sauce

1 tablespoon extra-virgin olive oil or avocado oil

½ teaspoon kosher salt

½ teaspoon garlic powder

½ teaspoon sweet paprika

¼ teaspoon dried dill

¼ teaspoon onion powder

1 pound boneless, skinless chicken breast

SALAD

6 cups shredded green cabbage

1½ cups fresh corn kernels (from 2 ears)

1 cup shredded carrots (from 2 medium carrots)

1 red bell pepper, diced

1 bunch of fresh cilantro, chopped (about 1 cup)

½ cup sliced scallions

1 jalapeño, seeded and diced

Pickled Jalapeño Ranch Dressing (page 234)

GRILLING AND TOPPINGS

2 tablespoons buffalo sauce

1½ cups tortilla strips or slightly crushed tortilla chips

2 avocados, diced

½ cup roasted and salted pepitas

2 ounces shredded Cheddar cheese (½ cup)

¼ cup chopped fresh cilantro

¼ cup sliced scallions

Crunch for days! This is one of my go-to recipes for when friends come over, because it stays crunchy for a while, entertains a big crowd with little work, and combines my need for spicy food with my husband Tony's need for ranch on everything. I especially love serving this to fans of traditional fried buffalo wings. They get their buffalo chicken fix, plus a healthy dose of fresh veggies while they're at it. It's both hearty and refreshing, so you can enjoy it in all seasons. P.S. If you love a good "fried" buffalo chicken salad, skip the grilled chicken and try topping this with my Crispy Cornflake Chicken Tenders (page 147) tossed with a few tablespoons of buffalo sauce! YUM.

1. **Make the marinade:** In a large bowl, whisk the buffalo sauce, olive oil, salt, garlic powder, paprika, dried dill, and onion powder.

2. **Prepare the chicken:** Place the chicken breasts on a cutting board and cover with plastic wrap. Use a meat mallet to pound the chicken until it is about ½ inch thick. Remove the plastic wrap and add the chicken to the marinade and use tongs to toss until well coated. Cover with plastic wrap and marinate for 20 minutes at room temperature or up to 2 hours in the fridge. Before cooking, remove the chicken from the fridge and bring to room temperature for 20 to 30 minutes.

3. Preheat the grill to 400°F and scrape off any leftover bits from the grates, or preheat the oven to 400°F.

4. **Make the salad:** In a large bowl, toss the cabbage, corn, carrots, bell pepper, cilantro, scallions, and jalapeño. Pour over about half of the dressing and toss to coat evenly. Transfer to a serving platter or large salad bowl.

5. **Cook the chicken:**
   - ▪ **TO GRILL:** Cook the chicken with the lid closed until a meat thermometer inserted into the center reads 165°F, 7 to 9 minutes per side.
   - ▪ **TO BAKE:** Place chicken on a greased baking sheet and bake until a meat thermometer inserted into the center reads 165°F, 15 to 20 minutes.

6. **Finish the salad:** Transfer the chicken to a cutting board, brush with the buffalo sauce, and allow to rest for at least 5 minutes to retain the juiciness of the chicken. Cut diagonally against the grain or chop into cubes. If serving immediately, place chicken on the salad, then drizzle with the remaining dressing, if desired. Top the salad with the tortilla strips, avocado, pepitas, Cheddar, cilantro, and scallions. If preparing the salad ahead of time, wait to add toppings until ready to serve.

7. **To store:** Keep any leftover salad in an airtight container and store in the fridge for up to 3 days.

make it your way

TO MAKE GLUTEN-FREE: Instead of soy sauce, use coconut aminos or tamari. Leave out the wonton strips and replace with roasted chickpeas, if desired.

TO MAKE VEGETARIAN AND VEGAN: Leave out the chicken.

sesame chicken cabbage crunch salad

SERVES 4 AS A MAIN DISH, 6 AS A SIDE SALAD ■ PREP TIME: 30 MINUTES, PLUS 20 MINUTES MARINATING TIME ■ COOK TIME: 15 MINUTES

Oh, cabbage. It's one of those veggies that seems to lurk in your fridge for weeks on end, which is exactly how it became the star of this crunchy, fresh, absolutely delicious salad. Soon I was tossing in a rainbow of veggies, juicy chicken that I marinated in my favorite flavors like soy sauce, garlic, and ginger, plus a number of outrageously crunchy toppings. I drizzled on a beautiful homemade sesame ginger dressing, and after each bite, I couldn't stop saying "WOW. This is so good!" It's also a great excuse to munch on those crispy little wonton strips.

1. **Make the marinade:** In a large bowl, whisk the soy sauce, brown sugar, garlic, tahini, sesame oil, rice vinegar, ginger, and red pepper flakes.

2. **Prepare the chicken:** Place the chicken breasts on a cutting board and cover with plastic wrap. Use a meat mallet to pound the chicken until it is about ½ inch thick. Remove the plastic wrap and add the chicken to the marinade and use tongs to toss until well coated. Cover with plastic wrap and marinate at room temperature for 20 minutes or up to 2 hours in the fridge. Before cooking, remove the chicken from the fridge and bring to room temperature for 20 to 30 minutes.

3. Preheat the grill to 400°F and scrape off any leftover bits from the grates, or preheat the oven to 400°F.

4. **Assemble the salad:** In a large bowl, combine the green and red cabbage, carrots, bell pepper, cilantro, scallions, and jalapeño. Cover and set aside until you're ready to serve.

5. **Cook the chicken:**
   - **TO GRILL:** Cook the chicken with the lid closed until a meat thermometer inserted into the center reads 165°F, 7 to 9 minutes per side.
   - **TO BAKE:** Place the chicken on a greased baking sheet and bake until a meat thermometer inserted into the center reads 165°F, 15 to 20 minutes.

6. Transfer the chicken to a cutting board, and allow it to rest for at least 5 minutes to retain the juiciness of the chicken, then cut diagonally against the grain.

7. **Finish the salad:** Add the dressing to the salad and toss with tongs until the veggies are well coated. Transfer the salad to a large platter or salad bowl and top with the sliced chicken. If serving immediately, garnish with wonton strips, almonds, cashews, cilantro, scallions, sesame seeds, and jalapeño slices. If preparing salad ahead of time, wait to add the toppings until ready to serve. Keep any leftover salad in an airtight container in the fridge for up to 3 days.

CHICKEN

¼ cup low-sodium soy sauce

2 tablespoons packed dark brown sugar

2 garlic cloves, grated

1 tablespoon tahini

1 tablespoon toasted sesame oil

1 tablespoon rice vinegar

1 tablespoon grated fresh ginger

½ teaspoon red pepper flakes

1 pound boneless, skinless chicken breast

SALAD

4 cups shredded green cabbage

2 cups shredded red cabbage

1 cup shredded carrots (from 2 medium carrots)

1 red bell pepper, thinly sliced

¾ cup chopped fresh cilantro

½ cup sliced scallions

1 jalapeño, seeded and diced

SERVING

Sesame Ginger Dressing (page 230)

½ cup crispy wonton strips

⅓ cup toasted sliced almonds

⅓ cup roasted cashew halves

2 tablespoons chopped fresh cilantro

2 tablespoons sliced scallions

1 tablespoon toasted sesame seeds

Fresh jalapeño slices

roasted carrot cauliflower quinoa salad with sunshine dressing

SERVES 4 AS A MAIN DISH, 6 AS A SIDE SALAD ■ PREP TIME: 20 MINUTES ■ COOK TIME: 30 MINUTES

ROASTED VEGGIES AND QUINOA

4 medium carrots, cut in half lengthwise and cut into 2-inch diagonal slices

2 cups cauliflower florets

1 tablespoon extra-virgin olive oil

1 teaspoon kosher salt

½ teaspoon ground cumin

½ teaspoon ground turmeric

½ teaspoon garlic powder

¼ teaspoon cayenne pepper (optional, for a kick of heat)

Freshly ground black pepper

1⅔ cups water

¾ cup uncooked white quinoa, rinsed and drained

MIX-INS

¾ cup thawed frozen peas

⅓ cup thinly sliced scallions

⅓ cup chopped fresh cilantro

⅓ cup chopped fresh parsley

⅓ cup pitted Medjool dates, chopped, or dried cherries

Sunshine Dressing (page 230)

GARNISHES

⅓ cup roasted and salted shelled pistachios or sliced, toasted almonds

4 ounces feta cheese, crumbled

Zest of 1 lemon (optional)

Extra chopped fresh parsley and cilantro

I'm all about a non-lettuce salad and you should be, too. I often make this for myself to devour all week long, but I also love layering all the beautiful, vibrant ingredients on a platter and wow-ing guests. Seriously, prepare for them to drop their jaws, then do a backflip on their first bite. Yes, it's that good, thanks to Moroccan-inspired spiced roasted carrots and cauliflower, fresh herbs, sweet chewy dates, crunchy pistachios, and a dressing that's sweet, bold, and vibrant. JUST MAKE IT ALREADY.

1. Preheat the oven to 400°F. Line a large baking sheet with parchment paper.

2. **Prepare the roasted veggies and quinoa:** Add the carrots and cauliflower to the prepared pan. Drizzle with the olive oil and sprinkle with ½ teaspoon of the salt, the cumin, turmeric, garlic powder, cayenne (if using), and a few grinds of pepper. Toss well to coat, then spread in a single layer. Roast until the veggies are tender and golden, flipping halfway, 25 to 30 minutes. Cool for 5 minutes.

3. **Meanwhile, cook the quinoa:** In a medium pot, combine the water, quinoa, and remaining ½ teaspoon salt. Place over high heat and bring to a boil. Cover, reduce the heat to low and simmer until tender, about 15 minutes. Remove from heat, fluff with a fork, then re-cover and steam until fluffy, 5 to 10 minutes. Allow quinoa to cool for 15 to 20 minutes before assembling the salad.

4. **Add the mix-ins:** In a large bowl, combine the cooked quinoa, roasted carrots and cauliflower, peas, scallions, cilantro, parsley, and dates. Pour the dressing over the salad and mix well to combine. Transfer to a serving platter, if desired.

5. **Add the garnishes:** Top with pistachios, feta, lemon zest (if using), and extra herbs. Serve warm or cold.

6. **To store:** Keep any leftover salad in an airtight container and store in the fridge for up to 5 days.

make it your way

TO MAKE DAIRY-FREE OR VEGAN: Leave out the cheese or use dairy-free feta.

damn good soup

When life feels chaotic and unsettled, making and eating these soups gives me the feeling of a hug in a bowl. There's something nostalgic and comforting about the aroma of cozy spices simmering away on the stovetop and perfuming my kitchen that brings me back down to Earth and feels like home. Each soup is unique and tells a story: about family, growth, and changing seasons. I hope you make them all year round!

gigi's comforting & healing root vegetable soup

SERVES 4 ■ PREP TIME: 20 MINUTES ■ COOK TIME: 40 MINUTES

2 tablespoons extra-virgin olive oil

1 small yellow onion, finely chopped

½ medium green bell pepper, finely chopped

½ medium orange bell pepper, finely chopped

2 to 3 cups cubed butternut squash (½-inch cubes)

1 medium sweet potato, peeled and cut into ½-inch cubes

2 medium carrots, sliced

1 medium parsnip, sliced

3 garlic cloves, minced

1 teaspoon adobo seasoning

1 teaspoon ground cumin

1 teaspoon ground coriander

1 teaspoon ground turmeric

½ teaspoon curry powder

½ teaspoon dried oregano

½ teaspoon kosher salt, plus more to taste

Freshly ground black pepper

6 cups vegetable broth

2 cups fresh spinach, chopped

1 cup frozen corn

⅓ cup chopped fresh cilantro

Meet one of the most restorative soups you'll ever try. When I was pregnant with my third son, Lachlan, and felt very ill, my mom swooped in with this soup full of nourishing root vegetables and healing spices. She also let me rest and helped take care of my older sons, who love their grandma "Gigi." After Lachlan was born, I continued to crave this comforting soup with its slightly sweetened broth, thanks to butternut squash and sweet potato. I sipped on it almost every week while writing this cookbook, and I know I'll make it regularly the second that sweater weather rolls around each fall. I hope you will, too! I highly recommend pairing it with my No-Knead Pumpkin Cranberry Walnut Harvest Bread (page 42).

1. In a large pot or Dutch oven, warm the olive oil over medium heat. Once the oil is hot, add the onion, and bell peppers and sauté, stirring occasionally, until softened, 5 to 7 minutes.

2. Stir in the butternut squash, sweet potato, carrots, parsnip, garlic, adobo, cumin, coriander, turmeric, curry powder, dried oregano, salt, and a few grinds of pepper. Cook for 1 minute, stirring frequently, then stir in the broth. Bring to a gentle boil, then cover, reduce the heat to medium-low so the soup simmers, and cook, stirring occasionally, until the vegetables are fork-tender, 15 to 20 minutes.

3. Stir in the spinach, corn, and cilantro and simmer, uncovered, to allow the flavors to combine, 5 to 10 minutes. Taste and adjust the seasonings as necessary. Ladle into bowls and serve immediately.

4. **To store:** Let the soup cool completely, then store it in an airtight container in the fridge for up to 5 days. For freezing instructions, see page 21.

make it your way

HEARTY HARVEST VEGETABLE & GRAINS SOUP: For an even heartier soup, add a heaping ½ cup (about 4 ounces) of uncooked pearl couscous or pearl barley with the squash.

MIX AND MATCH VEGETABLES: Try adding frozen green beans in addition to corn and/or potatoes instead of sweet potatoes.

make it nutrient-dense

FOR A BOOST OF PROTEIN: Stir in 2 cups of cooked, shredded chicken or 1 (15-ounce) can drained and rinsed chickpeas or white beans with the squash.

make it your way

TO MAKE DAIRY-FREE: Skip the yogurt and top with more coconut milk.

TO MAKE VEGAN: Use roasted peanuts or cashews instead of honey-roasted and skip the yogurt.

This soup works wonderfully with pumpkin or kabocha squash.

make it nutrient-dense

Stir in 1 cup of cooked green lentils and 2 cups of fresh spinach to the soup in step 4 for an additional boost of fiber and plant-based protein.

golden curry coconut butternut squash soup

SERVES 4 TO 6 ■ PREP TIME: 15 MINUTES ■ COOK TIME: 1 HOUR 30 MINUTES

I love a simple, silky-smooth butternut squash soup but I REALLY love pairing the sweet squash with rich, creamy coconut milk and a hint of peanut flavor. Add some warming curry spices and a sprinkling of honey-roasted peanuts, herbs, and a little hint of spice on top and I'm in love. Soak it all up with warm naan and you'll be in heaven, too.

1. Preheat the oven to 400°F. Line a baking sheet with parchment paper.

2. **Roast the butternut squash:** Place a towel on your counter and place a cutting board on top; this will help keep it from sliding. Use a sharp knife to cut off both ends of the butternut squash (about ½ inch off each end). Place the squash upright and cut vertically down the middle. Use a spoon to scoop out the seeds. Place the halves on the prepared pan, drizzle with 1 tablespoon of the olive oil, and use your hands to rub the squash all over with oil, then place flesh-side down and roast until the squash is very tender, about 1 hour (you should be able to pierce it easily with a fork). Cool for at least 10 minutes, then scoop out the flesh, transfer it to a high-powered blender, and set aside without blending (if you don't have a high-powered blender, put the squash in a medium bowl for now). Discard the peel.

3. **Cook and blend the soup:** In a large pot, warm the remaining 1 tablespoon of oil over medium heat. Once the oil is hot, add the onion and sauté, stirring occasionally, until softened, 3 to 5 minutes. Add the garlic, ginger, turmeric, curry powder, and cayenne (if using) and cook, stirring constantly, until fragrant, about 30 seconds. Transfer the mixture to the blender with the butternut squash, then add the broth, coconut milk, peanut butter, salt, and a few grinds of pepper. Protecting your hand with a dish towel, crack the lid slightly away from you to let the steam escape. Blend on low, then gradually increase the speed to high and blend until completely smooth and creamy, 1 to 2 minutes. (Alternatively, you can skip the blender and add the butternut squash, coconut milk, broth, peanut butter, salt, and pepper to the large pot with the onions and use an immersion blender to blend the soup until smooth.)

4. Pour the puree back into the large pot you used to cook the onions and place over medium heat. Bring to a simmer and cook until the soup reaches your desired thickness, 15 to 20 minutes. If the soup is too thick for your liking, stir in a little more broth a splash at a time. Taste and adjust the seasoning of the soup as necessary, adding another tablespoon of nut butter if you like, or a squeeze of fresh lime juice (if using).

5. **Top and serve:** Ladle the soup into bowls and top with cilantro, peanuts, a spoonful of Greek yogurt (if using), and hot sauce. Serve with naan.

6. **To store:** Cool completely, then store in an airtight container in the fridge for up to 5 days. Reheat in the microwave or on the stovetop. For freezing instructions, see page 21.

SQUASH

1 (2-pound) butternut squash

2 tablespoons extra-virgin olive oil

1 medium yellow onion, chopped

3 garlic cloves, minced

1 tablespoon grated fresh ginger

1 tablespoon grated fresh turmeric (or sub ½ teaspoon ground turmeric)

1 tablespoon curry powder

¼ teaspoon cayenne pepper (optional, for a kick of heat)

3 cups vegetable broth, plus more as needed

1 (15-ounce) can light coconut milk

2 tablespoons natural creamy peanut butter or cashew butter, plus more to taste

1 teaspoon kosher salt, plus more to taste

Freshly ground black pepper

Fresh lime juice (optional)

TOPPINGS AND SERVING

½ cup chopped fresh cilantro

¼ cup chopped honey-roasted peanuts or cashews

½ cup plain whole-milk Greek yogurt (optional)

Hot sauce or chile crisp

Warm naan (I like Stonefire)

roasty toasty tomato soup with herbed grilled cheese naan (PAGE 94)

VEGETARIAN

roasty toasty tomato soup with herbed grilled cheese naan

SERVES 4 ■ PREP TIME: 20 MINUTES ■ COOK TIME: 1 HOUR

VEGGIES AND GARLIC

2½ pounds Roma or plum tomatoes, cut in half vertically

2 medium yellow onions, cut into 1-inch chunks

1 large red bell pepper, cut in half vertically, stem and seeds removed

3 tablespoons extra-virgin olive oil

1½ teaspoons kosher salt, plus more to taste

Freshly ground black pepper

1 head of garlic

2 cups vegetable broth, plus more to taste

½ cup packed fresh basil leaves

2 teaspoons dried oregano

½ cup full-fat coconut milk or heavy cream

HERBED GRILLED CHEESE NAAN

4 tablespoons (57 grams) salted butter, softened

2 tablespoons chopped fresh herbs, such as thyme, rosemary, basil, and/or parsley

½ teaspoon garlic powder

¼ teaspoon kosher salt

4 pieces naan (I like Stonefire)

4 ounces shredded sharp Cheddar cheese (1 cup)

4 ounces shredded Gruyère cheese (1 cup)

Flaky sea salt (I like Maldon)

EXCUSE ME! AN HERB BUTTER GRILLED CHEESE NAAN that gets dipped into the best homemade tomato soup you will ever have in your freaking life. Garlicky, salty, herby: It's a total flavor explosion. The Indian flatbread makes splendid grilled cheese that's soft on the inside, crispy on the outside, and is a perfectly acceptable snack or quick dinner option when you have zero time. Tomato soup was, oddly, one of my biggest pregnancy cravings, and after I started to make this version, I never went back to boxed. The tomatoes get all roasty-toasty and golden in the oven with sweet onions. Make this any time of year, but it's best when tomatoes are ripe and in season and trust me: It's absolutely worth turning on your oven.

1. Put a rack in the middle of the oven and preheat to 400°F.

2. On a large baking sheet, combine the tomatoes, onions, and red bell pepper and drizzle with 2 tablespoons of the olive oil. Generously season with ½ teaspoon of kosher salt and a few grinds of pepper. Toss well to coat, then spread out in a single layer.

3. **Prep the garlic:** Peel and discard the outermost papery layers of the whole garlic head, leaving the skins intact. Using a sharp knife, cut ¼-inch off from the stem end of the head so that the individual cloves of garlic are exposed. Place the garlic in a medium square piece of foil, drizzle with the remaining 1 tablespoon of olive oil, then loosely wrap in the foil and place on the pan with the veggies.

4. **Roast the veggies and garlic:** Transfer the baking sheet to the middle rack and roast undisturbed in the oven until the tomatoes are tender and juicy and the peppers and onions are soft, about 45 minutes. Cool for 10 minutes.

5. Remove the garlic from the foil packet and discard the foil. Use your fingers to squeeze out the roasted garlic from the skin (discarding the skin) directly into a high-powered blender. (Put the garlic in a large pot if using an immersion blender.)

6. **Blend the soup:** Add the roasted vegetables, broth, basil, dried oregano, remaining 1 teaspoon of salt, and pepper to taste. Protecting your hand with a dish towel, crack the lid slightly away from you to let the steam escape. Blend until smooth, adding more broth as needed to achieve your desired soup consistency, about 2 minutes. (If using an immersion blender, add all the ingredients to the pot with the garlic and blend until smooth.)

4 tablespoons full-fat coconut milk or heavy cream

Julienned fresh basil or chopped fresh parsley

Red pepper flakes

7. **Cook the soup:** Gently pour the mixture into a large pot and place over medium heat. Gently stir in the full-fat coconut milk or heavy cream. Bring to a simmer, then cook uncovered to allow the flavors to combine, stirring occasionally, 15 to 20 minutes. Taste and adjust the seasonings as necessary.

8. **Prep the grilled cheese naan:** While the soup simmers, in a medium bowl, mix together the butter, herbs, garlic powder, and salt with a fork until well combined. Spread the butter on one side of each piece of naan. Flip each naan over so that the buttered side is on the bottom.

9. In a medium bowl, mix the Cheddar and Gruyère. Top half of each piece of naan with about ½ cup of the cheese mixture. Fold over the other half to close.

10. **Cook the naan grilled cheese:** Warm a large skillet over medium heat. Once the pan is hot, add the naan sandwiches, two at a time, and cook until the cheese is melted and the naan is golden brown on both sides, 3 to 5 minutes per side. (If your sandwiches are coming unfolded, it helps to place a heavy-bottomed skillet, like a cast-iron, on top to keep them closed and achieve maximum contact with the hot pan. This helps get an extra crispy crust!) Use a spatula to transfer the sandwiches to a cutting board. Repeat with the remaining sandwiches, wiping out the skillet between batches, if necessary. Sprinkle the sandwiches with flaky sea salt and cut into large triangles.

11. **Serve:** Ladle the hot soup into bowls and swirl a spoonful or two of the coconut milk on top. Garnish with basil and red pepper flakes. Serve right away alongside the naan grilled cheese for dipping.

12. **To store:** Cool completely, then store in an airtight container in the fridge for up to 5 days. Reheat in the microwave or on the stovetop. For freezing instructions, see page 21.

mini ginger cilantro chichen meatball soup
with peanut-curry broth (PAGE 98)

mini ginger cilantro chicken meatball soup with peanut-curry broth

SERVES 4 ■ PREP TIME: 30 MINUTES ■ COOK TIME: 40 MINUTES

CHICKEN MEATBALLS

1 pound 93% lean ground chicken (or sub ground turkey)

½ cup panko bread crumbs

¼ cup finely chopped scallions

¼ cup finely chopped fresh cilantro

1 jalapeño, seeded and finely diced

1 large egg

3 garlic cloves, minced

1 tablespoon packed dark brown sugar (or sub coconut sugar)

1 tablespoon grated fresh ginger

1 teaspoon kosher salt

¼ teaspoon cayenne pepper (optional, for a kick of heat)

Freshly ground black pepper

1 to 2 tablespoons toasted sesame oil, plus more as needed

What soup isn't more fun with the addition of cute mini chicken meatballs? Especially if they're swimming in a delicious, rich, Thai-influenced peanut-curry broth that's a little bit spicy, a little bit bright, and all lightened up with tons of fresh herbs. If you can get your hands on fresh turmeric, it will pay off in flavor and vibrant color. Ladle the meatballs and broth over rice or rice noodles for a satisfying, umami-rich meal!

1. **Make the chicken meatballs:** Fill a medium bowl with water and place it on the counter. In a large bowl, combine the ground chicken, bread crumbs, scallions, cilantro, jalapeño, egg, garlic, brown sugar, ginger, salt, cayenne (if using), and a few grinds of pepper. Use clean hands to mix until well combined; avoid overmixing, otherwise the meatballs will be tough. Form the mixture into meatballs about the size of a marble, 45 to 50 mini meatballs total. Dip your hands into the water between each meatball to prevent sticking.

2. In a large pot over medium-high heat, warm 1 to 2 tablespoons of sesame oil. Once the oil is hot, add the meatballs in batches, spacing the meatballs ½ inch apart, and brown on all sides, about 5 minutes total. Use a slotted spoon to transfer to a plate and set aside. Add more oil if necessary between batches, and repeat with the remaining meatballs.

SOUP

1 tablespoon toasted
sesame oil

2 medium carrots, thinly sliced

½ cup sliced scallions

6 garlic cloves, minced

1 tablespoon grated fresh
ginger

1 tablespoon grated fresh
turmeric (or ½ teaspoon
ground turmeric)

4 cups low-sodium chicken
broth

1 (15-ounce) can light coconut
milk

¼ cup natural creamy peanut
butter

¼ cup low-sodium soy sauce

1 tablespoon curry powder

1 tablespoon sambal oelek or
sriracha (optional)

6 bok choy ribs with leaves,
roughly chopped

1 to 2 teaspoons fish sauce,
to taste

Juice of 1 lime

SERVING

8 ounces cooked rice noodles
or 2 cups cooked rice

½ cup chopped fresh cilantro

½ cup torn fresh Thai basil
leaves (or sub regular basil)

¼ cup torn fresh mint leaves

¼ cup sliced scallions

¼ cup chopped peanuts

3. **Make the soup:** In the same pot, warm the sesame oil over medium heat. Once the oil is hot, add the carrots and scallions and sauté, stirring occasionally, until softened, 2 to 3 minutes. Stir in the garlic, ginger, and turmeric and sauté, stirring constantly, until fragrant, about 30 seconds. Add the broth, coconut milk, peanut butter, soy sauce, curry powder, and sambal oelek (if using); stir until well combined. Use a large spoon to gently drop in a few meatballs at a time until they are all in the pot. Bring the broth to a gentle boil, then reduce the heat and simmer uncovered until the meatballs are cooked through, about 15 minutes. Add the bok choy, fish sauce, and lime juice and simmer until bok choy is tender, about 5 minutes.

4. **Serve:** Divide the rice noodles or rice among 4 bowls. Ladle the soup over and top with cilantro, basil, and mint. Finish each bowl with 1 tablespoon of scallions and chopped peanuts. Serve immediately.

5. **To store:** Cool completely, then store it in an airtight container in the fridge for up to 5 days. Reheat in the microwave or on the stovetop. For freezing instructions, see page 22; do not freeze the soup with the rice or noodles.

make it your way

TO MAKE GLUTEN-FREE: Use gluten-free panko bread crumbs, coconut aminos or tamari instead of soy sauce, and gluten-free fish sauce.

Swap 2 cups of chopped spinach for the bok choy.

make it your way

CHEESY SKILLET BLACK BEAN DIP: Preheat the oven to 350°F. Skip the blending and use a slotted spoon to transfer 3½ cups of beans to a large oven-safe skillet. Mix in 2 ounces (½ cup) of shredded Cheddar cheese, ½ cup of salsa of your choice, and ½ cup of Greek yogurt and stir until well combined. Top with 4 ounces (1 cup) of shredded Cheddar cheese and bake until the cheese is melted, 20 to 25 minutes. Top with the garnishes and serve with tortilla chips for dipping.

NACHOS OR RICE TOPPING: Skip the blending and use a slotted spoon to top tortilla chips or rice. Add garnishes as desired.

black bean soup with creamy jalapeño cashew sauce

**SERVES 6 TO 8 ▪ PREP TIME: 15 MINUTES, PLUS 8 HOURS SOAKING TIME
▪ COOK TIME: 2 HOURS 25 MINUTES**

I truly, madly, deeply love a good black bean soup. I'm talking about the ones you find on a restaurant menu that have a silky-smooth black bean puree and some whole beans, too. You'll need to soak the dried beans overnight, then simmer them for a few hours, but I promise, this recipe is worth all of this time and effort; canned beans just won't be the same. Toppings like my Jalapeño Lime Cashew Sauce and salty, crunchy corn chips bring extra flavor and texture. You can also serve the beans over rice, or just melt cheese on top and scoop with chips for an irresistible cheesy bean dip.

1. **Prepare the black beans:** In a large pot, combine the water and beans and soak at room temperature for 8 to 10 hours. (After 10 hours, the beans will begin to absorb too much water and may lose some of their texture and flavor.)

2. Drain the beans and return them to the pot. Add the broth and bay leaves, place over high heat, and bring to a boil. Boil for 1 to 2 minutes, then reduce the heat to low, cover, and simmer gently, stirring occasionally, until the beans are tender and soft, 1 to 2 hours. Remove the bay leaves and keep the beans over low heat.

3. **Make the veggies:** In a medium skillet, warm the olive oil over medium heat. Once the oil is hot, add the onion, bell peppers, cilantro, jalapeño, and garlic and sauté, stirring occasionally, until softened, about 5 minutes. Reduce the heat to low, add the cumin, coriander, paprika, and dried oregano, and cook, stirring frequently, until the spices are toasted and smell fragrant, about 1 minute. Add the onion mixture to the pot of beans, then stir in the adobo and salt. Raise the heat to medium and continue simmering uncovered, stirring occasionally, until the beans thicken slightly, 20 to 25 minutes.

4. **Blend the soup:** Transfer 3 cups of soup to a blender. Protecting your hand with a dish towel, crack the lid slightly away from you to let the steam escape. Blend on low speed, then gradually increase the speed to high and blend until smooth and creamy, about 1 minute. (If you want a smoother, creamier soup, blend more whole beans.) Add the blended beans back to the pot and stir to combine. Stir in the lime juice, then taste and adjust the seasonings, if necessary.

5. **Top and serve:** Ladle the hot soup into bowls, swirl a spoonful or two of the Jalapeño Lime Cashew Sauce on top, then garnish with Pickled Red Onions, a small handful of corn chips, a few jalapeño slices, some diced avocado, scallions, cilantro, and a lime wedge on the side.

6. **To store:** Cool completely, then store in an airtight container in the fridge for up to 5 days. Reheat in the microwave or on the stovetop. For freezing instructions, see page 21.

BLACK BEANS

8 cups water

1 pound dried black beans

6 cups vegetable broth

2 bay leaves

VEGGIES

1 tablespoon extra-virgin olive oil

1 medium yellow onion, finely diced

1 orange bell pepper, finely diced

1 green bell pepper, finely diced

½ cup chopped fresh cilantro

1 jalapeño, finely diced

3 garlic cloves, minced

2 teaspoons ground cumin

1 teaspoon ground coriander

1 teaspoon sweet paprika

1 teaspoon dried oregano

1 teaspoon adobo seasoning

1 teaspoon kosher salt, plus more to taste

Juice of 1 lime

TOPPINGS

Jalapeño Lime Cashew Sauce (page 232)

Pickled Red Onions (page 237)

Corn chips, such as Fritos

Thinly sliced fresh jalapeños

Diced avocado

Sliced scallions

Chopped fresh cilantro

Lime wedges

spiced lentil chickpea stew with apricots & raisins

SERVES 4 TO 6 ▪ PREP TIME: 10 MINUTES ▪ COOK TIME: 30 MINUTES

VEGGIES AND SPICES

2 tablespoons extra-virgin olive oil

1 medium yellow onion, diced

1 jalapeño, seeded and diced

3 garlic cloves, minced

1 tablespoon grated fresh ginger

1 tablespoon garam masala

1 teaspoon sweet paprika

½ teaspoon ground turmeric

½ teaspoon curry powder

¼ teaspoon cayenne pepper

STEW

2 (15-ounce) cans chickpeas, drained and rinsed

1 (28-ounce) can crushed tomatoes or tomato puree (do not use tomato sauce)

1 (15-ounce) can light coconut milk

1 cup vegetable broth

½ cup dried green lentils

1 teaspoon kosher salt, plus more to taste

Freshly ground black pepper

⅓ cup chopped dried apricots

⅓ cup golden raisins

Juice of ½ lemon

SERVING

Plain whole-milk Greek yogurt

¼ cup chopped fresh cilantro

Torn fresh mint leaves (optional)

Warm naan (I like Stonefire)

On my way to make a vegetarian version of tikka masala with chickpeas, I threw in some lentils, apricots, and raisins and got this deliciously spiced vegan stew that combines the warm flavors of tikka masala with just a hint of sweetness from the dried fruit, which softens and plumps up in the sauce. The dish gets extra heartiness and texture by using both protein-packed chickpeas and smaller lentils. Dollop all of it with cooling Greek yogurt (or skip it to make a dairy-free and vegan dish) and fresh herbs. Serve this with warm naan for a fabulous, plant-based dinner.

1. **Cook the veggies and spices:** In a large pot, warm the olive oil over medium heat. Once the oil is hot, add the onion and jalapeño and sauté, stirring occasionally, until the onions soften, 3 to 5 minutes. Add the garlic, ginger, garam masala, paprika, turmeric, curry powder, and cayenne and stir until well combined. Cook, stirring frequently, until fragrant and the spices are toasted, about 1 minute.

2. **Cook the stew:** Add the chickpeas, crushed tomatoes, coconut milk, broth, and lentils, scraping up any browned bits off the bottom of the pan as the liquid deglazes it. Season with the salt and a few grinds of pepper. Bring to a boil, cover, and reduce the heat to medium-low. Cook, stirring occasionally, until the lentils are soft and tender and the stew is thickened, 20 to 25 minutes.

3. Stir in the dried apricots and raisins and cook, uncovered, until the raisins plump up, about 5 minutes. Add the lemon juice. Taste and add additional salt and pepper as needed.

4. **Serve:** Ladle the soup into bowls and top with a dollop of Greek yogurt, cilantro, and mint (if using). Serve immediately with warm naan for dipping.

5. **To store:** Cool completely, then store it in an airtight container in the fridge for up to 5 days. Reheat in the microwave or on the stovetop. For freezing instructions, see page 21.

make it your way

TO MAKE DAIRY-FREE AND VEGAN: Leave out the yogurt.

TO MAKE GLUTEN-FREE: Serve with gluten-free bread.

pasta e ceci with sweet potato & brown butter–fried rosemary

SERVES 4 ■ PREP TIME: 10 MINUTES ■ COOK TIME: 30 MINUTES

I adore a good simple soup. But what ya girl loves more is taking a simple concept to the next level with just a little bit of extra effort. Enter this Italian pasta and chickpea stew that gets a touch of sweetness thanks to our bestie, the sweet potato! You'll blend half of the soup to get it all nice and dreamy creamy (without the cream!) and then top it all off with fresh Parm and some beautiful, toasty, brown butter–fried rosemary. Bonus: It's all made in one pot. It's the most delicious soup you never knew you needed. Bonus points if you serve it with your favorite crackers crushed on top.

1. **Make the rosemary:** Line a plate with paper towels. In a large pot, melt the butter with the rosemary sprigs over medium heat. Once melted, whisk constantly; the butter will begin to crackle, then foam. After a few minutes, the butter will begin to turn a golden amber color. As soon as the butter turns brown and gives off a nutty aroma, immediately remove the rosemary sprigs and transfer them to the plate. This process should take about 5 minutes.

2. **Sauté the veggies:** To the same pot with the browned butter, add the onion, carrot, and sweet potato and cook, stirring occasionally, until the onion softens, about 5 minutes. Stir in the garlic and cook until fragrant, about 30 seconds.

3. **Cook the soup:** Add the broth, chickpeas, salt, and a few grinds of pepper and bring to a simmer. Cook, uncovered, until all the vegetables have softened, about 10 minutes. Remove from the heat.

4. Transfer half of the soup to a high-powered blender. Protecting your hand with a dish towel, crack the lid slightly away from you to let the steam escape. Blend on high speed until smooth. Return the puree to the pot, then stir in the pasta, place over medium heat, bring the soup to a gentle simmer, and cook until the pasta is al dente, 8 to 10 minutes. Stir in the spinach and lemon juice and cook until the spinach wilts, about 2 minutes. Taste and adjust the seasoning, adding more salt, if necessary.

5. **Serve:** Strip the fried rosemary leaves from their stems and discard the stems. Ladle the soup into bowls and top with a sprinkle of the rosemary leaves, Parmesan, and crushed crackers. Or just soak it all up with some toasted sliced bread! Serve immediately.

6. **To store:** Cool completely, then store in an airtight container in the fridge for up to 5 days. Reheat in the microwave or on the stovetop. I do not recommend freezing this soup.

BROWN BUTTER–FRIED ROSEMARY

2 tablespoons salted butter

3 sprigs of fresh rosemary

VEGGIES

1 small yellow onion, chopped

1 large carrot, chopped

1 medium to large sweet potato, peeled and cut into ½-inch cubes

3 garlic cloves, minced

SOUP

6 cups vegetable broth

1 (15-ounce) can chickpeas, drained and rinsed

1 teaspoon kosher salt, plus more to taste

Freshly ground black pepper

1 cup ditalini (or sub any other short pasta)

2 to 3 cups fresh spinach, chopped

Juice of ½ lemon

SERVING

Grated Parmesan cheese

Your favorite crackers, crushed

make it your way

TO MAKE DAIRY-FREE AND VEGAN: Replace the butter with extra-virgin olive oil. Cook the rosemary in olive oil until crisp, 1 to 2 minutes. Leave out the Parmesan cheese or replace with nutritional yeast.

TO MAKE GLUTEN-FREE: Use gluten-free short pasta.

knock-your-socks-off chipotle chicken pozole

SERVES 6 ▪ PREP TIME: 10 MINUTES ▪ COOK TIME: 40 MINUTES

VEGGIES AND SPICES

1 tablespoon extra-virgin olive oil

1 medium yellow onion, finely chopped

1 medium red bell pepper, finely chopped

3 garlic cloves, minced

1 teaspoon ground cumin

1 teaspoon ground coriander

½ teaspoon dried oregano

SOUP

3½ cups low-sodium chicken broth

1 (15-ounce) can diced fire-roasted tomatoes

1 pound boneless, skinless chicken thighs

1 (25-ounce) can hominy, drained and rinsed

1 teaspoon kosher salt, plus more to taste

CREAMY WHITE BEAN BASE

1 (15-ounce) can cannellini beans, drained and rinsed

2 to 3 chipotle peppers in adobo sauce, plus 1 to 2 tablespoons of the sauce, to taste

½ cup low-sodium chicken broth

MIX-INS

¾ cup frozen corn

Juice of 1 lime

½ cup finely chopped fresh cilantro

SERVING

Tortilla strips or chips

Plain whole-milk Greek yogurt

Shredded green cabbage

Sliced avocado

Thinly sliced fresh jalapeños

Chopped fresh cilantro

Lime wedges

During the holidays as a kid, I could always count on pozole being on the menu and I savored its warm, flavorful red chile broth and chewy hominy. Once I began cooking on my own, I couldn't always find the same dried chiles that my mom used in her broth, so I created my own shortcut version. Prepare for this one to go fast because IT IS GOOD. It uses widely available canned chipotle chiles to give a quick red chile flavor and a nutritious white bean base that miraculously adds creaminess with no actual cream required. The result may not be traditional, but it is incredibly flavorful and packed with protein. Under no circumstances should you skip the toppings, which really help to elevate every single bite! Pile on tortilla chips, cabbage, avocado, and Greek yogurt, then grab a spoon and get ready to knock your socks off!

1. **Cook the veggies and spices:** In a large pot, warm the olive oil over medium heat. Once the oil is hot, add the onion and bell pepper. Sauté, stirring occasionally, until the onion begins to soften, 5 minutes. Add the garlic, cumin, coriander, and dried oregano, and cook until fragrant, about 30 seconds.

2. **Cook the soup:** To the pot with the veggies, add the broth, tomatoes, chicken thighs, hominy, and salt. Raise the heat to high and bring to a boil, then reduce the heat to medium-low and simmer, uncovered, stirring occasionally, until the chicken is cooked through and no longer pink, 20 to 25 minutes. Remove the chicken with a slotted spoon and transfer to a cutting board. Use two forks to shred the chicken, then return it to the pot.

3. **Blend the bean base:** In a blender or food processor, add the cannellini beans, chipotle peppers, adobo sauce, and broth, and blend until mostly smooth, 1 minute. Pour the bean mixture into the pot with the chicken and veggies, then stir in the corn, lime juice, and cilantro. Simmer the soup to allow the flavors to combine, 10 to 15 minutes. Taste and adjust the seasonings as necessary.

4. **Serve:** Transfer the soup to bowls. Garnish with tortilla chips, Greek yogurt, cabbage, cilantro, and lime wedges for squeezing and serve immediately.

5. **To store:** Cool completely, then store in an airtight container in the fridge for up to 5 days. Reheat in the microwave or on the stovetop. For freezing instructions, see page 21.

make it your way

TO MAKE DAIRY-FREE: Leave out the Greek yogurt.

the best chicken soup you'll ever eat

SERVES 6 ■ **PREP TIME: 20 MINUTES** ■ **COOK TIME: 35 MINUTES**

My mom has always believed in the healing power of food. She's taught me how garlic has antiviral properties, how ginger can aid in digestion, and how turmeric helps with inflammation, especially when paired with a little hint of spicy black pepper. So one day when I was really sick, I set off on a mission to create a healing chicken soup with Mom's favorite ingredients, plus fresh herbs like rosemary and thyme and little cozy bites of pearl couscous. The result is nourishing, nostalgic, and guaranteed to make you feel a little bit better on your worst days. Trust me, you'll never go back to another chicken soup after you try this one. I was excited to see this become the number one chicken soup recipe on Google—literally!—but I am even more gratified that so many readers told me it helped them return to feeling their best.

1. **Cook the vegetables:** In a large Dutch oven or pot, warm the olive oil over medium heat. Once the oil is hot, add the onion, carrots, celery, and garlic. Cook, stirring frequently, until the onion becomes translucent, about 5 minutes.

2. Add the ginger and turmeric. Sauté, stirring constantly, until fragrant, about 30 seconds, then add the broth, chicken thighs, rosemary, thyme, salt, and pepper to taste.

3. **Cook the soup:** Bring the soup to a boil, then stir in the couscous. Use a spoon to press the chicken down so that it is completely covered in broth. Reduce the heat to medium-low and simmer, uncovered, until the chicken is fully cooked, 20 to 25 minutes.

4. Remove the chicken with a slotted spoon and transfer to a cutting board. Use two forks to shred the chicken, then return to the pot. Stir in the peas (if using) and simmer until tender, about 5 minutes. If you prefer a more brothy soup, feel free to add another cup of broth. Taste and adjust the seasonings, if necessary, and serve warm.

5. **To store:** Cool completely, then store in an airtight container in the fridge for up to 5 days. Reheat in the microwave or on the stovetop. For freezing instructions, see page 21.

1 tablespoon extra-virgin olive oil

1 medium yellow onion, diced

2 large carrots, thinly sliced

2 celery stalks, roughly chopped

6 garlic cloves, minced

1 tablespoon grated fresh ginger

1 tablespoon grated fresh turmeric (or sub 1 teaspoon ground turmeric)

6 cups low-sodium chicken broth, plus more as needed

1 pound boneless, skinless chicken thighs

1 teaspoon chopped fresh rosemary leaves

1 teaspoon fresh thyme leaves

1 teaspoon kosher salt, plus more to taste

Freshly ground black pepper

1 cup uncooked pearl couscous

⅔ cup frozen peas (optional, but recommended)

make it your way

TO MAKE GLUTEN-FREE: Use gluten-free orzo or another short gluten-free pasta instead of couscous.

make it nutrient-dense

Add any mixed frozen vegetables lurking in your freezer when you add the chicken thighs. I love this with a few cups of cubed butternut squash and parsnips, which add vitamin A and fiber.

nana aida's crazy good chicken stew (pollo guisado)

SERVES 6 ■ PREP TIME: 15 MINUTES ■ COOK TIME: 1 HOUR 10 MINUTES

2½ pounds bone-in, skin-on chicken thighs

1 teaspoon adobo seasoning

1 teaspoon kosher salt, plus more to taste

1 to 2 tablespoons extra-virgin olive oil, as needed

1 small yellow onion, chopped

1 small green bell pepper, diced

½ cup finely chopped fresh cilantro

3 garlic cloves, minced

1 (8-ounce) can tomato sauce

1 teaspoon ground cumin

1 teaspoon ground coriander

1 teaspoon ground turmeric

½ teaspoon dried oregano

3 cups low-sodium chicken broth

1 pound Yukon Gold potatoes, cut into 1-inch chunks

3 medium carrots, cut into 2-inch chunks

2 or 3 bay leaves

½ cup pimento-stuffed olives, plus 1 tablespoon of their brine

SERVING

Cooked jasmine rice or Arroz con Gandules (page 218)

Chopped fresh cilantro

Crispy Fried Tostones (page 221; optional)

My great-grandmother, Nana Aida, a Puerto Rican native, taught my grandmother Gloria (also known as G) to cook Pollo Guisado, a traditional Puerto Rican chicken stew. My grandmother then taught my mom, and together they taught me. Now it's my turn to share this beautiful, comforting stew full of rich, bold flavors with your family. This one always brings me back to my childhood, and I've tweaked the recipe here and there to achieve my ultimate one-pot comfort food. Serve it over rice, such as Arroz con Gandules, and add Crispy Fried Tostones for a festive meal.

1. **Prepare the chicken:** Pat the chicken dry with a paper towel to help it brown nicely. Sprinkle the adobo seasoning and ½ teaspoon of kosher salt all over the chicken and rub into the skin.

2. **Brown the chicken:** In a large pot or Dutch oven, warm 1 tablespoon of the olive oil over medium-high heat. Once the oil is hot, carefully place the chicken skin-side down in the pot and cook, undisturbed, until the skin is golden brown, has started to render, and the thighs easily release from the pan when moved, 4 to 5 minutes. Flip and brown chicken on the other side for another 4 to 5 minutes. Use tongs to transfer the chicken to a plate. (It doesn't need to be cooked all the way through.)

3. **Sauté the vegetables:** Reduce the heat to medium. If the pan seems dry, add the remaining 1 tablespoon of olive oil to the pot, then add the onion, bell pepper, cilantro, and garlic. Sauté, stirring occasionally, until the onions and bell peppers soften, 5 to 7 minutes. Reduce the heat to medium-low and stir in the tomato sauce, cumin, coriander, turmeric, dried oregano, and the remaining ½ teaspoon of kosher salt. Simmer, stirring occasionally, until the sauce comes together, about 2 minutes.

4. **Cook the stew:** Return the chicken to the pot, then add the broth, potatoes, carrots, bay leaves, olives, and olive brine. Raise the heat to high and bring to a boil, then reduce the heat to low, cover, and cook until chicken is cooked through and the vegetables are tender, 35 to 40 minutes. Uncover and simmer for another 10 minutes to thicken a bit. Taste and add more salt, if necessary.

5. **Serve:** Put a scoop of cooked rice into each bowl. Ladle the stew over the rice and serve with extra cilantro on top. Serve with crispy tostones on the side, if desired.

6. **To store:** Cool completely, then store in an airtight container in the fridge for up to 5 days. Reheat in the microwave or on the stovetop. For freezing instructions, see page 21; do not freeze the soup with the rice.

make it nutrient-dense

Instead of Yukon Gold potatoes, use sweet potatoes.

ADD EVEN MORE VEGETABLES: During the last 5 minutes of cooking, stir in 2 to 3 cups of chopped spinach or 1 cup of frozen peas or corn.

hearty vegetarian mains everyone will love

I went ALL. IN. on these recipes, which are designed to blow the minds of every person who sits at your table: Vegetable-lovers, for sure, but also people who claim they can't be satisfied if they don't eat meat. My mom cooked so many vegetarian meals when I was growing up, and many of these recipes are inspired versions of my childhood favorites. Others I created when I wanted hearty, satisfying, ultra-flavorful meals that helped me include more veggies in my diet. Throw these into your rotation when cooking for vegetarians. But don't stop there: Go ahead and cook one for your meat-loving friend or your "let's-add-bacon-to-everything" husband (looking at you, Tony). I promise this will change the way they see vegetarian meals.

cherry tomato, spinach & couscous stuffed peppers

SERVES 4 AS A MAIN DISH, 8 AS A SIDE ■ **PREP TIME: 10 MINUTES** ■ **COOK TIME: 1 HOUR 10 MINUTES**

Nonstick cooking spray

PEPPERS

4 large bell peppers, cut in half vertically and seeded

1 tablespoon extra-virgin olive oil

¼ teaspoon kosher salt

STUFFING

2 tablespoons extra-virgin olive oil

1 pint cherry tomatoes, halved

½ medium yellow onion, diced

3 garlic cloves, minced

1 teaspoon Italian seasoning

1¼ teaspoons kosher salt

Freshly ground black pepper

½ teaspoon red pepper flakes

1 cup pearl couscous

2 cups water or vegetable broth

4 cups fresh spinach, chopped

1 (15-ounce) can cannellini beans (or sub chickpeas), drained and rinsed

½ cup Easy Basil Pesto (page 232) or store-bought pesto

2 ounces grated Parmesan cheese (½ cup)

TOPPINGS

¼ cup Easy Basil Pesto (page 232) or store-bought basil pesto

4 ounces shredded mozzarella cheese (1 cup)

¼ cup julienned fresh basil

I try to use pearl couscous as much as possible and you should, too. People don't think of it as pasta because it's often sold in the rice section, but it's one of my favorites! It makes sauces starchier and creamier, it feels a bit like baby gnocchi, and soaks up sauces like no one's business. In this recipe, it makes a hearty stuffing reminiscent of risotto with gorgeous pops of cherry tomatoes and spinach. Truly one of my favorite freezer-friendly meals to keep on hand!

1. Preheat the oven to 350°F. Grease a 9 × 13-inch baking dish with cooking spray.

2. **Make the peppers:** Place the pepper halves in the prepared baking dish and drizzle with the olive oil. Use your hands to coat the peppers all over with the oil. Season with the salt. Place the peppers in the baking dish skin-side down. Set aside.

3. **Make the stuffing:** In a large, deep skillet, warm the oil over medium heat. Once the oil is hot, add the tomatoes, onion, garlic, Italian seasoning, ¼ teaspoon salt, and pepper to taste, and sauté, stirring occasionally, until the tomatoes start to break down and become juicy when pressed with the back of a wooden spoon, 5 to 8 minutes. Add the red pepper flakes and cook, stirring, for 30 seconds. Add the couscous, stirring well to allow the couscous to somewhat toast and absorb the flavors of the tomatoes, about 2 minutes. Add the water, bring to a gentle boil, then cover, reduce the heat to low, and cook until the couscous is cooked and the sauce has thickened, but some liquid still pools on the bottom of the pan, about 10 minutes. Uncover, stir in the spinach, and cook until wilted, 1 to 2 minutes. Stir in the beans, pesto, Parmesan, the remaining 1 teaspoon of salt, and pepper to taste, and cook on low, stirring frequently, until well combined and thickened, about 5 minutes. Remove from the heat.

4. **Assemble the peppers:** Divide the couscous mixture among the pepper halves, filling them all the way to the top. Top each pepper with 1 to 2 teaspoons of pesto and sprinkle with 2 tablespoons of mozzarella cheese. Coat a large piece of foil with cooking spray. Place spray-side-down on the baking dish and cover tightly (this will prevent the cheese from sticking to the foil).

5. **Bake the peppers:** Bake until the peppers are fork-tender, 35 to 40 minutes. Carefully remove the foil and transfer the pan back to the oven. Cook uncovered until the cheese is slightly golden, about 10 minutes. Garnish with basil. Cool the peppers for 10 minutes before serving.

6. **To store:** Keep any leftover peppers in an airtight container in the fridge for up to 5 days. Reheat in the microwave until heated through. For freezing instructions, see page 21.

make it your way

Amp up the flavor and texture
by topping these with my Herby
Golden Bread Crumbs (page 236)
before serving.

creamy baked butternut squash mac & cheese
with sage-walnut bread crumbs (PAGE 118)

creamy baked butternut squash mac & cheese with sage-walnut bread crumbs

SERVES 6 ▪ PREP TIME: 15 MINUTES ▪ COOK TIME: 1 HOUR 10 MINUTES

BUTTERNUT SQUASH AND PASTA

1 tablespoon extra-virgin olive oil, plus more for greasing

2 to 3 cups cubed butternut squash (½-inch pieces)

Kosher salt and freshly ground black pepper

12 ounces short pasta, such as cavatappi or fusilli

½ cup whole milk (or sub unsweetened almond milk)

CHEESE SAUCE

3 tablespoons salted butter

3 tablespoons all-purpose flour

2 cups whole milk (or sub unsweetened almond milk)

¾ teaspoon kosher salt, plus more to taste

½ teaspoon garlic powder

¼ teaspoon onion powder

¼ teaspoon sweet paprika

¼ teaspoon red pepper flakes

Ground nutmeg

Freshly ground black pepper

3 ounces shredded sharp Cheddar cheese (¾ cup)

3 ounces shredded Gruyère cheese (¾ cup)

2 ounces grated Parmesan cheese (½ cup)

Here's a vegetable-packed pasta dish that's perfect for entertaining (even for Thanksgiving), but easy enough to make for your little pasta eaters on a regular basis. It's a more sophisticated version of the pumpkin mac and cheese that my son, Sidney, gobbled up when he was a baby. I love how the toasted sage and walnut bread crumb topping adds a touch of savoriness and sophistication, while the butternut squash slightly sweetens the cheese sauce. Sometimes I find myself eating it straight out of the pot before baking, which you can totally do, too, if you're running short on time *or* are serving fussy eaters.

1. Preheat the oven to 375°F. Line a large baking sheet with parchment paper. Grease a 9-inch square pan with olive oil and set aside.

2. **Roast the butternut squash:** Place the butternut squash on the prepared baking sheet, drizzle with the oil, season with salt and pepper, and use your hands to toss together. Spread out in a single layer and roast undisturbed until the squash is fork-tender, 25 to 30 minutes. (Leave the oven on.)

3. **Cook the pasta:** Meanwhile, bring a large pot of generously salted water to a boil over high heat. Cook the pasta according to package directions until al dente. Drain and set aside.

4. When the squash is done roasting, add the cubes to a blender along with the milk. Blend until completely smooth, about 1 minute.

5. **Make the sauce:** In another large pot, melt the butter over medium heat, then whisk in the flour, cooking and whisking constantly until a paste forms, about 30 seconds. Slowly stream in the milk, constantly whisking away any lumps, until smooth and combined. Raise the heat to medium-high, bring to a rapid simmer, then reduce the heat to medium-low and simmer, stirring occasionally, until the sauce thickens to the consistency of gravy, 3 to 5 minutes. Once the sauce has thickened, reduce the heat to low and stir in the salt, garlic powder, onion powder, paprika, red pepper flakes, a pinch of nutmeg, and lots of pepper (don't be shy!). Fold in the Cheddar, Gruyère, and Parmesan cheeses and stir until completely melted. Stir in the squash purée until well combined and smooth. Taste and add more salt and pepper, if necessary.

6. Add the pasta to the sauce and stir well to combine, then pour the mixture into the prepared baking dish and spread into an even layer. (If you're in a hurry, you can skip the baking part and serve the mac and cheese warm, straight out of the pot!)

2 tablespoons salted butter

6 to 8 fresh sage leaves, chopped

½ cup panko bread crumbs

⅓ cup chopped walnuts

7. **Prepare the topping:** In the same large pot in which you cooked the pasta (no need to wash), warm the butter and sage over medium heat. Once the butter is melted, start whisking; the butter will first crackle, then foam, then it will turn golden brown and the sage will become crispy, 3 to 5 minutes. Add the panko and walnuts to the pan and cook, stirring occasionally, until the panko is toasted and turns a light golden brown, 2 to 4 minutes. Sprinkle the bread crumbs on top of the casserole.

8. **Bake the pasta:** Bake until the topping is golden brown and the mac and cheese is bubbling, 20 to 25 minutes. Cool for 5 to 10 minutes before serving.

9. **To store:** Keep any leftovers in an airtight container in the fridge for up to 5 days. Reheat in the microwave with an extra splash of milk until heated through.

10. **To make ahead:** Prepare the mac and cheese as directed, but before baking, cover the baking dish with foil and place it in the fridge for up to 1 day before serving. When you're ready to serve, bake as directed, adding 10 minutes to the baking time.

tip

The mac and cheese is best when you roast your squash, but if you are short on time, you can boil the butternut squash cubes until fork-tender, 5 to 8 minutes, then remove with a slotted spoon and cook your pasta in the same water.

make it your way

TO MAKE GLUTEN-FREE: Use gluten-free pasta, a 1:1 gluten-free all-purpose flour in the sauce, and gluten-free panko bread crumbs.

ADD PROTEIN: Stir in 8 ounces (about ½ cup) of chopped cooked bacon to the pasta and sauce mixture before baking.

CREAMY PUMPKIN MAC & CHEESE: Instead of butternut squash, skip the roasting step and stir 1 cup of canned pumpkin puree into the sauce.

make it nutrient-dense

Amp up the veggies by stirring in 1 cup of frozen spinach or frozen peas to the pasta and sauce mixture before baking.

magical sweet potato black bean enchiladas with creamy roasted poblano jalapeño sauce

MAKES 8 TO 10 ENCHILADAS ■ PREP TIME: 40 MINUTES ■ COOK TIME: 1 HOUR

CREAMY ROASTED POBLANO JALAPEÑO SAUCE

2 medium poblano peppers

1 jalapeño, halved and seeded (or keep the seeds if you like it spicy!)

½ large yellow onion, cut into large chunks

3 garlic cloves

1 tablespoon extra-virgin olive oil

¾ cup fresh cilantro

¾ cup vegetable broth

½ cup sour cream or plain whole-milk Greek yogurt

2 ounces plain cream cheese

2 tablespoons fresh lime juice

1 teaspoon ground cumin

1 teaspoon kosher salt, plus more to taste

My mom is famous for making the most amazing enchiladas layered with beautiful, colorful veggies, beans, and the most delicious lip-smacking sauce, and these slightly spicy enchiladas are inspired by all of the various versions she has made over the years. While they do take a bit of love and time to make, the result is bound to impress just about anyone. The slow burn of the creamy poblano sauce will have you coming back for more . . . and more . . . and more!

make it your way

SHORTCUT ENCHILADAS: To switch up the flavors or to save time, use 1 (28-ounce) can of your favorite red or green enchilada sauce (gluten-free, if desired) in place of the homemade poblano sauce.

CREAMY CHICKEN POBLANO ENCHILADAS: For a boost of protein, add 1 to 2 cups of shredded or cubed cooked chicken to the filling in step 3 when you stir in the black beans. You may end up with extra to fill more tortillas!

FILLING

1 tablespoon extra-virgin olive oil

1 medium sweet potato, peeled and diced into ¼-inch pieces

1 medium zucchini, diced into ¼-inch pieces

1 red bell pepper, diced

½ medium red onion, finely diced

1½ cups fresh or frozen sweet corn

1 teaspoon ground cumin

1 teaspoon ground coriander

½ teaspoon ground turmeric

½ teaspoon garlic powder

½ teaspoon kosher salt, plus more to taste

1 (15-ounce) can black beans, drained and rinsed

⅓ cup finely chopped fresh cilantro

ENCHILADAS

Extra-virgin olive oil, for greasing the pan

12 to 16 (6-inch) soft corn tortillas (gluten-free) or 8 to 10 (8-inch) medium-sized soft taco flour tortillas

4 ounces shredded pepper Jack cheese (1 cup)

4 ounces shredded Monterey Jack cheese (1 cup)

GARNISH AND SERVING

Pickled Red Onions (page 237)

Chopped fresh cilantro

1 avocado, sliced

Sour cream or plain whole-milk Greek yogurt

Roasted and salted pepitas

1. Preheat the oven to 400°F. Line a baking sheet with parchment paper.

2. **Make the poblano sauce:** On the prepared baking sheet, combine the poblanos, jalapeño, onion, and garlic. Drizzle with the olive oil and use your hands to toss the mixture. Roast until charred, flipping the peppers halfway through, about 20 minutes. Place the poblanos in a reusable silicone bag or a sealable plastic bag, seal, and let steam for 10 minutes; this will make it easier to remove the skin and stems. Use a paper towel to rub off the poblano skins, then remove the stems and seeds. Reduce the oven to 350°F.

3. Transfer the roasted vegetables to a high-powered blender or food processor and add the cilantro, broth, sour cream, cream cheese, lime juice, cumin, and salt and blend until completely smooth. Taste and add more salt, if necessary. Pour the sauce into a large bowl while you prepare the filling.

4. **Cook the filling:** In a large skillet, warm the oil over medium heat. Once the oil is hot, add the sweet potato, zucchini, bell pepper, onion, and corn and sauté, stirring often, until the veggies soften, about 10 minutes. Stir in the cumin, coriander, turmeric, garlic powder, and salt and cook, stirring for 30 seconds to toast the spices. Stir in the black beans, cilantro, and ¾ cup of the poblano sauce. Remove from the heat.

5. **Assemble and top the enchiladas:** Grease a 9 × 13-inch baking dish with oil and spread ¾ cup of the poblano sauce on the bottom of the baking dish. Dip a tortilla into the bowl of poblano sauce to fully coat, allow the excess to drip off, and transfer to a clean plate. If using corn tortillas: Place about ¼ cup of the filling on each tortilla and sprinkle 1 tablespoon of cheese on top. If using flour tortillas: place ½ cup of the filling on each tortilla and sprinkle 2 tablespoons of cheese on top. Roll up tightly and place seam-side down in the dish. Repeat with the remaining tortillas, filling, and pepper Jack cheese until you fill up the entire pan. (If there is any filling leftover, sprinkle it on top of the tortillas after covering them in the poblano sauce.)

6. Cover the enchiladas with the remaining sauce and sprinkle with the Monterey Jack cheese. Bake until the cheese is melted and the sauce is slightly bubbling, 20 to 25 minutes. Allow the enchiladas to cool for 10 minutes before serving.

7. **Garnish and serve:** Top with the Pickled Red Onions and cilantro. Serve warm with avocado slices, sour cream, and a sprinkle of pepitas.

8. **To store:** Keep any leftovers in an airtight container in the fridge for up to 5 days. Reheat in the microwave in 1-minute intervals until heated through. For freezing instructions, see page 21.

9. **To make ahead:** Assemble the enchiladas as directed, but before baking, cover with foil and place in the fridge for up to 1 day before serving. When you're ready to serve, bake as directed, adding 5 to 10 minutes to the baking time.

caramelized corn brown butter pasta with feta & jalapeño

SERVES 4 TO 6 ▪ PREP TIME: 15 MINUTES ▪ COOK TIME: 30 MINUTES

From the moment I tried this pasta, I knew it was going in my cookbook. The creamy caramelized corn sauce is truly one of the best things I've ever had. Even when I tested this recipe various ways—with goat cheese instead of feta and different shapes of pasta—I found myself practically licking the plate clean every single time. It's a seriously creamy, tangy, sweet, and salty situation that is bound to become a staple in your kitchen. This is one of those dishes that's absolutely perfect on its own, but you can make it even heartier by adding some bacon, ground sausage, shrimp, or grilled chicken. One of my favorite weeknight dinners EVER.

1. **Brown the butter:** Melt the butter in a small saucepan over medium heat. Once melted, start whisking; the butter will first crackle, then foam. After a few minutes, the butter will begin to turn a golden amber color. As soon as the butter turns brown and gives off a nutty aroma, 5 to 8 minutes total, remove from the heat and set aside to cool.

2. **Cook the pasta:** Bring a large pot of generously salted water to a boil over high heat. Once the water boils, cook the pasta according to package directions until al dente. Reserve 1 cup of the pasta water, then drain the pasta and return to the pot.

3. **Cook the corn:** In a large, deep skillet, warm the olive oil over medium heat. Add the corn, jalapeños, garlic, and ½ teaspoon salt and sauté, stirring occasionally, until the corn begins to caramelize and turn slightly golden brown, 10 to 15 minutes.

4. **Blend with the feta:** Transfer half of the caramelized corn and jalapeño mixture (reserve the remaining half) to a high-powered blender and add the feta, reserved pasta water, and remaining ½ teaspoon salt. Blend until the mixture is mostly smooth, 1 minute.

5. Add the creamy corn and feta sauce, the reserved half of the corn mixture, and the brown butter to the pot of pasta. Stir well to coat. Taste and add more salt and pepper, if necessary.

6. **Top and serve:** Top with the basil, sliced jalapeño, and more crumbled feta. Serve immediately.

7. **To store:** Keep any leftover pasta in an airtight container in the fridge for up to 4 days. Reheat in the microwave with an extra splash of water until heated through.

BROWN BUTTER AND PASTA

4 tablespoons (57 grams) salted butter, cut into 4 equal pieces

Kosher salt

12 ounces pasta of choice (my favs are fusilli col buco, fettuccine, or cavatelli)

1 cup reserved pasta water

Freshly ground black pepper

CORN AND FETA

1 tablespoon extra-virgin olive oil

3 cups fresh sweet corn, cut off the cob (from about 4 ears)

1 to 2 jalapeños, seeded and finely diced

1 garlic clove, minced

1 teaspoon kosher salt, plus more to taste

4 ounces feta cheese (or sub goat cheese), crumbled, plus more for topping

TOPPINGS

½ cup julienned fresh basil

1 jalapeño, thinly sliced

make it your way

TO MAKE GLUTEN-FREE: Use gluten-free pasta.

ADD PROTEIN: Stir in 8 ounces of cooked and chopped bacon, 8 ounces of cooked ground sausage, or 1 pound of grilled shrimp or chicken breast.

next-level weeknight peanut-tahini noodles with toasted sesame, chile & basil

SERVES 4 ▪ PREP TIME: 15 MINUTES ▪ COOK TIME: 10 MINUTES

SAUCE

¼ cup low-sodium soy sauce

3 to 4 tablespoons water, as needed

3 tablespoons natural creamy peanut butter

3 tablespoons tahini

1 to 2 tablespoons packed dark brown sugar (or sub coconut sugar), to taste

2 tablespoons sambal oelek (or another hot chile paste)

2 tablespoons fresh lime juice or rice vinegar

1 tablespoon grated fresh ginger

2 garlic cloves, grated

NOODLES

10 ounces rice noodles or 3 (3-ounce) ramen noodle packs

1 tablespoon toasted sesame oil

GARNISH AND SERVING

½ cup sliced scallions

½ cup chopped fresh cilantro

½ cup julienned fresh basil

⅓ cup roasted and salted peanuts (or sub honey-roasted peanuts), chopped

Toasted sesame seeds

2 to 3 Persian cucumbers, sliced or cut into matchsticks

Say hello to a super fast, fresh weeknight meal that's a little spicy, a little sweet, and endlessly versatile. I use tahini, a sesame paste popular in the Middle East, to make these peanut noodles extra creamy and earthy. Herbs and scallions add freshness, and cool mini cucumbers add crunch. You can easily add your favorite protein, whatever veggies are in the fridge, or just wolf them down as they are.

1. **Make the sauce:** In a medium bowl, whisk the soy sauce, 3 tablespoons of water, the peanut butter, tahini, brown sugar, sambal oelek, lime juice, ginger, and garlic. The sauce should be pourable and fairly thin, similar to a salad dressing; add an extra tablespoon of water if needed. (It will thicken as it sits, too.) Set aside.

2. **Cook the noodles:** Make the noodles according to the package directions, then drain and return to the pot. Toss with the toasted sesame oil, then pour in the peanut-tahini sauce. Use tongs to toss and coat the noodles with sauce.

3. **Serve:** Divide the noodles among serving bowls and garnish with scallions, cilantro, basil, peanuts, and a sprinkle of sesame seeds. Serve warm with sliced cucumbers on the side.

4. **To store:** Store any leftovers in an airtight container in the fridge for up to 5 days. It's wonderful warm or cold. The sauce will dry up, so I recommend reheating in the microwave or on the stove with a splash of water until heated through.

make it your way

TO MAKE GLUTEN-FREE: Use coconut aminos or tamari instead of soy sauce and rice noodles.

USE YOUR PASTA OF CHOICE: Instead of rice or ramen noodles, sub udon, spaghetti, linguine, or fettuccine.

make it nutrient-dense

ADD PROTEIN: Boost the protein by adding 1 pound of any of the following: pan-fried cubed tofu, cooked ground chicken or cubed chicken, cooked ground pork, or cooked shrimp.

Add extra veggies by tossing the noodles with stir-fried broccoli and red bell pepper, or veggies of your choosing.

comforting portobello, poblano & pepper jack cheese enchilada skillet

SERVES 6 ▪ PREP TIME: 15 MINUTES ▪ COOK TIME: 25 MINUTES

If you've never experienced the joy of mushrooms and enchilada sauce together, I implore you to make these right away. Portobello mushrooms have a meat-like heartiness that pairs beautifully with the earthy, smoky heat of poblanos; add sweet corn and broiled pepper Jack cheese and OMG. These are inspired by one of my go-to Mexican restaurants in Chicago, but I've made it a little easier by skipping the rolling and just throwing everything into one skillet for one delicious hot mess.

1. **Make the sauce:** In a large, deep, oven-safe skillet, warm the olive oil over medium heat. Once the oil is hot, add the onion and jalapeño and sauté, stirring occasionally, until the onion softens, 3 to 5 minutes. Add the garlic and sauté, stirring frequently, until fragrant, about 30 seconds. Transfer the mixture to a blender or food processor. Add the tomato sauce, broth, cilantro, chili powder, cumin, dried oregano, salt, and chipotle chili powder. Blend on high speed until the sauce is smooth, about 1 minute.

2. Preheat the broiler to high.

3. **Prepare the filling:** In the same skillet, warm the oil over medium heat. Once the oil is hot, add the mushrooms, poblanos, corn, onion, salt, and pepper to taste. Sauté, stirring occasionally, until all of the liquid has evaporated and the mushrooms are golden brown, 8 to 10 minutes. Reduce the heat to medium-low and add the enchilada sauce, tortilla strips, and ½ cup of the cheese. Stir again to combine and simmer for a few minutes to integrate the flavors.

4. Sprinkle the remaining cheese over the top of the enchilada mixture. Place the skillet in the oven under the broiler and broil until the cheese melts and is slightly golden brown in places, watching carefully to avoid burning, 2 to 4 minutes.

5. **Garnish and serve:** Remove from the oven and allow to cool for at least 10 minutes before serving, then top with cilantro and Pickled Red Onions. Serve warm with a dollop of yogurt.

6. **To store:** Keep any leftovers in an airtight container in the fridge for up to 5 days. Reheat in the microwave in 30-second intervals until heated through. For freezing instructions, see page 21.

ENCHILADA SAUCE

1 tablespoon extra-virgin olive oil

½ medium yellow onion, diced

1 jalapeño, seeded and diced

3 garlic cloves, minced

1 (15-ounce) can tomato sauce

½ cup vegetable broth

⅓ cup chopped fresh cilantro

1 teaspoon chili powder

1 teaspoon ground cumin

1 teaspoon dried oregano

1 teaspoon kosher salt

½ teaspoon chipotle chili powder

FILLING

1 tablespoon extra-virgin olive oil

3 portobello mushroom caps, sliced into strips

2 poblano peppers, seeded and cut into thin strips

1½ cups fresh corn kernels (from 2 ears)

½ medium yellow onion, sliced

1 teaspoon kosher salt

Freshly ground black pepper

8 (6-inch) corn tortillas, cut into 1-inch strips

8 ounces shredded pepper Jack cheese (2 cups)

GARNISH AND SERVING

2 tablespoons chopped fresh cilantro

Pickled Red Onions (page 237)

Plain whole-milk Greek yogurt

mom's puerto rican rice & beans (PAGE 130)

mom's puerto rican rice & beans

SERVES 6 TO 8 ■ PREP TIME: 20 MINUTES, PLUS 8 HOURS SOAKING TIME ■ COOK TIME: 2 HOURS

BEANS

8 cups water

1 pound dried pink or pinto beans (about 2 cups)

2 bay leaves

SOFRITO

2 tablespoons extra-virgin olive oil

½ cup finely diced yellow onion

½ cup finely diced green bell pepper

¼ cup finely chopped fresh cilantro

3 garlic cloves, minced

1 cup no-salt-added tomato sauce (from one 15-ounce can; reserve extra sauce for the rice)

1 tablespoon (2 packets) Goya Sazón Culantro y Achiote (or Homemade Sazón, page 237)

Kosher salt and freshly ground black pepper

SERVING

Arroz con Gandules (page 218)

Sliced avocado

Fresh cilantro

Hot sauce (optional)

Crispy Fried Tostones (page 221; optional)

Nothing reminds me of home more than this recipe that was passed down through generations of my mother's family to her, and now to me. Growing up, my mom was always working and trying to provide for us, so we needed easy, nutritious meals that could quickly be reheated. She'd make a big pot of these rice and beans to have on hand so we could serve ourselves until our bellies were content. The beans are cooked in sofrito, a flavorful base of aromatics, and paired with Arroz con Gandules (rice with pigeon peas). They always provide me with the warmest dose of comfort and I love how flavorful and saucy the beans get. Plus, they make awesome leftovers to throw into burritos, quesadillas, tacos, whatever you'd like! I find myself coming back to this recipe when I want a nourishing vegetarian meal for my own family, or to be reminded of my mom.

1. **Prepare the beans:** In a large pot, combine the water and beans and soak at room temperature for 8 to 10 hours (after 10 hours, the beans will begin to absorb too much water and may lose some of their texture and flavor). DO NOT drain the water; it will add crucial flavor to the final dish.

2. After you soak the beans, add the bay leaves and bring the beans to a boil over high heat. Boil for 1 to 2 minutes, then reduce the heat to low, cover, and simmer gently, stirring occasionally, until beans are tender and soft, 1 to 2 hours. Once beans are done cooking, remove the bay leaf but DO NOT drain the liquid from the beans! Set aside.

3. **Make the sofrito:** In a medium skillet, warm the olive oil over medium heat. Once the oil is hot, add the onion, bell pepper, cilantro, and garlic. Sauté, stirring occasionally, until the onions and peppers soften, about 5 minutes. Reduce the heat to low, add the tomato sauce and sazón, and simmer until the sauce comes together, 2 to 3 minutes.

4. Pour the sofrito into the cooked beans. Place the pot over medium-low heat, bring to a simmer, and cook uncovered, stirring occasionally, until the liquid reduces by about half, 20 to 30 minutes. Taste and season with salt and pepper as necessary. Remove from the heat and cover the beans until you are ready to serve. They should stay hot for an hour or so.

5. **To serve:** In a large bowl, or in individual serving bowls, place the Arroz con Gandules alongside the beans and as much of their sauce as you like. Top with avocado and cilantro. You can also add hot sauce if you like a little heat. Serve warm with Crispy Fried Tostones, if using.

6. **To store:** Keep any leftovers (rice and beans separated) in an airtight container in the fridge for up to 5 days. Reheat in the microwave until heated through.

7. **To freeze:** Cool beans completely and place in an airtight container. Freeze for up to 3 months. Thaw overnight in the fridge before reheating on the stovetop or in the microwave until heated through.

make it your way

TO MAKE GLUTEN-FREE: Use coconut aminos or tamari in place of the soy sauce.

TO MAKE VEGAN: Use brown sugar instead of honey.

CRISPY, STICKY ORANGE CHICKEN: Cube 1 pound of boneless, skinless chicken breast and use in place of the tofu, cooking over medium-high heat until no longer pink in the center, 5 to 7 minutes total.

crispy, sticky orange tofu stir-fry

SERVES 4 ■ PREP TIME: 20 MINUTES ■ COOK TIME: 20 MINUTES

My favorite way to eat tofu is when it's super crispy, and one way to achieve that is to coat it in cornstarch and salt, then pan-fry until golden brown. This crispy tofu is served in a sticky, sweet, and slightly spicy orange sauce that will have you licking the plate clean. It's a quick, easy weeknight meal that tastes like takeout and is even better with my Coconut Rice.

1. **Prepare the tofu:** Wrap the tofu in two layers of paper towels and set on a plate. Place a heavy skillet or pot on top and let sit for 15 to 20 minutes to squeeze out the excess liquid.

2. **Meanwhile, make the orange sauce:** In a medium bowl, whisk the orange zest, orange juice, soy sauce, honey, rice vinegar, ginger, cornstarch, garlic, and red pepper flakes until well combined. Set aside.

3. Unwrap the tofu, discard the paper towels, and cut into 1-inch cubes. Transfer the tofu to a medium bowl or gallon-size zip-top bag and sprinkle with the cornstarch and salt. Gently toss the tofu in the mixture using your hands, or seal the bag and gently shake until the tofu is well coated.

4. **Cook the tofu:** Line a large plate with paper towels. In a large nonstick skillet, warm the avocado oil over medium-high heat. Once the oil is hot, add the tofu in a single layer, making sure not to crowd the pan and working in batches if necessary, and cook until brown and crispy, 2 to 3 minutes per side, adding more oil between batches if the pan becomes dry. Transfer the tofu as it finishes to the prepared plate and repeat with the remaining tofu.

5. **Cook the stir-fry:** In the same skillet, warm the oil over medium heat. Once the oil is hot, add the onion, carrot, red bell pepper, green beans, and cashews. Cook, stirring frequently, until the green beans are slightly tender but still have a bite, 6 to 8 minutes. Stir in the cooked tofu. Pour in the orange sauce, bring to a gentle simmer, then reduce the heat to low and cook, stirring frequently, until the sauce begins to thicken, 2 to 4 minutes.

6. **Garnish and serve:** Top with the scallions and sesame seeds and serve immediately with Coconut Rice on the side.

TOFU

1 (16-ounce) package extra-firm tofu, drained

2 tablespoons cornstarch (or sub arrowroot starch)

1 teaspoon kosher salt

2 tablespoons avocado oil, plus more as needed

SAUCE

Zest of 1 large orange

¾ cup fresh orange juice (from 2 to 3 oranges)

¼ cup low-sodium soy sauce

2 tablespoons honey

1 tablespoon rice vinegar

1 tablespoon grated fresh ginger

1 tablespoon cornstarch (or sub arrowroot starch)

3 garlic cloves, grated

½ teaspoon red pepper flakes

STIR-FRY

1 tablespoon avocado oil

½ medium yellow onion, sliced

1 medium carrot, cut into matchsticks

1 large red bell pepper, thinly sliced

8 ounces fresh green beans, ends trimmed (or sub 3 to 4 cups broccoli florets)

½ cup raw cashews

GARNISH AND SERVING

4 scallions, thinly sliced

Toasted sesame seeds

Coconut Rice (page 217)

creamy garlic mushroom orecchiette with lemon ricotta

SERVES 4 ■ PREP TIME: 10 MINUTES ■ COOK TIME: 20 MINUTES

If the golden, herbed mushrooms weren't reason enough to make this, how about a pasta that's cooked in both broth and milk to create a creamy base for savory mozzarella and Parmesan cheeses—and finished with dollops of bright, creamy lemon ricotta? Dreamy. Add grilled chicken or shrimp if that's your thing!

1. **Make the lemon ricotta:** In a medium bowl, combine the ricotta, lemon zest and juice, salt, and pepper to taste. Stir with a spoon or a whisk until incorporated. Set aside.

2. **Cook the mushrooms:** In a large, deep skillet, melt the butter over medium heat. Add the mushrooms, thyme, salt, and pepper to taste and cook, stirring occasionally, until the pan is dry and the mushrooms are cooked down and starting to brown, 8 to 10 minutes. Stir in the garlic and cook until fragrant, about 1 minute. Transfer to a medium bowl.

3. **Cook the pasta:** In the same skillet, heat the broth and milk, stirring and scraping up any yummy mushroom bits leftover on the bottom of the pan. Stir in the pasta and bring to a gentle simmer. Cook, stirring occasionally, adding another ¼ cup broth if necessary so the consistency stays moist, until the pasta is al dente, about 10 minutes.

4. Reduce the heat to low and stir in the mozzarella, Parmesan, salt, and lots of black pepper. Add a splash more broth if you'd like a saucier consistency. Stir in the mushrooms.

5. Remove from the heat and dollop 4 heaping tablespoons of lemon ricotta on top of the pasta.

6. **Add topping and garnishes:** Add about 1 heaping tablespoon of the lemon ricotta to each plate and use a spoon to spread in a sweeping motion. Serve the pasta on the other side of the plate and enjoy extra ricotta with each bite of pasta. Serve warm, garnished with thyme leaves, lemon zest, and red pepper flakes (if using).

7. **To store:** Keep any leftover pasta and/or ricotta in an airtight container in the fridge for up to 5 days. Reheat in the microwave with an extra splash of milk until heated through.

make it your way

BOOST THE PROTEIN: Serve with grilled or baked chicken breast or sautéed Italian or garlic chicken sausage.

TO MAKE GLUTEN-FREE: Use gluten-free brown rice pasta.

LEMON RICOTTA

½ cup whole-milk ricotta cheese

1 teaspoon lemon zest, plus more for garnish

1 tablespoon fresh lemon juice

¼ teaspoon kosher salt

Freshly ground black pepper

MUSHROOMS

2 tablespoons salted butter

1 pound baby bella mushrooms, sliced

2 teaspoons fresh thyme leaves

½ teaspoon kosher salt

Freshly ground black pepper

3 garlic cloves, minced

PASTA AND GARNISHES

3½ cups vegetable broth, plus more as needed

1 cup whole milk (or sub unsweetened almond milk)

1 pound orecchiette (bowties or penne also work great)

3 ounces shredded mozzarella cheese (¾ cup)

2 ounces grated Parmesan cheese (½ cup)

½ teaspoon kosher salt, plus more to taste

Freshly ground black pepper

1 teaspoon fresh thyme leaves, for garnish

Red pepper flakes, for garnish (optional)

hand-helds every night!

Who doesn't like to eat with their hands? These recipes start with classic handhelds and finger food (chicken tenders, meatballs, pizza), then take them out for a fun ride with toppings, coatings, and flavors you might not expect. These recipes can be party food, shareable dishes for potlucks, or, if you just need a quick family dinner that makes a weeknight better than average, well, they're here for that, too.

baked sticky hot gochujang ginger & apricot chicken wings

SERVES 6 AS A MAIN DISH, 8 AS A STARTER ■ PREP TIME: 15 MINUTES ■ COOK TIME: 45 MINUTES

Nonstick cooking spray

CHICKEN

3½ to 4 pounds chicken wingettes and drumettes

2 tablespoons baking powder

2 teaspoons sweet paprika

2 teaspoons garlic powder

1 teaspoon kosher salt

Freshly ground black pepper

SAUCE

¾ cup apricot jam or preserves

2 tablespoons low-sodium soy sauce

2 to 3 tablespoons gochujang, depending on your heat tolerance

3 garlic cloves, minced

1 tablespoon packed dark brown sugar (or sub coconut sugar)

1 tablespoon rice vinegar

1 tablespoon grated fresh ginger

GARNISH

¼ cup sliced scallions

2 to 3 tablespoons toasted sesame seeds

Chicken wings that are sticky, hot, and *dripping* with flavor. My game-day guests always gasp after they taste these and ask for the recipe. My husband can't stop eating them and I can never stop licking the sauce off my fingers. (Kinda weird, but just being honest.) To serve this as a main meal, I suggest pairing these with "The Slaw" (page 206) or my butternut squash mac and cheese (page 118). OKAY MAKE THEM BYE!

1. Preheat the oven to 425°F. Line a large baking sheet with aluminum foil and place a wire rack on top. Generously spray the wire rack with cooking spray to prevent sticking.

2. **Prep the chicken:** Pat the wingettes and drumettes very dry with a paper towel, then place in a large bowl. Add the baking powder, paprika, garlic powder, salt, and a few grinds of pepper and use your hands to rub the spices into the skin of the chicken. Place the chicken on the wire rack at least ½ inch apart.

3. **Cook the chicken:** Bake for 25 minutes, then flip the chicken. Bake until cooked through, another 15 to 20 minutes. Allow to cool for at least 5 minutes.

4. **Make the sauce:** While the chicken cooks, in a large bowl, whisk the apricot jam, soy sauce, 2 tablespoons of the gochujang, the garlic, brown sugar, rice vinegar, and ginger until well combined. Taste and add another tablespoon of gochujang if you want to increase the heat level. Add the chicken to the sauce and use tongs to toss until the chicken is fully coated.

5. **To serve:** Transfer the wings to a platter and top with the scallions and sesame seeds. Enjoy immediately.

6. **To store:** Keep any leftovers in an airtight container in the fridge for up to 4 days. Reheat in the microwave in 30-second intervals until heated through, or preheat the oven to 350°F and bake on a parchment-lined baking sheet until heated through, about 10 minutes.

make it your way

TO MAKE GLUTEN-FREE: Use coconut aminos or tamari instead of soy sauce and use gluten-free sambal oelek or a hot chile paste in place of the gochujang.

holiday empanadas

**MAKES 15 LARGE EMPANADAS ■ PREP TIME: 40 MINUTES, PLUS 30 MINUTES CHILLING TIME
■ COOK TIME: 30 MINUTES**

DOUGH

3 cups (360 grams) all-purpose flour, plus more for dusting

1 teaspoon kosher salt

1 cup (226 grams) cold salted butter, diced into small pieces

1 large egg

4 to 6 tablespoons whole milk, as needed

FILLING AND EGG WASH

3¾ cups Weeknight Chicken Picadillo (page 156) or an equivalent amount of your favorite filling, cooled to room temperature

8 ounces shredded pepper Jack, sharp Cheddar, or Monterey Jack cheese (2 cups)

1 large egg, lightly beaten

SERVING SUGGESTIONS

Jalapeño Lime Cashew Sauce (page 232)

Spicy Cilantro Yogurt Sauce (page 236)

Your favorite hot sauce or salsa

Holidays at my mom's house always meant empanadas served alongside a big pot of pozole and a tray of enchiladas or tostadas. I looked forward to the empanadas in particular because my mom often didn't have time to make them, so they felt special. Feel free to use this dough as a starting point and stuff them with leftover taco meat or any other leftovers, including roasted veggies.

1. **Make the dough:** In a food processor, combine the flour and salt, pulse a few times, then add the butter. Pulse a few more times until the dough forms pea-size pieces. Add the egg and 4 tablespoons of milk and process again until the dough is damp and forms a few big clumps, adding an additional 1 to 2 tablespoons of milk, if necessary. (Stop before it turns into a big, cohesive dough ball; that means it's overmixed.)

2. Generously flour a surface, or lay out a piece of plastic wrap. Dump the dough onto the surface and divide into three equal parts (roughly 266 grams each). Press each piece of dough into a cohesive disk then wrap tightly in plastic wrap and place in the fridge for at least 30 minutes or up to 48 hours. (If making the dough ahead of time, you can refrigerate it for up to 1 week, or wrap in plastic wrap and foil, place in a reusable silicone bag or a plastic freezer storage bag, and freeze for up to 3 months. Thaw in the fridge overnight, then proceed.)

3. Line two large baking sheets with parchment paper and set aside. Divide each disc into 5 equal portions for a total of 15 equal dough balls (53 grams each). Work with one dough ball at a time, keeping the rest covered with a damp towel so they don't dry out. Add flour to a clean surface, then use a rolling pin generously dusted with flour to roll each dough ball into an approximately 6-inch circle.

4. **Fill, egg wash, and bake:** Immediately add 3 to 4 tablespoons of filling to one half of a dough round. Then add 1 to 2 tablespoons of cheese on top. (Resist the urge to add any more filling; overstuffing makes empanadas hard to seal.) Fold the other half of the dough over and press the edges together, using a fork to crimp and seal the edges shut. Transfer empanadas to the prepared baking sheets, 1 to 2 inches apart. Repeat with the remaining dough and filling. Refrigerate the empanadas for 30 minutes, or if making ahead, cover with plastic wrap and chill for up to 48 hours before baking (this will improve the dough's texture and help it stay sealed).

5. Preheat the oven to 375°F.

6. Use a pastry brush to brush each empanada with the beaten egg. Bake until the empanadas are golden brown, 25 to 35 minutes. Serve warm with sauce on the side for dipping.

7. **To store:** Keep in an airtight container or wrap leftover empanadas tightly in plastic wrap and store in the fridge for up to 3 days. To reheat, place them on a parchment paper–lined baking sheet and bake at 300°F until heated through, 10 to 15 minutes. To freeze empanadas, skip the egg wash and pop the baking sheet with the filled unbaked empanadas in the freezer until solid, about 2 hours, then transfer to a reusable silicone bag or plastic freezer storage bag and place back in the freezer. Bake frozen empanadas straight from frozen at 375°F for 30 to 40 minutes.

naughty lil' spinach & artichoke stuffed mushrooms with schmoozy ritzy crunch

SERVES 6 ▪ PREP TIME: 20 MINUTES ▪ COOK TIME 25 MINUTES

Your girl loves to put her favorite foods together, so this is the glorious product of my obsession with spinach and artichoke dip and my love of stuffed mushrooms. So good, they're a little bit naughty. I might have stopped there, but then my husband Tony swooped in with his beloved Ritz crackers and convinced me we needed a buttery crunch to go with our shrooms. Oh yes, yes, we did.

1. Preheat the oven to 400°F. Line a large baking sheet with parchment paper.

2. **Make the filling:** In a medium skillet, warm the olive oil over medium heat. Once the oil is hot, add the onion and sauté, stirring occasionally, until it begins to soften, about 5 minutes. Stir in the garlic, salt, and pepper to taste and cook until fragrant, about 30 seconds.

3. Reduce the heat to low, add the spinach, and cover the pan until the spinach wilts, about 2 minutes. Remove the lid and stir in the cream cheese, breaking it apart with a wooden spoon until it melts. Remove from the heat and stir in the Greek yogurt, mixing until well combined, then stir in the artichoke hearts, mozzarella, and Parmesan until well incorporated. Taste and season with more salt and pepper as needed.

4. **Make the mushrooms and topping:** Pat the mushroom caps dry with a paper towel and place top-down on the prepared baking sheet. Evenly fill each cap with a heaping scoop of filling and sprinkle the tops with the crushed crackers. (If you have a little filling leftover, that's okay, just enjoy it while the mushrooms bake.) Gently spray the tops with cooking spray.

5. Bake until the cracker topping is golden brown and the mushrooms are tender, 20 to 25 minutes. Serve warm.

6. **To store:** Keep any leftovers in an airtight container in the fridge for up to 3 days. To reheat, put the mushrooms on a parchment paper–lined baking sheet and bake at 350°F until heated through, about 10 minutes.

FILLING

1 tablespoon extra-virgin olive oil

½ medium yellow or white onion, diced

3 garlic cloves, minced

½ teaspoon kosher salt, plus more to taste

Freshly ground black pepper

2 cups fresh spinach

4 ounces plain cream cheese, softened

¼ cup plain whole-milk Greek yogurt

1 (8-ounce) jar marinated artichoke hearts, drained and chopped into ½-inch pieces

1 ounce shredded mozzarella cheese (¼ cup)

1 ounce grated Parmesan cheese (¼ cup)

MUSHROOMS AND TOPPING

16 ounces baby bella mushrooms, stems discarded or saved for another use

12 Ritz crackers, crushed into crumbs (or ⅓ cup Herby Golden Bread Crumbs, page 236)

Nonstick cooking spray

make it your way

SPINACH & ARTICHOKE DIP: Not into mushrooms? Forget about them and double the filling for a delicious dip. You can even transfer it to a 9-inch square baking dish (or bake it directly in the skillet if it's oven-safe!), top it with an extra 4 ounces (1 cup) of mozzarella cheese, and bake until golden brown, about 20 minutes, if ya feelin' fancy. And of course, you can use Ritz for dipping.

TO MAKE GLUTEN-FREE: Use ⅓ cup of gluten-free panko bread crumbs in place of the Ritz crackers.

sizzlin' hot jalapeño corn dip

SERVES 8 ■ PREP TIME: 10 MINUTES ■ COOK TIME: 30 MINUTES

DIP

1 tablespoon extra-virgin olive oil

3 cups corn kernels (fresh, frozen, or canned and drained)

1 red bell pepper, diced

⅓ cup sliced scallions

½ cup drained pickled jalapeños, chopped, plus 1 tablespoon of their brine

1 teaspoon garlic powder

¾ teaspoon kosher salt

8 ounces cream cheese, softened

½ cup plain whole-milk Greek yogurt

2 ounces shredded pepper Jack cheese (½ cup; or sub Monterey Jack cheese)

4 ounces shredded Monterey Jack cheese (1 cup)

TOPPING AND SERVING

¼ cup thinly sliced scallions

2 tablespoons chopped fresh cilantro

Tortilla or corn chips, for scooping

CORN LOVA HERE. I'm in favor of corn in every way possible: In salsa, mixed with pasta, baked atop pizza. I can't resist creamed corn and don't even get me started on corn on the cob right off the grill. After all, I grew up amid cornfields in the Midwest, and some of my happiest childhood memories took place on a picnic blanket sitting next to my dad, slathering salty butter on the sweetest corn. I sought to replicate that feeling of warmth in this dip—a tribute to my love for corn in creamy, cheesy form. It's perfectly enhanced by pickled jalapeños and their brine (trust me here). Make it any time of year: Frozen and canned corn will always be there for you.

1. Preheat the oven to 375°F.

2. **Make the dip:** In a deep, 10-inch oven-safe skillet, warm the olive oil over medium heat. Once the oil is hot, add the corn, bell pepper, and scallions and sauté, stirring occasionally, until the corn begins to turn golden brown, about 10 minutes. Stir in the pickled jalapeños and brine, garlic powder, and salt. Cook, stirring for 30 seconds to infuse the jalapeño flavor into the corn.

3. Reduce the heat to low and stir in the cream cheese, breaking it apart with a spoon until it melts. Stir in the yogurt and mix until well combined. Stir in the pepper Jack. Spread the mixture evenly in the skillet, then top with the Monterey Jack.

4. **Bake the dip:** Bake until golden brown and bubbling, 20 to 25 minutes. Let cool for 5 to 10 minutes.

5. **Top and serve:** Sprinkle with the scallions and cilantro, then serve warm with chips for scooping.

6. **To store:** Keep any leftovers in an airtight container in the fridge for up to 5 days. Reheat in the microwave until heated through.

---

make it your way

FOR A PROTEIN BOOST: Stir in 2 cups of shredded cooked chicken breast or 1 (15-ounce) can of drained and rinsed black beans with the pepper Jack cheese.

crispy cornflake chicken tenders

SERVES 4 ■ PREP TIME: 10 MINUTES ■ COOK TIME: 20 MINUTES

Ummm, hello! I'm here to offer you a quick weeknight meal that will truly please everyone. These are not your average chicken tenders thanks to a crispy cornflake coating that adds some serious crunch. Kids love them, adults love them, and they make the best appetizer or last-minute dinner. Dip in honey mustard or drizzle with hot honey for some grown-up comfort food. These are delicious paired with sweet potato fries, or just throw them on your favorite salad (I'm looking at you, Southwestern Brussels Sprouts Salad, page 74) for some extra protein and crunch!

1. Preheat the oven to 400°F. Place an oven-safe metal wire rack on a large baking sheet. Spray the rack with cooking spray.

2. **Make the cornflake coating:** In a food processor, pulse the cornflakes until they resemble fine bread crumbs. Transfer to a medium bowl and whisk in the paprika, onion powder, garlic powder, salt, and pepper until well combined.

3. **Prepare the chicken:** In another medium bowl, whisk the eggs and milk until well combined. Dip a chicken tender into the egg mixture, coating both sides. Use tongs to grab it and transfer to the cornflake mixture. Toss to completely coat both sides, then use tongs to transfer the chicken to the prepared wire rack on the baking sheet. Repeat with remaining chicken tenders.

4. **Cook the chicken:** Generously spray the tops of the chicken tenders with cooking spray. Bake until golden brown on the outside and a meat thermometer inserted into the thickest part of the tender reads 165°F, 15 to 20 minutes.

5. **To serve:** Transfer to a serving platter, drizzle Quick Hot Honey over the chicken or serve the Honey Mustard Sauce on the side for dipping. Serve immediately.

6. **To store:** Keep any leftovers in an airtight container or reusable silicone bag in the fridge for up to 3 days. To reheat, place the chicken tenders on a baking sheet and bake them at 375°F until heated through and crispy, 8 to 10 minutes.

7. **To freeze:** Put the completely cooled chicken tenders in a single layer on a baking sheet and place in the freezer to ensure they don't stick together. Freeze for 1 hour, then transfer to an airtight container or reusable silicone bag and store in the freezer for up to 3 months. To reheat from frozen, place the frozen chicken tenders on a baking sheet and bake at 375°F until heated through and crispy, 15 to 20 minutes.

Nonstick cooking spray

CRUNCHY CORNFLAKE COATING

6 cups cornflakes

1 teaspoon sweet paprika

½ teaspoon onion powder

½ teaspoon garlic powder

½ teaspoon kosher salt

½ teaspoon freshly ground black pepper

CHICKEN

2 large eggs

2 tablespoons milk of choice, dairy-free if desired

1½ pounds boneless, skinless chicken tenders

SERVING

Quick Hot Honey (page 231), or 1 or 2 batches Honey Mustard Sauce (page 236)

make it your way

CRISPY CORNFLAKE CHICKEN NUGGETS: Cut 1½ pounds of boneless, skinless chicken breast into 1-inch cubes and bread the same way. Bake as directed.

scoop 'em up mini pesto turkey meatballs with herb garlic butter toasts

SERVES 4 TO 6 AS A MAIN DISH, 6 TO 8 AS A STARTER ▪ **PREP TIME: 20 MINUTES**
▪ **COOK TIME: 25 MINUTES**

MEATBALLS AND SAUCE

1 pound 93% lean ground turkey (or sub ground chicken)

½ cup panko bread crumbs

1 large egg

2 tablespoons Easy Basil Pesto (page 232) or store-bought basil pesto

½ teaspoon red pepper flakes

1 teaspoon Italian seasoning

½ teaspoon garlic powder

½ teaspoon kosher salt

Freshly ground black pepper

2 tablespoons extra-virgin olive oil

1 (25-ounce) jar marinara sauce

8 ounces fresh whole-milk mozzarella cheese, shredded

GARLIC TOASTS

1 (1-pound) loaf of Italian or French bread, cut diagonally into ¼-inch slices

6 tablespoons (85 grams) salted butter, softened

4 garlic cloves, finely minced

1 tablespoon finely chopped fresh parsley

1 to 2 teaspoons chopped fresh thyme leaves or rosemary

¼ teaspoon kosher salt

TOPPINGS

⅓ cup Easy Basil Pesto (page 232) or store-bought basil pesto

Fresh basil leaves

Mini meatballs, meet tie dye pizza—that colorful pie topped with swirls of red and green sauce, and my inspiration for this recipe. This dish is the best of both worlds: Pesto and red sauce, swirled together to create magical, irresistible flavors. Meatballs smothered in cheese. Herby, garlicky toast. Could be an appetizer, could be an entrée—your choice! (My boys would vote for both on the same night.)

1. Preheat the oven to 400°F. Line a large baking sheet with parchment paper and set aside.

2. **Make the meatballs and sauce:** Fill a medium bowl with water and place it on the counter. In a large bowl, place the turkey, panko, egg, pesto, red pepper flakes, Italian seasoning, garlic powder, salt, and a few grinds of pepper. Use clean hands to mix until well combined; avoid overmixing, otherwise the meatballs will become tough. Form the mixture into 45 to 50 mini meatballs, about the size of a marble. Dip your hands into the water between each meatball if they become too sticky.

3. In a large, deep oven-safe skillet, warm the olive oil over medium-high heat. Once the oil is hot, add the meatballs in batches (don't crowd the pan!) and brown on all sides, about 5 minutes total (they will finish cooking in the sauce). Use tongs to transfer the meatballs to a plate as they finish. Repeat with the remaining meatballs. Return all the meatballs to the skillet, pour in the marinara, and gently stir so the meatballs are coated in sauce. Top evenly with the mozzarella. Reduce the heat to medium-low and cover. Simmer until the meatballs are cooked through, 5 to 10 minutes. (Don't stir—we want the mozzarella to stay on the surface!) Keep warm.

4. **Meanwhile, make the garlic toasts:** Place the bread slices on the prepared baking sheet. In a medium bowl, mix the butter, garlic, parsley, thyme, and salt until well combined. Spread evenly over both sides of bread slices. Bake undisturbed until slightly golden brown on the edges, 10 to 15 minutes. Remove from the oven and set aside.

5. **Finish the meatballs and sauce:** Switch the oven to the broiler setting on high. Uncover the skillet, transfer to the broiler, and broil until the sauce is bubbly and the cheese is slightly golden brown, 2 to 4 minutes.

6. **Top and serve:** Remove from the oven and dollop tablespoonfuls of pesto on top of the meatballs and cheese. Garnish with the basil. Serve immediately with the garlic toasts on the side for scooping.

7. **To store:** Keep any leftovers in an airtight container in the fridge for up to 5 days. Reheat in the microwave in 30-second intervals or on the stovetop until heated through. For freezing instructions, see page 21.

make it your way

MINI PESTO TURKEY MEATBALLS
AND PASTA: Serve the meatballs
and sauce with cooked spaghetti or
penne instead of toast.

make it nutrient-dense

Stir 1 to 2 cups of chopped spinach
into the marinara before topping
with mozzarella.

make it your way

MOMMY'S VEGGIE-LOADED CHICKEN TAQUITOS: Use the filling from Everyone's Favorite Baked Chicken Tacos (page 152) and pair with my Spicy Cilantro Yogurt Sauce (page 236).

baked crispy mango jalapeño black bean chicken taquitos

SERVES 4 TO 6 ■ PREP TIME: 30 MINUTES ■ COOK TIME: 30 MINUTES

This recipe is the result of my quest to create taquitos that we can enjoy at home that are easy to make (no deep-frying needed!). If you are short on time, feel free to use store-bought rotisserie chicken instead of chicken thighs.

1. Preheat the oven to 400°F. Line a baking sheet with parchment paper.

2. **Prepare the chicken:** Place the chicken on the prepared baking sheet and drizzle with the olive oil. In a small bowl, whisk the adobo, salt, cumin, chili powder, paprika, garlic powder, and a few grinds of pepper. Rub the seasoning all over the chicken. Bake until a meat thermometer inserted into the thickest part of the thigh reads 165°F, 15 to 20 minutes. (Don't turn off the oven: you'll need it in a few minutes!) Cool the chicken for at least 5 minutes, then chop or shred using two forks.

3. **Prepare the filling:** Transfer the shredded chicken to a large bowl and add the black beans, mango, jalapeño, and red onion, and stir well to combine. Gently fold in half of the mango jalapeño sauce, reserving the rest for serving. Taste and add more salt as needed.

4. **Assemble the taquitos:** Line a separate large baking sheet with parchment paper. Wrap a stack of 4 tortillas in a damp paper towel and microwave for 30 seconds to make the tortillas pliable. Transfer the tortillas to the prepared baking sheet and spread in a single layer. If using corn tortillas, add 2 heaping tablespoons of filling and 2 tablespoons of cheese to the middle of each one. If using flour tortillas, add ¼ cup of filling and ¼ cup of cheese to the middle of each one. Roll up the tortillas and place seam-side down at least 1 inch apart on the baking sheet, then generously spray with cooking spray. Repeat with the remaining tortillas and filling.

5. Bake until the taquitos are crispy and golden, 15 to 20 minutes.

6. **Make the yogurt drizzle and serve:** In a small bowl, whisk the Greek yogurt, lime juice, and salt until it can easily be drizzled. Transfer the taquitos to a platter, drizzle with the yogurt lime sauce and the reserved mango jalapeño sauce. Sprinkle cilantro on top and serve immediately.

7. **To store:** Keep any leftovers in an airtight container in the fridge for up to 3 days. To reheat, put the taquitos on a baking sheet and spray with cooking spray or brush with olive oil to help re-crisp them. Bake at 350°F until warm and crispy, about 10 minutes.

8. **To freeze:** Prepare the taquitos as directed but before baking, place them on a baking sheet and freeze for 2 hours. Once frozen, transfer to a reusable silicone bag or airtight container and freeze for up to 1 month. Bake as directed, being sure to coat them with cooking spray, and add 5 minutes of baking time, if necessary.

CHICKEN

1 pound boneless, skinless chicken thighs

1 tablespoon extra-virgin olive oil

1 teaspoon adobo seasoning

1 teaspoon kosher salt

1 teaspoon ground cumin

1 teaspoon chili powder

1 teaspoon sweet paprika

½ teaspoon garlic powder

Freshly ground black pepper

FILLING

1 (15-ounce) can black beans, drained and rinsed

1 large ripe mango, diced

1 jalapeño, seeded and diced

¼ cup diced red onion

Mango Jalapeño Sauce (page 233)

Kosher salt

ASSEMBLY

16 (6-inch) soft corn tortillas (gluten-free) or 8 (8-inch) flour tortillas

8 ounces shredded Monterey Jack cheese (2 cups)

Nonstick cooking spray

YOGURT DRIZZLE AND SERVING

¼ cup plain whole-milk Greek yogurt

2 teaspoons fresh lime juice

⅛ teaspoon kosher salt

Chopped fresh cilantro

everyone's favorite baked chicken tacos (packed with veggies!)

SERVES 4 TO 6 ■ PREP TIME: 20 MINUTES ■ COOK TIME: 30 MINUTES

FILLING

1 tablespoon extra-virgin olive oil

½ medium yellow onion, diced

1 small orange bell pepper, very finely diced

1 medium zucchini, very finely chopped

¾ cup fresh corn kernels (from 1 ear)

1 pound 93% lean ground chicken (or sub ground turkey)

1 teaspoon adobo seasoning

1 teaspoon ground cumin

1 teaspoon sweet paprika

1 teaspoon chili powder

1 teaspoon garlic powder

½ teaspoon kosher salt, plus more to taste

Freshly ground black pepper

¾ cup salsa of your choice

¼ cup chopped fresh cilantro

TACOS

18 (6-inch) soft corn tortillas

¼ cup extra-virgin olive oil, for brushing, plus more as needed

5 ounces shredded Monterey Jack or Cheddar cheese (1¼ cups)

4 ounces shredded pepper Jack cheese (1 cup)

36 pickled jalapeño slices (optional)

Spicy Cilantro Yogurt Sauce (page 236) or Jalapeño Lime Cashew Sauce (page 232), for serving

When we were going through our kitchen renovation, I began making this veggie-packed filling for nachos, quesadillas, and rice bowls. It really shines in these amazing baked tacos, which quickly became one of my kids' favorite meals. They adorably call it "Mommy's Nachos."

1. Preheat the oven to 425°F. Line two large baking sheets with parchment paper.

2. **Make the filling:** In a large, deep skillet, warm the olive oil over medium heat. Once the oil is hot, add the onion, bell pepper, zucchini, and corn, and sauté, stirring occasionally, until softened, 5 to 8 minutes. Move the veggies to the edges of the pan.

3. Add the chicken to the middle of the pan, breaking apart the meat with a wooden spoon, and cook, stirring frequently, until no longer pink, about 5 minutes. Stir in the adobo, cumin, paprika, chili powder, garlic powder, salt, and a few grinds of pepper Cook, stirring frequently, until the spices are toasted and smell fragrant, about 1 minute. Stir in the salsa and cilantro and cook, stirring occasionally, until the excess liquid cooks off, 5 minutes. Remove from the heat, taste, and adjust the seasonings.

4. **Make the tacos:** Wrap 4 tortillas in a damp paper towel and microwave for 30 to 45 seconds to make the tortillas pliable.

5. Lightly brush each tortilla with about 1 teaspoon of olive oil and place oil-side down on the prepared baking sheets. In a medium bowl, mix together the Monterey Jack and the pepper Jack. Add 1 tablespoon of the cheese mixture to one side of the tortilla, then top with ¼ cup of the filling, 2 pickled jalapeño slices (if using), and another 1 tablespoon of cheese. Fold the tortilla over, pushing down to adhere shut and make a taco. Repeat with the remaining tortillas, filling, and cheese.

6. **Bake the tacos:** Bake for 4 minutes, then check to see if any of the tortillas have popped open. If so, press the top of the tortilla down with a spatula; the melted cheese will help seal them shut. Bake for another 5 minutes, then remove the pans, flip the tacos, and rotate the pans to ensure even cooking. Bake until the tacos are crispy and golden brown, 6 to 8 minutes. Allow the tacos to cool on the pan until cool enough to handle, 5 to 10 minutes. Serve immediately with Spicy Cilantro Yogurt Sauce or Jalapeño Lime Cashew Sauce.

7. **To store:** Keep leftover tacos in an airtight container in the fridge for up to 5 days. To reheat, place tacos on a baking sheet and bake at 375°F for 5 to 10 minutes, or until heated through.

8. **To freeze:** Allow tacos to cool completely after baking, then place them on a baking sheet and freeze for 2 hours. Once frozen, transfer the tacos to a reusable silicone bag or an airtight container and freeze for up to 3 months. To reheat from frozen, place the tacos on a baking sheet and bake at 375°F for 10 to 15 minutes, or until heated through.

make it your way

TO MAKE DAIRY-FREE: Leave out the cotija cheese and use Jalapeño Lime Cashew Sauce (page 232) instead of the Spicy Cilantro Yogurt Sauce.

honey chipotle lime shrimp tacos with avocado mango salsa

SERVES 4 ▪ PREP TIME: 20 MINUTES ▪ COOK TIME: 10 MINUTES

I've had a lot of shrimp tacos, but these are my favorite: Sweet avocado and mango salsa and seasoned shrimp, all wrapped in a charred corn tortilla makes a dish that's bright and herbal with just a bit of heat. It's important to use mangoes that are firm but just slightly tender—not super ripe, soft ones. The goal is for the mangoes to stay cubed and not get too mushy in the salsa, so that you get sweet little pops of fruit in every bite. The salsa can also be doubled or tripled and used for chip-dipping all summer long. And here's another way to switch it up: Throw the salsa, slaw, and shrimp over cooked rice for an easy, delicious meal!

1. **Make the salsa:** In a medium bowl, gently toss the avocado, mango, corn, cilantro, onion, jalapeño, lime juice, and salt. Taste and adjust the seasoning. Set aside.

2. **Make the slaw:** In another medium bowl, toss the cabbage and ⅓ cup of Spicy Cilantro Yogurt Sauce (reserve the remaining sauce for serving) until the sauce coats all of the cabbage. Set aside.

3. **Prepare the shrimp:** Pat the shrimp dry with a paper towel and transfer to a large bowl with the salt, chipotle chili powder, garlic powder, paprika, and lime zest. Toss well to combine so that the shrimp are fully coated in the spices.

4. **Cook the shrimp:** In a large nonstick skillet, warm the olive oil over medium heat. Once the oil is hot, add the shrimp and cook, stirring and flipping occasionally, until pink and cooked through, 6 to 8 minutes. Remove the pan from the heat and immediately toss with the lime juice and honey. (Alternatively, roast the shrimp in the oven: Preheat the oven to 400°F. Line a baking sheet with parchment paper. Toss the shrimp with the olive oil and spices. Spread the shrimp in a single layer on the baking sheet and bake undisturbed until fully cooked, about 10 minutes. Finish by tossing shrimp with lime juice and honey.)

5. **Warm the tortillas:** Turn a gas burner on your stove to the lowest heat possible. Carefully place a tortilla directly on the burner until charred, 45 seconds to 1 minute, then use tongs to flip the tortilla and repeat on the other side. If using an electric stove, place a nonstick skillet over medium heat. Warm each tortilla for 1 minute on each side. Stack each tortilla as it finishes in a warm towel on a plate, then close the towel around the tortillas to keep warm.

6. **Assemble the tacos:** Top the tortillas with slaw, shrimp, salsa, jalapeño slices, a drizzle of the remaining Spicy Cilantro Yogurt Sauce, and cotija cheese and serve immediately.

SALSA

1 avocado, diced

1 large ripe mango, diced

¾ cup fresh corn kernels (from 1 ear)

2 tablespoons chopped fresh cilantro

2 tablespoons finely chopped red onion

½ jalapeño, finely diced

1 tablespoon fresh lime juice

¼ teaspoon kosher salt, plus more to taste

SLAW

3 cups shredded green cabbage

Spicy Cilantro Yogurt Sauce (page 236)

SHRIMP

1 pound large raw shrimp, peeled, deveined, tails removed

1 teaspoon kosher salt

½ teaspoon chipotle chili powder

½ teaspoon garlic powder

½ teaspoon sweet paprika

Zest of 1 lime

2 tablespoons extra-virgin olive oil

1 tablespoon fresh lime juice

1 tablespoon honey

ASSEMBLY

8 (6-inch) corn tortillas

½ jalapeño, sliced

4 ounces cotija cheese, crumbled

weeknight chicken picadillo (my favorite empanada filling)

SERVES 4, MAKES ABOUT 3¾ CUPS ■ PREP TIME: 10 MINUTES ■ COOK TIME: 25 MINUTES

POTATOES, VEGGIES, AND CHICKEN

2 tablespoons extra-virgin olive oil

1 cup finely diced Yukon Gold potatoes

½ medium yellow onion, diced

½ green bell pepper, finely diced

½ cup chopped fresh cilantro

3 garlic cloves, minced

1 pound 93% lean ground chicken (or sub ground turkey)

SPICES

1 teaspoon adobo seasoning

1 teaspoon ground coriander

1 teaspoon ground cumin

½ teaspoon ground turmeric

½ teaspoon garlic powder

½ teaspoon dried oregano

½ teaspoon kosher salt, plus more to taste

Freshly ground black pepper

MIX-INS

1 (8-ounce) can tomato sauce

½ cup pimento-stuffed olives, plus 2 tablespoons of their brine

SERVING OPTIONS

Holiday Empanadas (page 140)

Arroz con Gandules (page 218) or your favorite rice

Crispy Fried Tostones (page 221)

Sliced avocado

Everyone in my family has a different version of this picadillo: Nana added raisins; Mom sometimes likes to add sweet potatoes; I adore the saltiness of olives but otherwise keep it simple with my own sazón mixture. Heck, sometimes I even skip the potatoes and still find it just as fabulous. It's my fav filling for Holiday Empanadas, but try it in tacos, taquitos, burritos, or quesadillas, or you can serve it with Crispy Fried Tostones or rice—I especially love it with Arroz con Gandules. There's no wrong way to eat it.

1. **Make the potatoes, veggies, and chicken:** In a large pot or deep skillet, warm the olive oil over medium heat. Once the oil is hot, add the potatoes, onion, bell pepper, cilantro, and garlic and sauté, stirring occasionally, until the onion and pepper are softened, about 5 minutes. Add the chicken and cook, stirring occasionally and breaking up the meat with a wooden spoon, until cooked almost all the way through with just a little pink left, about 5 minutes.

2. **Stir in the spices:** Add the adobo, coriander, cumin, turmeric, garlic powder, dried oregano, salt, and a few grinds of pepper and cook, stirring frequently, until fragrant, about 30 seconds.

3. **Add the mix-ins:** Immediately stir in the tomato sauce, olives, and brine, bring the mixture to a simmer, then cover, reduce the heat to low, and cook, stirring occasionally, until the potatoes are fork-tender, 10 to 15 minutes. Taste and adjust the salt and spices as necessary.

4. **To serve:** If using for empanada stuffing, cool to room temperature first. Otherwise, serve immediately with Arroz con Gandules or your favorite rice, Crispy Fried Tostones, and/or sliced avocado.

5. **To store:** Keep any leftovers in an airtight container in the fridge for up to 5 days. Reheat in the microwave in 30-second intervals until heated through.

6. **To freeze:** Keep the picadillo in an airtight container or freezer-safe reusable silicone bag and place in the freezer for up to 3 months. To reheat, let the picadillo thaw in the fridge before microwaving in 30-second intervals. Alternatively, you can reheat the picadillo on the stovetop over medium-low heat, stirring occasionally, until heated through, about 10 minutes.

make it your way

SWEET AND SALTY PICADILLO:
Stir in ½ cup dark or golden raisins
with the olives.

make it nutrient-dense

Sub diced sweet potatoes for the
Yukon Gold potatoes.

make it your way

TO MAKE DAIRY-FREE: Use vegan butter instead of regular butter and all vegan ingredients in the Bangin' Sauce (page 232). Make sure your hamburger buns are dairy-free, too.

TO MAKE GLUTEN-FREE: Use gluten-free panko bread crumbs. Use coconut aminos or tamari instead of soy sauce. Serve in lettuce wraps or on gluten-free hamburger buns.

hot chile basil lime chicken burgers with bangin' sauce

SERVES 4 ■ PREP TIME: 20 MINUTES ■ COOK TIME: 10 MINUTES

OMG THESE ARE A MUST-MAKE. The trick to keeping these chicken burgers extra juicy is to add a little mayo to the burger mixture before cooking. I'm a big fan of burgers all year round, so I've included options for grilling and pan-frying. Load them up with my famous slaw and a cool, creamy, spicy Bangin' Sauce, and you're set.

1. If grilling, preheat the grill to medium-high heat (about 400°F). Line a baking sheet with parchment paper.

2. **Make the burgers:** In a large bowl, combine the chicken, panko, garlic, scallions, basil, cilantro, sambal oelek, brown sugar, mayo, soy sauce, ginger, lime zest, salt, and a few grinds of pepper. Mix with clean hands just until evenly combined. If time allows, cover the bowl with plastic wrap and allow the mixture to rest in the fridge for 30 minutes.

3. Divide the meat mixture into 4 equal portions. Using slightly damp hands, shape into ¼-inch-thick patties and place on the prepared baking sheet. (This will allow for easy transfer to the grill or pan.)

4. **Cook the burgers:**

   ■ **TO GRILL:** Brush the grates with avocado oil to prevent sticking. Transfer the patties to the hot grill and cook until a meat thermometer inserted into the thickest part of the burger reads 165°F, 4 to 5 minutes per side. You'll know the burgers are ready to flip if they release from the grill easily when you try to move them with a spatula. This means a good crust has formed.

   ■ **TO PAN-FRY:** Warm about 1 tablespoon of avocado oil in a large skillet over medium-high heat. Once the oil is hot, but not smoking, carefully transfer the patties into the pan. Sear until a golden brown crust has formed and a meat thermometer inserted into the thickest part reads 165°F, 4 to 5 minutes per side.

5. **Toast the buns:** Spread the butter over the cut side of the bun halves, then place on the grill (away from direct flames) until the bread is toasted, about 1 minute. Alternatively, toast the buns on the stove: In a large skillet, melt the butter over medium heat, then place the buns face-down and cook until toasted, about 1 minute.

6. **Assemble the burgers:** Add 1 heaping tablespoon Bangin' Sauce to each half of the toasted buns. Top each bottom bun with lettuce, then add the burger patty, about ¼ cup of slaw, and avocado slices. Top with the remaining bun and serve immediately.

7. **To store:** Keep cooked burger patties in an airtight container or reusable silicone bag in the fridge for up to 4 days. Reheat in the microwave in 30-second intervals or in a pan on the stovetop over medium heat until heated through. For freezing instructions, see page 21.

BURGERS

1 pound 93% lean ground chicken (or sub ground turkey)

½ cup panko bread crumbs

3 garlic cloves, minced

2 scallions, finely chopped

3 tablespoons finely chopped fresh basil

2 tablespoons finely chopped fresh cilantro

2 tablespoons sambal oelek (or sriracha)

2 tablespoons packed dark brown sugar (or sub coconut sugar)

1½ teaspoons mayonnaise

1 tablespoon low-sodium soy sauce

1 tablespoon grated fresh ginger

1 teaspoon lime zest

½ teaspoon kosher salt

Freshly ground black pepper

Avocado oil, for grilling or frying

ASSEMBLY

1 tablespoon salted butter

4 whole-grain hamburger buns

Bangin' Sauce (page 232)

Butter lettuce leaves

"The Slaw" (page 206)

1 large avocado, thinly sliced

it's a

← **the zinger** (PAGE 165)

← holy poblano!
(PAGE 165)

getting figgy
with it →
(PAGE 165)

pizza party!

← the morgan (PAGE 164)

matt's famous no-knead pizza dough

MAKES 2 (½-POUND) DOUGH BALLS ■ **PREP TIME: 20 MINUTES, PLUS RISING TIME**

My brother-in-law, Matt, has been working on his pizza dough recipe for as long as I can remember. Every year, he produces a tantalizing array of thin, chewy pizzas for Christmas dinner. This no-knead dough needs at least 3 to 4 hours to rise—or an overnight stay in the fridge—but it can be rolled instead of stretched, making it much more accessible to those of us without professional pizzeria experience! This recipe will take you from a bowl of flour, water, and yeast to a festive celebration, any night of the week. For best results, use a scale to weigh your ingredients and use a pizza peel and stone; it really does make all the difference!

2½ cups (300 grams) all-purpose flour or bread flour, plus more for dusting

¾ teaspoon instant yeast

1½ teaspoons kosher salt

1 cup (240 grams) lukewarm water, warmed to 115°F

1 tablespoon extra-virgin olive oil

1. **Make the dough:** In a large bowl, whisk the flour, yeast, and salt. Add the warm water. Mix with a wooden spoon until a sticky dough comes together and no dry flour can be seen.

2. Grease another large bowl with the olive oil. Transfer the dough to the bowl, turn the dough to coat it with oil, then cover with plastic wrap and a towel. Allow the dough to rise until doubled in size, 3 to 4 hours at room temperature (this will depend on the temperature and humidity in your home) or up to 24 hours in the fridge (bring the dough to room temperature 90 minutes before baking).

3. Generously flour a clean surface. Turn the dough out, cut it in half, and use your hands to cup the dough into 2 rounds, using as much flour as needed. Cover with plastic wrap and a towel and allow dough to sit for at least 45 minutes, if baking right away. (This allows the dough to continue to proof—the dough will stay good at room temperature for hours.) If not baking the same day, see Make-Ahead Pizza Dough, or freezing instructions on page 21.

make-ahead pizza dough

Shape the risen dough into 2 rounds as directed in step 3, then immediately transfer each round to a quart-size container, cover with an airtight lid and transfer to the fridge for up to 4 days. Remove the dough from the fridge at least 90 minutes before baking to allow it to come to room temperature. Transfer dough to a well-floured surface then shape or roll out dough and bake as directed.

pizza, your way

MAKES 1 PIZZA ■ PREP TIME: 10 MINUTES
■ COOK TIME: 8 TO 10 MINUTES

All-purpose flour or bread flour, for dusting

Cornmeal, for dusting (optional)

1 (½ pound) ball Matt's Famous No-Knead Pizza Dough (page 163) or store-bought pizza dough

Extra-virgin olive oil, for greasing (optional)

Toppings of choice (see pages 164 to 165)

FOUR different options for finished pizzas. Double the toppings when using a full pound of dough, or make two different pizzas. Or, freestyle your pizzas and add whatever toppings you like!

1. Place a rack in the upper-middle of the oven and add a pizza stone. Preheat the oven to 500°F for at least 45 minutes to 1 hour. This is very important; a hot pizza stone makes all the difference!

2. Lightly dust a pizza peel with 1 to 2 tablespoons flour, then 1 tablespoon cornmeal, and use your hands or a well-floured rolling pin to stretch or roll the dough ball into an approximate 9-inch round, about ¼ inch thick. It can really be any shape you'd like, so don't worry too much about getting it perfect. Assemble the pizza on the pizza peel before using it to transfer the pizza to the pizza stone. When using a pizza peel, make sure the pizza dough can move easily by giving it a gentle shake on the dusted peel before adding toppings—if it sticks, you'll never be able to transfer it to the stone!

3. Work quickly to assemble the pizza with your toppings of choice and transfer the pizza onto the pizza stone. Use a quick back-and-forth wrist movement to release the pizza from the peel onto the stone. Try to keep the pizza peel flat so that none of the toppings fall off during transfer. This takes practice, but you'll get the hang of it quickly!

4. Bake for 8 to 10 minutes, until the cheese is melted and the crust is golden. Add any garnishes then cut into slices and serve immediately.

VEGETARIAN

THE MORGAN

Mushroom lovers, this one's for you.

2 tablespoons extra-virgin olive oil

8 ounces baby bella mushrooms, stemmed and finely chopped

½ teaspoon kosher salt

Freshly ground black pepper

4 garlic cloves, grated

4 ounces shredded fresh whole-milk mozzarella cheese (1 cup)

2 ounces goat cheese (optional)

1 ounce grated Parmesan cheese (¼ cup)

¼ cup Pickled Red Onions (page 237)

Flaky sea salt (I like Maldon)

1. In a medium skillet, warm 1 tablespoon of the olive oil over medium-high heat. Add the mushrooms, season with salt and pepper to taste, and sauté, stirring occasionally, until the mushrooms become golden brown, 6 to 8 minutes.

2. Brush the pizza dough with the remaining 1 tablespoon of olive oil, then sprinkle with the garlic, using a spoon to spread the garlic evenly over the dough, leaving a ¾-inch border for the crust. Top with the mushrooms, mozzarella, goat cheese (if using), Parmesan, and Pickled Red Onions.

3. Bake as directed. Remove from the oven and sprinkle with a little sea salt. Serve immediately.

THE ZINGER

Here to prove that pineapple belongs on pizza.

⅓ cup pizza sauce

4 ounces shredded fresh whole-milk mozzarella cheese (1 cup)

½ cup fresh pineapple chunks

12 to 15 pepperoni slices (about 1 ounce)

12 pickled jalapeño slices

1 ounce grated Parmesan cheese (¼ cup)

1. Spread the pizza sauce over the rolled-out pizza dough, leaving a ¾-inch border for the crust. Sprinkle with the mozzarella, then top with the pineapple, pepperoni, and pickled jalapeños.

2. Bake as directed. Garnish with the Parmesan cheese. Serve immediately.

VEGETARIAN

HOLY POBLANO!

Bring a little sweet heat to the party.

2 tablespoons extra-virgin olive oil, plus more for drizzling

1 poblano pepper, julienned

½ cup fresh corn kernels (or sub thawed frozen corn)

½ teaspoon kosher salt

4 ounces shredded fresh whole-milk mozzarella cheese (1 cup)

2 ounces goat cheese, crumbled

2 to 3 tablespoons Quick Hot Honey (page 231)

Flaky sea salt (I like Maldon)

1. In a medium skillet, warm 1 tablespoon of the olive oil over medium heat. Once the oil is hot, add the poblano and corn and season with the salt. Sauté, stirring occasionally, until the corn is slightly golden brown, 6 to 8 minutes.

2. Brush the rolled-out pizza dough with the remaining 1 tablespoon of olive oil and top with the poblano and corn mixture, leaving a ¾-inch border for the crust, then top with the mozzarella and goat cheese. Drizzle with a little more oil.

3. Bake as directed. Drizzle the hot honey over the pizza and sprinkle with sea salt. Serve immediately.

GETTING FIGGY WITH IT

A surprisingly delicious mix of toppings.

4 slices thick-cut bacon

¼ cup fig preserves

4 ounces goat cheese, crumbled

2 ounces shredded fresh whole-milk mozzarella cheese (½ cup)

1 to 2 cups fresh arugula

Extra-virgin olive oil, for drizzling

Flaky sea salt (I like Maldon)

1. **Cook the bacon on the stovetop:** Place the bacon in a large skillet or pan over medium heat. Cook the bacon on both sides until crispy and golden brown, about 8 minutes total. If the pan starts to smoke at any point, reduce the heat. Use tongs to transfer the bacon to a cutting board, blot with a paper towel to absorb excess grease, then chop the bacon into bite-sized pieces. Set aside.

2. Use a spoon to spread the fig preserves all over the rolled-out pizza dough, leaving a ¾-inch border for the crust. Top with the goat cheese, mozzarella, and bacon.

3. Bake as directed. Remove from the oven, then top with arugula, a drizzle of olive oil, and sprinkle with a little sea salt. Serve immediately.

dreamy dinners

My favorite dinners involve cozying up in the kitchen and experimenting with different cooking techniques to create something flavorful and comforting. I designed these dishes with flavors from a variety of cultures, such as Moroccan, Latin, and Asian, to leave you in a good mood in many ways. Sure, your body will be fueled by the nourishing ingredients (you'll find plenty of feel-good veggies), but, more important, your soul will be comforted by the process of chopping, cooking, and presenting something beautiful and delicious to family and friends. Dreamy, indeed.

chicken couscous with crushed pistachio olive dressing & feta

SERVES 4 TO 6 ▪ PREP TIME: 15 MINUTES, PLUS 20 MINUTES MARINATING TIME
▪ COOK TIME: 35 MINUTES

CHICKEN AND MARINADE

4 tablespoons extra-virgin olive oil

Zest and juice of 1 lemon

2 tablespoons olive brine (I use Castelvetrano olives, which are in the dressing)

3 garlic cloves, minced

1 teaspoon sweet paprika

1 teaspoon dried oregano

1 teaspoon kosher salt

Freshly ground black pepper

1½ pounds bone-in, skin-on chicken thighs (about 4 large)

COUSCOUS

3 medium carrots, cut diagonally into ¼-inch slices

1 lemon, sliced

1 medium shallot, thinly sliced

1¼ cups pearl couscous

3 garlic cloves, minced

2 cups low-sodium chicken broth

½ teaspoon kosher salt

Freshly ground black pepper

TOPPINGS

Crushed Pistachio Olive Dressing (page 230)

4 ounces feta cheese, crumbled

¼ cup chopped fresh parsley

1 to 2 tablespoons honey

Flaky sea salt (I like Maldon)

Freshly ground black pepper

I love olives, but I might love olive brine even more (which is likely why I adore a good dirty martini!). Olive brine is an ingredient that too many people just pour down the drain, but little did you know, it gives chicken a nice salty, olive-y flavor! Best. Chicken. Marinade. Ever! Throw it into a pot with my beloved pearl couscous, and you'll have a one-pot meal that will make you feel like you're on a Mediterranean vacation.

1. **Marinate the chicken:** In a large bowl, whisk 2 tablespoons of the olive oil, the lemon zest and juice, brine, garlic, paprika, dried oregano, salt, and a few grinds of pepper until combined. Add the chicken and turn over to coat. Cover with plastic wrap and marinate for 30 minutes at room temperature or up to 2 hours in the fridge. Before cooking, bring to room temperature for 20 to 30 minutes.

2. Position a rack in the middle of the oven and preheat to 425°F.

3. **Brown the chicken:** In a deep, large, oven-safe skillet or Dutch oven, warm the remaining 2 tablespoons of olive oil over medium-high heat. Remove the chicken from the marinade, allowing any excess to drip off. Once the oil is hot, carefully place the chicken skin-side down into the pan and cook, undisturbed, until the skin is golden brown and starts to render and the thigh easily releases from the pan when moved, 4 to 5 minutes. Turn the chicken over and cook until browned on the other side, 4 to 5 minutes. Use tongs to transfer the chicken to a plate (it will finish cooking in the oven).

4. **Make the couscous:** Return the skillet to the stove and place over medium heat. Add the carrots, lemon, and shallot and cook, stirring occasionally to allow the lemons to deglaze the pan, until the shallots are tender, 3 to 5 minutes. Use tongs to remove the lemons and transfer to the plate with the chicken. Stir in the couscous and garlic and cook, stirring frequently, until the couscous is golden and toasted, 1 to 2 minutes. Immediately add the broth, salt, and a few grinds of pepper, stirring to combine. Bring the mixture to a simmer and add the chicken skin-side up on top of the couscous, then nestle in the lemon slices.

5. **Bake the chicken and couscous:** Transfer the skillet to the oven and bake on the middle rack until the chicken is fully cooked and reads 165°F on a meat thermometer when inserted into the thickest part, about 20 minutes.

6. **Top and serve:** Spoon the Crushed Pistachio Olive Dressing on top of the chicken and couscous. Top with the feta, parsley, a drizzle of honey, and a sprinkle with flaky sea salt and pepper. Serve immediately.

7. **To store:** Keep any leftovers in an airtight container in the fridge for up to 3 days, preferably without the toppings. Reheat in the microwave until warm and garnish with toppings as desired.

make it your way

TO MAKE DAIRY-FREE: Leave out
the feta or use dairy-free feta.

make it nutrient-dense

Stir in any (or all) of the following with the orzo: 2 cups of chopped spinach, 1 cup of shredded or chopped zucchini, and/or 1 (15-ounce) can of white beans, drained and rinsed.

pepperoni pizza baked orzo with basil & quick hot honey

SERVES 4 ■ PREP TIME: 15 MINUTES ■ COOK TIME: 30 MINUTES

Have you ever topped your pepperoni pizza with hot honey? If not, let me introduce you to the best sweet and spicy combo. At my house, Tony is always up for pepperoni pizza and my kids can't get enough pasta, so the whole family tears into this one-dish pasta that hits every craving (and can easily be bulked up with more meat or vegetables). I love to serve this with romaine salad tossed with Greek-Inspired Lemon Vinaigrette (page 235) and some Parmesan on top. So simple, so good!

1. Preheat the oven to 400°F.

2. **Cook the orzo:** In a large oven-safe skillet, warm the olive oil over medium heat. Once the oil is hot, add the onion and bell pepper and sauté, stirring occasionally, until the onions begin to soften, 3 to 5 minutes. Add the orzo, garlic, and red pepper flakes and stir until the orzo is toasted and the mixture is fragrant, about 2 minutes. Stir in the water, pizza sauce, Italian seasoning, salt, and pepper to taste.

3. Transfer the skillet to the oven and bake uncovered until the liquid is mostly absorbed and the orzo is cooked through, 12 to 15 minutes.

4. Stir ½ cup of the mozzarella into the orzo. Sprinkle the remaining 1 cup of mozzarella on top, then evenly arrange pepperoni slices on top. Place the skillet back in the oven and bake until the cheese is melted, about 5 minutes. Switch the oven to the broiler setting on high and broil until the cheese is slightly golden in places, 1 to 3 minutes.

5. **Top and serve:** Drizzle with the hot honey, then sprinkle with the Parmesan, basil, and a little flaky sea salt. Serve immediately.

6. **To store:** Keep any leftovers in an airtight container in the fridge for up to 5 days. Reheat in the microwave until heated through.

ORZO

1 tablespoon extra-virgin olive oil

½ medium white onion, finely diced

1 red bell pepper, diced

1 pound orzo

3 garlic cloves, minced

½ teaspoon red pepper flakes

2½ cups water or low-sodium chicken broth

1½ cups pizza sauce (or sub marinara)

1 teaspoon Italian seasoning

½ teaspoon kosher salt

Freshly ground black pepper

6 ounces shredded mozzarella or Italian cheese blend (1½ cups)

3 ounces pepperoni slices (mini pepperoni is great, too!)

TOPPINGS

2 tablespoons Quick Hot Honey (page 231)

2 tablespoons grated Parmesan cheese

6 to 8 fresh basil leaves, julienned

Flaky sea salt (I like Maldon)

make it your way

TO MAKE GLUTEN-FREE: Use gluten-free orzo (I like the DeLallo brand).

AMP UP THE PEPPERONI: Stir in 3 ounces of chopped pepperoni slices with the orzo.

SAUSAGE & SPINACH BAKED ORZO: Skip the pepperoni and hot honey. Cook 8 to 12 ounces of Italian sausage (preferably spicy!) with the onion and bell pepper until nicely browned and the onion

has softened, 5 to 8 minutes. Stir in 2 to 3 cups of chopped spinach with the orzo.

skillet chicken pasta with pistachio pesto, corn & zucchini

SERVES 4 ■ PREP TIME: 15 MINUTES ■ COOK TIME: 30 MINUTES

CHICKEN

1 pound boneless, skinless chicken breasts

1 teaspoon garlic powder

1 teaspoon kosher salt

Freshly ground black pepper

1 tablespoon extra-virgin olive oil

PASTA

Kosher salt

12 ounces pasta, such as spaghetti, gemelli, or bowtie pasta, but use anything you'd like! (gluten-free, if desired)

Cilantro Pistachio Pesto (page 235)

VEGGIES

1 tablespoon extra-virgin olive oil

¾ cup fresh corn kernels (from 1 ear)

1 medium zucchini, quartered lengthwise and sliced

½ teaspoon kosher salt

Freshly ground black pepper

2 ounces goat cheese, crumbled

TOPPINGS

2 ounces goat cheese, crumbled

¼ cup chopped roasted shelled pistachios

Zest of 1 lemon

Kosher salt

Freshly ground black pepper

Red pepper flakes

When summer corn is at its peak, grab an ear and run home to make this flavorful meal that's so easy to throw together. Cut those lovely kernels right off the cob for some sweetness that complements the tender chicken, bites of fresh zucchini, and tangy goat cheese. TRUST me, the Cilantro Pistachio Pesto is the magic that brings it all together. This pasta is so good that I don't even bother to reheat the leftovers—they're super tasty cold!

1. **Prepare the chicken:** Place the chicken breasts on a cutting board and cover with plastic wrap. Use a meat mallet to pound the chicken until it is about ½-inch thick. Remove the plastic wrap and season the chicken on both sides with the garlic powder, salt, and a few grinds of pepper Set aside.

2. **Make the pasta:** Bring a large pot of generously salted water to a boil over high heat. Add the pasta and cook according to the package directions until al dente. Reserve ½ cup of pasta water, then drain the pasta and return to the pot. Stir the pesto into the pasta.

3. **Cook the chicken:** In a large skillet, warm the olive oil over medium-high heat. Once the oil is hot, add the chicken and sear until golden brown on both sides and cooked through and no longer pink inside, 3 to 4 minutes per side. Remove the chicken from the skillet, transfer to a cutting board, and set aside to rest.

4. **Cook the veggies:** Return the skillet to the stove and warm the oil over medium heat, Once the oil is hot, add the corn and zucchini, season with the salt and a few grinds of pepper, and sauté, stirring occasionally, until the zucchini is tender and the veggies are slightly golden brown, 5 to 8 minutes. Add the veggies to the pasta and stir in the goat cheese, adding the reserved pasta water a splash at a time to make the sauce creamier, if desired.

5. **Top and serve:** Slice the chicken diagonally against the grain. Divide the pasta among serving bowls or plates, top with sliced chicken, and garnish with goat cheese, pistachios, lemon zest, salt and pepper to taste, and red pepper flakes. Serve immediately.

6. **To store:** Keep any leftovers in an airtight container in the fridge for up to 4 days. Reheat in the microwave in 30-second intervals, stirring in between, until heated through.

make it your way

TO MAKE GLUTEN-FREE: Use gluten-free pasta.

Sub 1 pound shrimp, deveined, shelled, and tails removed, for the chicken.

Sub feta cheese for the goat cheese (the flavor will be milder).

it's a sheet pan honey mustard chicken, sweet potato & bacon situation

SERVES 4 ■ **PREP TIME: 15 MINUTES** ■ **COOK TIME: 45 MINUTES**

Sheet pan meals make dinner such a breeze, but sometimes they can feel a little boring. Well, there's two ways I love to elevate them: bacon and FUN toppings. This one's a bit unexpected—chicken topped with an arugula-pecan-date-feta crumble—resulting in SO MANY TEXTURES. It's crispy, chewy, tender, crunchy. A beautiful dinner in just an hour from start to finish (with minimal cleanup)! If you really love honey mustard, I suggest doubling the sauce and serving some on the side or drizzled over the chicken and veggies.

1. **Cook the bacon:** Line a baking sheet with parchment paper. Place the bacon slices in a single layer on the prepared baking sheet and transfer to the middle rack of a cold oven. (This helps the bacon render more evenly and yields flat and crispy bacon.) Heat the oven to 425°F and cook until the bacon has reached your desired crispiness, 15 to 25 minutes. Use tongs to transfer the bacon to a cutting board, blot with a paper towel to absorb excess grease, then chop the bacon into bite-sized pieces. Set aside. (Alternatively, cook the bacon on the stovetop: Place the bacon in a large skillet or pan over medium heat. Cook on both sides until crispy and golden brown, about 8 minutes total. If the pan starts to smoke at any point, reduce the heat. Chop into bite-size pieces. Set aside.)

2. **Bake the chicken and veggies:** Line another large baking sheet with parchment paper. Place the chicken thighs in a large bowl, season with the salt and a few grinds of pepper and toss well to coat, then add the sweet potato and onion. Pour the Honey Mustard Sauce all over and use clean hands to thoroughly coat the chicken and veggies. Pour the chicken and potato mixture onto the prepared baking sheet and spread in an even layer.

3. Bake, stirring the vegetables halfway through but leaving the chicken undisturbed, until the sweet potatoes are fork-tender and a meat thermometer inserted into the thickest part of the chicken reads 165°F, 25 to 35 minutes, depending on the size of the chicken.

4. **Make the crumble:** Meanwhile, in a medium bowl, toss the arugula, pecans, feta, dates (if using), and lemon zest until well combined.

5. Scatter the arugula crumble mixture over the hot chicken and veggies, then top with the crispy bacon and salt and pepper to taste. Serve immediately.

BACON, CHICKEN, AND VEGGIES

4 slices thick-cut bacon

1½ pounds boneless, skinless chicken thighs

½ teaspoon kosher salt

Freshly ground black pepper

1 large sweet potato, cut into ½-inch cubes (about 2 cups)

1 medium yellow onion, cut into 1-inch chunks

Honey Mustard Sauce (page 236)

CRUMBLE

2 cups fresh arugula, finely chopped

½ cup toasted pecans, finely chopped

4 ounces feta cheese, finely crumbled or chopped

4 large pitted Medjool dates, finely chopped (about ⅓ cup; optional)

Zest of 1 lemon

Kosher salt and freshly ground black pepper

make it your way

TO MAKE DAIRY-FREE: Leave out the feta or sub dairy-free feta.

If you're a bacon lover, double the bacon.

one-pot coconut yellow curry chicken couscous

SERVES 6 ■ **PREP TIME: 20 MINUTES** ■ **COOK TIME: 30 MINUTES**

CHICKEN

1 tablespoon virgin coconut oil

1 pound boneless, skinless chicken breasts, cubed

1 teaspoon kosher salt

Freshly ground black pepper

VEGGIES

1 tablespoon virgin coconut oil

3 to 4 cups cauliflower florets

2 large carrots, thinly sliced

1 medium sweet potato, peeled and cut into ½-inch cubes

1 bunch of scallions, sliced

3 garlic cloves, minced

1 tablespoon grated fresh ginger

1 tablespoon curry powder

½ teaspoon ground turmeric

¼ teaspoon cayenne pepper

1 (15-ounce) can coconut milk

1 cup low-sodium chicken broth

2 tablespoons natural creamy peanut butter

2 tablespoons low-sodium soy sauce

COUSCOUS

1 cup pearl couscous

1 teaspoon kosher salt

Freshly ground black pepper

1 red bell pepper, julienned

½ cup frozen peas

Juice of 1 lime

GARNISH

Chopped fresh cilantro

Torn fresh mint and basil

I love this curry for so many reasons: You can cook it in just thirty minutes; a little nut butter gives it a wonderful umami richness; pearl couscous makes it super hearty and creamy by soaking up the sweet coconut milk broth; and you can throw a ton of vegetables in it—practically empty your fridge. The best part? It always, always comes out great! Plus it's a great excuse to include a ton of fresh herbs because they make the perfect topping.

1. **Prepare the chicken:** In a large, deep skillet or large pot, warm the coconut oil over medium heat. Once the oil is hot, add the chicken, season with the salt and a few grinds of pepper, and sear on all sides until golden brown, 5 to 7 minutes total. Transfer the chicken to a bowl or plate and set aside (the chicken will finish cooking later).

2. **Prepare the veggies:** In the same pot, warm the coconut oil over medium heat. Once the oil is hot, add the cauliflower, carrots, sweet potato, and scallions (reserve ¼ cup of the green parts for topping). Sauté, stirring occasionally, until slightly softened, about 5 minutes. Stir in the garlic, ginger, curry powder, turmeric, and cayenne and cook until fragrant, about 30 seconds. Add the coconut milk, broth, peanut butter, and soy sauce and cook, stirring until well combined and the peanut butter has melted, about 1 minute.

3. **Cook the couscous:** Stir in the couscous, salt, and pepper to taste, then return the chicken to the pot and raise the heat to high. Bring to a gentle boil, then cover, reduce the heat to low, and simmer, stirring occasionally to prevent the couscous from sticking to the bottom of the pan. Cook until the couscous is tender, about 15 minutes. Remove the lid, stir in the bell pepper, peas, and lime juice, and gently simmer, uncovered, until the excess liquid is soaked up, 5 to 10 minutes.

4. **Garnish and serve:** Top with the reserved scallion greens and generous amounts of cilantro, mint, and basil. Serve immediately.

5. **To store:** Keep any leftovers in an airtight container in the fridge for up to 5 days. Reheat in the microwave in 30-second intervals, stirring in between, until heated through.

make it your way

TO MAKE GLUTEN-FREE: Use coconut aminos or tamari in place of the soy sauce. Reduce the broth by ½ cup, omit the couscous, and serve the chicken and veggies over jasmine or Coconut Rice (page 217).

TO MAKE VEGAN AND VEGETARIAN: Leave out the chicken and stir in 1 (15-ounce) can chickpeas, drained and rinsed, with the couscous. Use vegetable broth in place of the chicken broth.

sweet & spicy hot chile chicken noodles

SERVES 4 ■ PREP TIME: 10 MINUTES ■ COOK TIME: 25 MINUTES

Umami, tang, sweetness, heat—it's all there! A collection of pantry sauces combined with some fresh Thai basil gives you so many flavors in one dish. It's one of my go-tos when I want something both satisfying and nutritious: I just load up this easy noodle dish with lots of veggies and get my slurp on. Experiment with different long noodles each time you make this dish!

1. **Cook the chicken:** In a large pot, warm the sesame oil over medium-high heat. Once the oil is hot, add the chicken, salt, and a few grinds of pepper. Use a wooden spoon to break up the chicken and cook, stirring occasionally, until nice and golden, about 5 minutes. Stir in the garlic, ginger, and coconut sugar and continue to cook the meat, breaking it up into smaller chunks, until it's cooked through, 2 to 3 minutes.

2. Add the sambal oelek and tomato paste. Sauté, stirring to fully incorporate the pastes with the meat mixture, until the chili paste is toasted and fragrant, 30 seconds to 1 minute. Once combined, add the broth, soy sauce, basil, and rice vinegar. Bring to a simmer, then reduce the heat to low and cook, uncovered and stirring every so often, until the sauce begins to thicken, 20 to 25 minutes. Remove from the heat.

3. **Cook the noodles:** While the sauce cooks, bring a large pot of generously salted water to a boil over high heat. Add the noodles and cook according to the package directions until al dente. Before draining, reserve 1 cup of the pasta water, then drain the pasta and add the cooked noodles to the pot with the meat sauce. Using tongs, toss the noodles with the chicken mixture, adding in the pasta water a few tablespoons at a time until your sauce is glossy and the noodles are well coated.

4. **Top and serve:** Divide the noodles into bowls and serve warm, topped with lots of basil, cashews, and red pepper flakes (if using).

5. **To store:** Keep any leftovers in an airtight container in the fridge for up to 4 days. Reheat in the microwave with an extra splash of water until heated through.

make it your way

TO MAKE GLUTEN-FREE: Use rice noodles. Use coconut aminos or tamari in place of the soy sauce.

TO MAKE VEGETARIAN AND VEGAN: Use crumbled tofu and vegetable broth in place of ground chicken and chicken broth and salted roasted peanuts if you're vegan.

make it nutrient-dense

Add a few cups of sautéed veggies, such as broccoli, spinach, snow peas, bell pepper, mushrooms, bok choy, and/or matchstick-cut carrots when you stir in the noodles.

CHICKEN

1 tablespoon toasted sesame oil

1 pound 93% lean ground chicken (or sub ground turkey)

1 teaspoon kosher salt

Freshly ground black pepper

6 garlic cloves, thinly sliced

1 tablespoon grated fresh ginger

1 tablespoon coconut sugar

3 tablespoons sambal oelek (or sub another hot chili paste)

2 tablespoons tomato paste

2 cups low-sodium chicken broth

3 tablespoons low-sodium soy sauce

2 tablespoons julienned fresh Thai basil (or sub regular basil)

2 tablespoons rice vinegar or black vinegar

NOODLES AND TOPPINGS

10 ounces long noodles, such as fettuccine or pappardelle, or 6 ounces ramen or rice noodles

Julienned fresh Thai basil (or sub regular basil)

Chopped roasted cashews or peanuts (I love honey-roasted!)

Red pepper flakes (optional)

sazón-seasoned roast chicken with green sauce

SERVES 4 TO 6 ■ **PREP TIME: 15 MINUTES** ■ **COOK TIME: 45 MINUTES**

Ease into your week with my favorite comforting Sunday-night meal, a flavorful roasted chicken seasoned with a homemade sazón spice blend. Spatchcocking the chicken is more than worth the effort; it allows the chicken to lie flat and pays off in even cooking and beautifully bronzed skin. My kids gobble this up every single time and prefer it without the Spicy Cilantro Yogurt Sauce, while I love to smother mine in it. Try serving this with Mom's Puerto Rican Rice & Beans (page 130).

1. Preheat the oven to 425°F, or preheat a gas grill to 400°F for direct cooking (turn all the burners on).

2. **Prep the chicken:** Place the chicken breast-side down on a sturdy cutting board and pat dry with paper towels. Using sharp, strong kitchen shears, cut closely along one side of the backbone, then repeat with the other side of the backbone. Be sure to cut as close to the spine as possible so you do not remove excess meat. Remove the backbone and discard, or save it to make homemade stock.

3. Flip the chicken breast-side up and firmly press down on the breast to flatten it until you hear the small crack of the breastbone breaking, which will allow the chicken to lie flat. Alternatively, with the legs facing away from you, you can make two 1-inch incisions on either side of the breastbone along the neck to help flatten the chicken.

4. In a small bowl, mix together the avocado oil, cumin, coriander, paprika, garlic powder, dried oregano, salt, adobo, turmeric, cayenne (if using), and pepper to taste. Generously brush the mixture over all sides of the chicken and rub it under the skin. (If time allows, coat the chicken up to 24 hours in advance, cover, and refrigerate. Let the chicken come to room temperature for 20 minutes before cooking.)

5. **Cook the chicken:**
   ■ **TO ROAST:** Place the chicken skin-side up in a large cast-iron skillet or place on a wire rack set in a foil-lined rimmed baking sheet. Roast until a meat thermometer inserted in the thickest part of the breast reads 160°F, 45 to 50 minutes.

   ■ **TO GRILL:** Place the chicken breast-side down over the middle burner, close the lid, and grill for 10 minutes. Flip the chicken, turn off the middle burner so the chicken is over indirect heat from the two side burners only. Close the lid and grill until a meat thermometer inserted in the thickest part of the breast reads 160°F, 45 minutes to 1 hour.

6. Transfer the chicken to a clean cutting board or large plate and allow to rest for 20 minutes before cutting it into quarters.

7. **To serve:** Sprinkle the chicken with cilantro and serve warm with Cilantro Yogurt Sauce and lime wedges on the side.

CHICKEN

1 (4-to 5-pound) whole chicken

¼ cup avocado oil

1½ teaspoons ground cumin

1½ teaspoons ground coriander

1 teaspoon sweet paprika

1 teaspoon garlic powder

1 teaspoon dried oregano

1 teaspoon kosher salt

½ teaspoon adobo seasoning

½ teaspoon ground turmeric or ground annatto seeds

¼ teaspoon cayenne (optional, for a kick of heat)

Freshly ground black pepper

SERVING

Chopped fresh cilantro

Spicy Cilantro Yogurt Sauce (page 236)

Lime wedges

make it your way

TO MAKE DAIRY-FREE: Serve with Jalapeño Lime Cashew Sauce (page 232) instead of Spicy Cilantro Yogurt Sauce.

moroccan-inspired chicken meatball bowls with whipped feta yogurt sauce & couscous

SERVES 4 ■ PREP TIME: 20 MINUTES ■ COOK TIME: 20 MINUTES

MEATBALLS

1 pound 93% lean ground chicken (or sub ground turkey)

½ cup panko bread crumbs (gluten-free, if desired)

½ cup finely shredded carrots

¼ cup finely chopped scallions

1 large egg

2 tablespoons chopped fresh mint

2 tablespoons chopped fresh cilantro

½ tablespoon grated fresh ginger

2 garlic cloves, minced

1 teaspoon packed dark brown sugar (or sub coconut sugar)

1 teaspoon kosher salt

½ teaspoon ground cumin

½ teaspoon sweet paprika

½ teaspoon ground turmeric

¼ teaspoon ground cinnamon

¼ teaspoon cayenne pepper

Freshly ground black pepper

1 to 2 tablespoons avocado oil or extra-virgin olive oil, as needed

make it your way

LAMB MEATBALLS: While any type of ground meat will work for these meatballs, lamb is particularly flavorful.

I'm a meatball fanatic for good reason: My kids always gobble them up and my husband loves just about anything that involves meat. Win! I load these up with the spices from some of my favorite Moroccan dishes: cumin, turmeric, and cinnamon. Don't skip the protein-packed Whipped Feta Yogurt Sauce or the fresh mint and cilantro that top this dish. The combo will keep you coming back for more.

1. **Prepare the meatballs:** Fill a small bowl with water and place it on the counter. In a large bowl, combine the chicken, panko, carrots, scallions, egg, mint, cilantro, ginger, garlic, brown sugar, salt, cumin, paprika, turmeric, cinnamon, cayenne, and a few grinds of pepper. Use clean hands to mix until well combined; avoid overmixing, otherwise the meatballs will become tough. Form into 16 golf ball–size meatballs, dipping your hands in water between each meatball to prevent sticking, and place them on a plate as you finish.

2. **Cook the meatballs:**
   - ■ **TO PAN-FRY:** In a large, deep skillet, warm 1 tablespoon of oil over medium-high heat. Once the oil is hot, add the meatballs, leaving about ½ inch between each (you may need to do this in batches, depending on how many meatballs you can fit in your skillet without overcrowding them), and brown on all sides until cooked through (a meat thermometer should register 165°F), 10 to 12 minutes. Transfer to a plate and repeat with the remaining meatballs, adding more oil, if necessary.
   - ■ **TO BAKE:** Preheat the oven to 400°F. Line a large baking sheet with parchment paper. Place the meatballs at least 1 inch apart on the parchment paper. Bake until a meat thermometer registers 165°F, 18 to 23 minutes.

3. **Cook the couscous:** In a large pot, bring the broth to a boil over medium heat. Stir in the couscous, salt, cumin, cinnamon, turmeric, and pepper to taste and return to a boil. Once boiling, reduce the heat to low, cover, and cook until all of the liquid is absorbed and the couscous is tender, 8 to 10 minutes. Remove from the heat and stir in the dried cherries, pistachios, and cilantro. Allow the mixture to sit for 5 minutes to plump up and rehydrate the cherries.

4. **To serve:** Spread one-quarter of the feta sauce onto each plate or shallow bowl, then top with the couscous and finally the meatballs. Garnish with mint, cilantro, and a drizzle of tahini (if using) before serving.

5. **To store:** Keep any leftovers in an airtight container in the fridge for up to 5 days. Reheat in the microwave in 30-second intervals until heated through. For freezing instructions, see page 21.

COUSCOUS

2¼ cups low-sodium chicken broth

1½ cups pearl couscous

½ teaspoon kosher salt

¼ teaspoon ground cumin

¼ teaspoon ground cinnamon

¼ teaspoon ground turmeric

Freshly ground black pepper

⅓ cup dried cherries (or sub chopped Medjool dates)

⅓ cup chopped roasted shelled pistachios (or sub toasted sliced almonds)

¼ cup chopped fresh cilantro

SERVING

Whipped Feta Yogurt Sauce (page 233)

Torn fresh mint

Torn fresh cilantro

Tahini (optional)

unbelievable mini chicken meatloaves with nana's whipped potatoes

SERVES 4 TO 6 ■ **PREP TIME: 20 MINUTES** ■ **COOK TIME: 50 MINUTES**

Nonstick cooking spray

WHIPPED POTATOES

1 pound yellow or Yukon Gold potatoes, peeled and quartered

2 medium carrots, cut into ¼-inch slices

2 teaspoons kosher salt, plus more to taste

¼ cup plain whole-milk Greek yogurt

3 to 6 tablespoons whole milk or unsweetened almond milk, as needed

2 tablespoons salted butter

Freshly ground black pepper

Okay, I get it. These might not look that appealing, or maybe you just find them incredibly old-school, but let me tell you . . . they are truly UNBELIEVABLE. You'd never guess that these little flavor bombs are packed with vitamin-rich sweet potato, spinach, and cilantro, not to mention tons of flavor from adobo seasoning. The whipped potato-carrot topping is inspired by Nana, my great-grandmother, who used to make mashed potatoes with carrots for my grandmother when she was a little girl. I'm a fan of the carrots because they add an irresistible sweetness. I could probably eat these every single day for the rest of my life and never get sick of them. Keep a few in your freezer for busy weeks; you won't regret it.

make it your way

TO MAKE DAIRY-FREE: Use vegan butter, dairy-free sour cream instead of Greek yogurt, and dairy-free milk.

TO MAKE GLUTEN-FREE: Use gluten-free panko bread crumbs.

Use shredded carrots instead of sweet potatoes in the meatloaves and/or use mashed sweet potatoes on top.

CHICKEN MEATLOAVES

1 tablespoon extra-virgin olive oil

½ small orange or red bell pepper, finely diced

½ medium yellow onion, finely diced

3 garlic cloves, minced

1 medium sweet potato, peeled and grated

2 cups fresh spinach, finely chopped

1 pound 93% lean ground chicken (or sub ground turkey)

⅔ cup finely chopped fresh cilantro

½ cup panko bread crumbs (gluten-free, if desired)

1 large egg

1 teaspoon adobo seasoning

1 teaspoon ground cumin

1 teaspoon ground coriander

¾ teaspoon kosher salt

½ teaspoon ground turmeric or ground annatto seeds

½ teaspoon dried oregano

Freshly ground black pepper

1. Preheat the oven to 350°F. Grease a 12-cup muffin tin with cooking spray. Set aside.

2. **Cook the potatoes:** Place the potatoes and carrots in a large pot, cover with water by at least 1 inch, and add 1 teaspoon of the salt. Bring to a boil over high heat and cook until fork-tender, 20 minutes. Drain and return to the pot. Add the Greek yogurt, 3 tablespoons of the milk, the butter, the remaining 1 teaspoon of salt, and pepper to taste.

3. **Whip the potatoes:** Use a handheld electric mixer to whip the potato and carrot mixture until smooth and creamy, about 2 minutes. (Alternatively, transfer the mixture to the bowl of a stand mixer fitted with the paddle attachment and whip on medium speed, or beat by hand.) If you'd like creamier potatoes, add an additional 2 to 3 tablespoons of milk and whip again for 30 seconds. Taste and adjust the salt and pepper, if necessary. Cover and set aside.

4. **Prepare the meatloaves:** While the potatoes and carrots are cooking, cook the veggies for your meatloaves. In a large skillet, warm the olive oil over medium heat. Once the oil is hot, add the bell pepper, onion, and garlic and sauté, stirring occasionally, until the onions are softened, 5 to 8 minutes. Add the sweet potato and spinach and cook, stirring occasionally, until the sweet potato softens, 2 to 3 minutes. Allow the mixture to cool for 5 minutes.

5. Transfer the cooked veggies to a large bowl. Add the chicken, cilantro, panko, egg, adobo seasoning, cumin, coriander, salt, turmeric, dried oregano, and a few grinds of pepper. Mix with a rubber spatula until well combined, then evenly divide the mixture among the prepared muffin cups. Use the spatula to smooth the tops.

6. **Bake:** Bake the meatloaves for 15 minutes, then use a ¼-cup measuring cup or large ice cream scoop to add the mashed potato and carrot mixture on top of each meatloaf. Transfer back to the oven and bake until a meat thermometer inserted into the center of a meatloaf reads 165°F, 5 to 10 minutes more. Let cool for 10 minutes before removing from the tin. To remove, run a butter knife along the sides of the tins and gently lift out the meatloaves. Serve warm.

7. **To store:** Keep any leftover meatloaves in an airtight container in the fridge for up to 4 days. Reheat in the microwave until warmed through, 1 to 2 minutes.

8. **To freeze:** Cool the meatloaves to room temperature, then place into reusable silicone bags or a freezer-safe container and freeze for up to 3 months. Thaw in the fridge overnight, then reheat in the microwave until warmed through, 1 to 2 minutes.

chipotle gouda pumpkin turkey enchiladas (PAGE 190)

chipotle gouda pumpkin turkey enchiladas

SERVES 6 TO 8 ■ PREP TIME: 30 MINUTES ■ COOK TIME: 40 MINUTES

Nonstick cooking spray

CHIPOTLE PUMPKIN SAUCE

1 (15-ounce) can pumpkin puree

1 (15-ounce) can tomato sauce

½ cup plain whole-milk Greek yogurt

2 to 3 chipotle peppers in adobo, depending on your heat preference

2 tablespoons chili powder

2 teaspoons ground cumin

2 garlic cloves, roughly chopped

1 teaspoon sweet paprika

½ teaspoon kosher salt, plus more to taste

FILLING AND TOPPING

1 tablespoon extra-virgin olive oil

1 medium yellow onion, finely diced

1 jalapeño, seeded and diced

3 garlic cloves, minced

1 pound 93% lean ground turkey (or sub ground chicken)

1 teaspoon kosher salt

Freshly ground black pepper

2 cups fresh spinach, chopped

1 (15-ounce) can black beans, drained and rinsed

It wouldn't really be an Ambitious Kitchen cookbook without my favorite enchiladas! I grew up eating my mom's enchiladas and now they are my favorite way to spoil my family and friends. These babies are a nutrient powerhouse—there's an entire can of pumpkin puree in there, along with turkey, black beans, and spinach. Good luck not licking the smoky, spicy-sweet sauce off your plate like my husband did, who apparently "doesn't like pumpkin."

1. Preheat the oven to 350°F. Spray a 9 × 13-inch baking dish with cooking spray.

2. **Make the chipotle pumpkin sauce:** In the bowl of a food processor or blender, combine the pumpkin, tomato sauce, Greek yogurt, chipotle peppers, chili powder, cumin, garlic, paprika, and salt; blend or process until smooth, about 1 minute. Taste and season with additional salt, if necessary. Add 1 cup of the pumpkin sauce to the bottom of the prepared dish and use a spatula to spread out evenly.

3. **Make the filling and topping:** In a large, deep skillet, warm the olive oil over medium heat. Once the oil is hot, add the onion and jalapeño and cook, stirring occasionally, until the onions begin to soften, about 5 minutes. Stir in the garlic and cook until fragrant, about 30 seconds. Add the turkey, season with the salt and a few grinds of pepper, and cook, breaking the meat apart with a wooden spoon, until no longer pink, about 5 minutes. Add the spinach and stir frequently until wilted, about 2 minutes. Stir in the black beans and 1½ cups of the chipotle pumpkin sauce until incorporated. Remove from the heat.

CHEESE AND ASSEMBLY

6 ounces shredded sharp Cheddar cheese (1½ cups)

6 ounces shredded Gouda cheese (1½ cups)

12 to 16 (6-inch) soft corn tortillas (gluten-free) or 8 (8-inch) medium-sized soft taco flour tortillas

YOGURT DRIZZLE

½ cup plain whole-milk Greek yogurt

1 to 2 tablespoons fresh lime juice, as needed

¼ teaspoon kosher salt

SERVING

1 avocado, sliced

¼ cup Pickled Red Onions (page 237)

2 tablespoons chopped fresh cilantro

4. **Mix the cheese:** In a large bowl, toss the Gouda and Cheddar together.

5. **Assemble the enchiladas:** Wrap a stack of 4 tortillas in a damp paper towel and microwave for 30 seconds to make the tortillas pliable. Transfer the tortillas to a cutting board in a single layer. Repeat with the rest of the tortillas.

6. If using corn tortillas: Place about ¼ cup of the filling on each tortilla and sprinkle 1 tablespoon of cheese on top. If using flour tortillas: place ½ cup of the filling on each tortilla and sprinkle 2 tablespoons of cheese on top.

7. Roll up each tortilla and place seam-side down in the baking dish. Pour the remaining chipotle pumpkin sauce over all the enchiladas and then sprinkle the remaining cheese mixture on top.

8. **Bake the enchiladas:** Bake the enchiladas until the cheese is melted and the edges of the tortillas begin to turn slightly golden brown, 25 to 30 minutes. Allow the enchiladas to cool for 10 minutes before serving.

9. **Make the yogurt drizzle:** In a small bowl, mix together the Greek yogurt, 1 tablespoon of the lime juice, and salt until well combined. Stir in more lime juice, if necessary, to make a pourable consistency.

10. **To serve:** Drizzle the enchiladas with the yogurt and garnish with avocado slices, Pickled Red Onions, and cilantro. Serve warm.

11. **To store:** Keep any leftovers in an airtight container in the fridge for up to 4 days. Reheat in the microwave in 30-second intervals until heated through. For freezing instructions, see page 21.

12. **To make ahead:** Assemble the enchiladas as directed, but before baking, cover with foil, and place it in the fridge up to 1 day before serving. When you're ready to serve, bake as directed, adding another 10 minutes to the baking time. You can make the sauce up to 2 days in advance to save time on prep, too. Store in an airtight container in the fridge.

hot honey-glazed salmon that goes with everything

SERVES 4 ■ **PREP TIME: 10 MINUTES** ■ **COOK TIME: 15 MINUTES**

Hot! Honey! Glazed! Salmon! I'm in love with hot honey (for proof, see the recipes on pages 165, 171, 211 . . . you get the idea) and I can't think of a better, faster way to put dinner on the table than to drizzle a little sweet heat on salmon that's baked with a spice rub and caramelizes beautifully in the oven. Serve on salads, pastas, in tacos, with rice, or just eat it straight off the pan if it's that kind of night.

1. Preheat the oven to 400°F. Line a large baking sheet with parchment paper.

2. **Prep the salmon:** Place the salmon skin-side down on the prepared baking sheet and drizzle with the olive oil and lime juice. In a small bowl, mix the brown sugar, paprika, garlic powder, chili powder, chipotle chili powder, salt, and a few grinds of pepper. Evenly sprinkle the spice mixture on the salmon and use your fingertips to rub it all over the fish.

3. **Bake the salmon:** Bake until the salmon reaches your desired doneness, 10 to 12 minutes. Switch the oven to the broiler setting on high. Broil until the salmon is crispy, watching carefully to avoid burning, about 2 minutes.

4. Immediately brush each filet with 1 tablespoon of Quick Hot Honey.

5. **To serve:** Transfer the salmon to serving plates and serve with any of the following: Coconut Rice, Spicy Cilantro Yogurt Sauce (leave it out if you want a dairy-free dinner), Farmers' Market Arugula Peach Pasta Salad, and/or avocado slices. Serve immediately.

6. **To store:** Keep any leftovers in an airtight container in the fridge for up to 3 days. Reheat in the microwave in 30-second intervals until heated through.

SALMON

4 (6-ounce) salmon filets

1 tablespoon extra-virgin olive oil

Juice of 1 lime

1 tablespoon packed dark brown sugar (or sub coconut sugar)

1 teaspoon sweet paprika

1 teaspoon garlic powder

½ teaspoon chili powder

½ teaspoon chipotle chili powder

½ teaspoon kosher salt

Freshly ground black pepper

¼ cup Quick Hot Honey (page 231)

SERVING OPTIONS

Coconut Rice (page 217)

Spicy Cilantro Yogurt Sauce (page 236)

Farmers' Market Arugula Peach Pasta Salad (page 78)

1 avocado, sliced

make it nutrient-dense

Toss 8 to 10 ounces of fresh asparagus spears or trimmed green beans with 1 tablespoon of extra-virgin olive oil, ½ teaspoon of garlic powder, ½ teaspoon of kosher salt, and freshly ground black pepper to taste. Spread evenly alongside the salmon on the baking sheet and bake as directed.

sheet pan sesame gochujang salmon bowls

SERVES 4 ▪ PREP TIME: 20 MINUTES ▪ COOK TIME: 15 MINUTES

MARINADE

2 to 3 tablespoons gochujang (or sub sambal oelek), depending on your heat tolerance

2 tablespoons toasted sesame oil

2 tablespoons packed dark brown sugar (or sub coconut sugar)

2 tablespoons rice vinegar

2 tablespoons low-sodium soy sauce

3 garlic cloves, minced

1 tablespoon grated fresh ginger

1 tablespoon sesame seeds

SALMON AND GREEN BEANS

4 (6-ounce) salmon filets

10 ounces fresh green beans, ends trimmed

SERVING

Coconut Rice (page 217)

¼ cup sliced scallions

¼ cup chopped fresh cilantro

Toasted sesame seeds

This sheet-pan meal looks elegant enough to be served at a restaurant and was inspired by my love for gochujang, a spicy Korean fermented paste that packs a ton of flavor into the salmon and veggies. It is so simple to make, and once you try the incredible sweet-spicy glaze, you'll end up making this one weekly.

1. **Make the marinade:** In a large bowl, whisk the gochujang, sesame oil, brown sugar, rice vinegar, soy sauce, garlic, ginger, and sesame seeds until well combined. Reserve ¼ cup of the marinade in a separate bowl to use as a finishing glaze.

2. **Marinate the salmon and green beans:** Place the salmon and green beans in the bowl with the marinade, and stir gently to coat. Marinate at room temperature for 20 to 30 minutes. (This can also be done up to 1 day in advance and refrigerated, covered, until ready to bake.)

3. Meanwhile, preheat the oven to 400°F. Line a large baking sheet with parchment paper.

4. **Bake:** Use tongs to transfer the salmon and green beans to the prepared baking sheet, placing the fish skin-side down and discarding the excess marinade. Bake until the salmon reaches your desired doneness, 10 to 12 minutes. Switch the oven to the broiler setting on high. Broil until the salmon is crispy, watching carefully to avoid burning, about 2 minutes.

5. Remove from the oven and immediately brush the reserved ¼ cup of marinade over the salmon filets; if desired, brush some of the marinade over the green beans as well.

6. **To serve:** Scoop the Coconut Rice onto each plate or bowl, top with a piece of salmon and some of the green beans, and garnish with scallions, cilantro, and sesame seeds. Serve immediately.

7. **To store:** Keep any leftovers in an airtight container in the fridge for up to 3 days. Reheat in the microwave in 30-second intervals until heated through.

make it your way

TO MAKE GLUTEN-FREE: Use sambal oelek or another hot chile paste instead of gochujang and coconut aminos or tamari instead of soy sauce.

hot maple bacon carbonara
with sweet potato & herby golden bread crumbs

SERVES 4 ■ **PREP TIME: 15 MINUTES** ■ **COOK TIME: 1 HOUR 15 MINUTES**

Hmm, how can we make the wonderful egg-and-bacon pasta known as carbonara taste even better? How about adding nutritious, creamy sweet potatoes and a sweet and spicy bacon garnish? Oh yes!

1. Preheat the oven to 375°F. Line a large baking sheet with parchment paper.

2. **Cook the sweet potato:** Use a fork to poke holes all over the sweet potato. Place on one side of the prepared baking sheet and bake for 30 minutes.

3. **Cook the bacon:** In a small bowl, whisk the maple syrup and cayenne. Remove the baking sheet with the sweet potato from the oven but keep the heat on. Carefully place the bacon in a single layer on the other side of the sheet and use a pastry brush to brush the bacon with the maple syrup and cayenne mixture. Bake until the bacon has reached your desired level of crispiness and the sweet potato is fork-tender, 20 to 30 minutes. Cool on the baking sheet for at least 5 minutes.

4. Use tongs to transfer the bacon to a cutting board, blot with a paper towel to absorb excess grease, then chop the bacon into bite-size pieces. Set aside. Move the sweet potato to a cutting board, cut it open, scoop out the flesh, and transfer to a high-powered blender. Add the milk and salt and blend until smooth, about 1 minute.

5. Bring a large pot of generously salted water to a boil over high heat.

6. **Meanwhile, make the sauce:** In a medium bowl, whisk the Parmesan, eggs, 1 teaspoon of salt, and lots of pepper until well combined. Set aside.

7. **Cook the pasta:** Add the pasta to the pot of boiling water and cook according to the package directions until al dente. Reserve 1 cup of pasta water, then remove from the heat and drain. Return the pasta to the pot, immediately add the egg and cheese mixture and ½ cup of the pasta water. Use tongs to thoroughly coat the pasta in the sauce, stirring quickly and constantly to avoid the egg curdling. The warmth of the pasta will transform the eggs into a creamy sauce. Stir in the sweet potato puree and toss again to coat the noodles. If the pasta seems dry or not creamy enough, pour in the additional pasta water a few tablespoons at a time until the sauce is glossy and the noodles are well coated. Taste and season with more salt, as needed.

8. **Top and serve:** Divide the pasta among bowls or plates. Top with the bacon pieces and sprinkle each bowl with 1 to 2 tablespoons of the Herby Golden Bread Crumbs and extra black pepper. Serve immediately.

9. **To store:** Keep in an airtight container in the fridge for up to 4 days. Reheat in the microwave with an extra splash of milk until heated through.

SWEET POTATO AND BACON

1 medium sweet potato

2 tablespoons pure maple syrup

½ teaspoon cayenne pepper

1 (8- to 10-ounce) package thick-cut bacon

½ cup whole milk or unsweetened almond milk

½ teaspoon kosher salt

PASTA AND SERVING

3 ounces grated Parmesan cheese (¾ cup)

2 large eggs

1 teaspoon kosher salt, plus more for pasta

Freshly ground black pepper

12 ounces bucatini pasta

1 cup reserved pasta water

¼ to ½ cup Herby Golden Bread Crumbs (page 236), to taste

make it your way

TO MAKE GLUTEN-FREE: Use gluten-free panko bread crumbs and your favorite gluten-free pasta (I recommend brown rice pasta).

tip

Save time by roasting your sweet potato up to 2 days in advance. Refrigerate until ready to use.

bacon, spinach & pumpkin lasagna roll-ups (PAGE 200)

bacon, spinach & pumpkin lasagna roll-ups

SERVES 6 TO 8 ▪ PREP TIME: 25 MINUTES ▪ COOK TIME: 1 HOUR

BACON AND NOODLES

8 ounces thick-cut bacon

Kosher salt

Nonstick cooking spray

1 pound lasagna noodles
(not no-boil)

FILLING AND ROLLUPS

1 (15-ounce) can pumpkin
puree

1 (15-ounce) container whole-
milk or part-skim ricotta cheese

1 large egg

¾ teaspoon kosher salt

½ teaspoon ground cinnamon

¼ teaspoon ground nutmeg

¼ teaspoon ground ginger

¼ teaspoon ground allspice

Freshly ground black pepper

10 ounces frozen chopped
spinach, thawed and excess
moisture squeezed out

6 ounces shredded mozzarella
cheese (1½ cups)

I am obsessed with using pumpkin in cozy, savory dishes. Not only is it available all year round in cans, but it packs such great nutrition, pairs so well with cheese, *and* adds a wonderful creaminess when mixed with ricotta. These roll-ups take some time, but can easily be prepped ahead, and the result is a total showstopper that's a little sweet from the pumpkin, a little salty from the bacon, and brought together with a silky garlic-Parmesan sauce. Make it for the holidays or anytime you want something cozy. (P.S. It freezes beautifully, so make a double batch if you're feeling ambitious!)

1. **Cook the bacon:** Line a large baking sheet with parchment paper. Place the bacon slices in a single layer on the prepared baking sheet and transfer to the middle rack of a cold oven. (This helps the bacon render more evenly and yields flat and crispy bacon.) Heat the oven to 425°F and cook until the bacon has reached your desired crispiness, 15 to 25 minutes. Use tongs to transfer the bacon to a cutting board, blot with a paper towel to absorb excess grease, then chop the bacon into bite-sized pieces. Set aside. Reduce the oven to 375°F.

2. **Meanwhile, cook the noodles:** Bring a large pot of generously salted water to a boil. Grease a baking sheet or cutting board, or line with parchment paper and set aside; you will use this surface to assemble your lasagna rolls. Grease a 9 × 13-inch baking dish with cooking spray and set aside.

3. Boil the lasagna noodles for 5 to 6 minutes, until pliable but still slightly firm, then drain and immediately lay the noodles flat in a single layer on the prepared surface. Do not let the lasagna noodles touch or they'll stick together.

4. **Make the filling:** In a large bowl, whisk the pumpkin, ricotta, egg, salt, cinnamon, nutmeg, ginger, allspice, and pepper to taste until well combined. Add the spinach and mix well to combine. (This can be made a day in advance and stored in an airtight container in the fridge, if desired.)

5. **Make the roll-ups:** Spread a heaping ¼ cup of filling on top of each lasagna noodle. Add 2 tablespoons of mozzarella on top, then roll up each lasagna noodle and place seam-side down in the prepared baking dish. Repeat until all of your roll-ups are arranged in the dish. Set aside.

CHEESE SAUCE

3 tablespoons salted butter

¼ cup all-purpose flour or white whole-wheat flour

2 cups whole milk or unsweetened almond milk

2 ounces grated Parmesan cheese (½ cup)

½ teaspoon garlic powder

½ teaspoon kosher salt

Freshly ground black pepper

TOPPINGS

4 ounces shredded mozzarella cheese (1 cup)

2 tablespoons chopped fresh sage leaves

1 ounce grated Parmesan cheese (¼ cup)

6. **Make the cheese sauce:** In a large skillet, melt the butter over medium heat, then whisk in the flour and cook, whisking constantly, until a paste forms, about 30 seconds. Slowly stream in the milk, constantly whisking away any lumps, until smooth and combined. Increase the heat to medium-high, bring the mixture to a rapid simmer, then reduce the heat to medium-low and simmer, stirring occasionally, until the sauce thickens and coats the back of a spoon, 3 to 5 minutes. Stir in the Parmesan, garlic powder, salt, and lots of pepper. Pour the sauce over the lasagna roll-ups, ensuring each roll is covered.

7. **Top and serve:** Top the roll-ups with the mozzarella, bacon, and sage. Bake until the sauce is bubbling and the topping is slightly golden brown, 30 to 35 minutes. (For an extra golden brown top, you can broil the roll-ups on high until the edges are crispy, 1 to 2 minutes.) Cool the roll-ups in the dish for at least 10 minutes before serving warm with the Parmesan sprinkled over top..

8. **To store:** Keep any leftovers in an airtight container in the fridge for up to 4 days. Reheat in the microwave until heated through. For freezing instructions, see page 21.

9. **To make ahead:** Assemble the lasagna roll-ups as directed, but before baking, cover with foil and place it in the fridge up to 1 day before serving. When you're ready to serve, bake the lasagna as directed, adding 10 minutes to the baking time.

make it your way

TO MAKE GLUTEN-FREE: Use gluten-free lasagna noodles and 1:1 gluten-free all-purpose flour.

TO MAKE VEGETARIAN: Leave out the bacon and garnish with as much Herby Golden Bread Crumbs (page 236) as you'd like.

marry me ropa vieja

SERVES 8 ▪ **PREP TIME: 30 MINUTES** ▪ **COOK TIME: 3 HOURS**

When Tony and I decided to get married, we wanted to honor my mom and her Puerto Rican family with our wedding menu, and I knew just how to do it. One of my favorite dishes has always been ropa vieja, a braised beef that is the national dish of Cuba and popular across Latin America. My nana used to make her own version with the same sofrito and sazón that she used for other Puerto Rican dishes. On a rainy November afternoon, guests arrived at our cozy reception site and were greeted with rice and beans, tostones, and piping hot ropa vieja. So many people told us that they had never eaten such delicious food at a wedding. Whenever I make this tender, low-and-slow meat dish, I think of our wedding, and the warmth and happiness that filled the room.

1. **Prep the beef:** Pat the beef dry with a paper towel and season all sides with the salt and pepper to taste. Allow the meat to rest at room temperature for 30 minutes.

2. Meanwhile, preheat the oven to 275°F.

3. **Cook the beef:** In a large oven-safe pot or Dutch oven, warm the olive oil over medium-high heat. Once the oil is hot, add the beef and brown on all sides, 7 to 10 minutes per side. Use large tongs to (carefully!) transfer the beef to a large plate and set aside.

4. In the same pot, sauté the onion and bell peppers, stirring occasionally, until tender and softened, about 10 minutes. Add the garlic, coriander, cumin, adobo seasoning, turmeric, paprika, garlic powder, and dried oregano and cook until fragrant, about 30 seconds. Stir in the tomato paste with a wooden spoon and cook, stirring frequently, until it becomes a deep red color, 1 to 2 minutes. (This helps to develop an even richer tomato flavor.) Add the crushed tomatoes and broth and stir until well combined. Stir in the olives, cilantro, and bay leaves, then nestle in the seared beef.

5. Cover the pot and transfer to the oven. Roast until the beef is tender and shreds easily, 2½ to 3 hours.

6. Carefully transfer the beef to a baking sheet to help catch any liquid. Use two forks to shred the beef. Discard the excess liquid.

7. Remove and discard the bay leaves from the sauce. Place the pot over medium-low heat, bring the sauce to a simmer, and cook until the sauce is slightly thickened, 10 to 20 minutes. Use a spoon to skim the fat off the top.

8. Fold the shredded beef back into the sauce and simmer for another 5 to 10 minutes to combine the flavors and heat the beef through.

9. **To serve:** Tuck the warm ropa vieja into tortillas or serve over rice, such as Arroz con Gandules, and/or with Crispy Fried Tostones. Garnish with onion, cilantro, a spoonful of yogurt (if using), and a squeeze of lime juice.

BEEF

2½ to 3 pounds beef chuck, trimmed of excess fat

1½ teaspoons kosher salt

Freshly ground black pepper

2 tablespoons extra-virgin olive oil

1 medium white onion, sliced

1 red bell pepper, sliced

1 yellow bell pepper, sliced

1 green bell pepper, sliced

6 garlic cloves, minced

2 teaspoons ground coriander

2 teaspoons ground cumin

1½ teaspoons adobo seasoning

1 teaspoon ground turmeric or ground annatto seeds

1 teaspoon sweet paprika

1 teaspoon garlic powder

1 teaspoon dried oregano

¼ cup tomato paste

1 (15-ounce) can crushed tomatoes (or sub tomato sauce)

1½ cups low-sodium chicken broth

½ cup pimento-stuffed olives, sliced

½ cup chopped fresh cilantro

2 bay leaves

SERVING OPTIONS

Tortillas of choice

Cooked rice or Arroz con Gandules (page 218)

Crispy Fried Tostones (page 221)

Finely diced white onion

Chopped fresh cilantro

Plain whole-milk Greek yogurt (optional)

Lime wedges

ambitious sides

Why stop at an entrée? Add a bit more pop to your table with this gorgeous collection of showstopping sides that will round out any meal nicely. Or, hey, make them the star of the show and plan your entire meal around them. I promise you they are worth it.

"the slaw"

SERVES 6 TO 8 ■ PREP TIME: 15 MINUTES, PLUS 30 MINUTES CHILLING TIME
■ COOK TIME: NO COOKING REQUIRED!

SLAW

3 cups shredded red cabbage

3 cups shredded green cabbage

2 cups shredded carrots

1 cup finely chopped fresh cilantro

½ cup sliced scallions (green parts only)

1 jalapeño, thinly sliced

DRESSING

3 tablespoons toasted sesame oil

2 tablespoons rice vinegar

2 tablespoons pure maple syrup

1 tablespoon fresh lime juice

1 garlic clove, minced

½ teaspoon kosher salt, plus more to taste

Freshly ground black pepper

GARNISH

Kosher salt and freshly ground black pepper

½ cup roasted pepitas (optional)

1 to 2 tablespoons toasted sesame seeds (optional)

Yes, you'll put this on everything! This crunchy slaw brightens all of my favorite dishes. Tacos. Burgers. Fried or grilled chicken sandwiches. Fish. As a side dish or straight out of the bowl. No mayo required. Just loads of flavor thanks to cilantro, scallions, and a slightly sweet toasted sesame dressing. Bring it to the next BBQ and you'll likely be asked to bring it to every gathering you attend for the rest of your life. Just sayin'.

1. **Prepare the slaw:** In a large bowl, toss together the red and green cabbage, carrots, cilantro, scallions, and jalapeño.

2. **Make the dressing:** In a small bowl, whisk the sesame oil, vinegar, maple syrup, lime juice, garlic, salt, and pepper to taste. Pour over the slaw and toss well to combine. Taste and adjust the seasonings as necessary. Cover and place in the fridge for at least 30 minutes and up to 2 hours to allow flavors to combine.

3. **Garnish:** Taste the slaw again and add more salt and pepper, if necessary. Before serving, garnish with pepitas and/or sesame seeds (if using).

4. **To store:** Keep any leftovers in an airtight container in the fridge for up to 2 days.

spiced butternut squash with feta, pecan & date crumble

SERVES 4 TO 6 ■ **PREP TIME: 15 MINUTES** ■ **COOK TIME: 30 MINUTES**

A beautiful side dish that comes together in a snap, but looks like you spent all day on it? Yes, please! I've topped this sweet, spicy, caramelized butternut squash with an elegant "crumble" of finely chopped nuts, salty cheese, chewy sweet dates, zesty zippy greens, and a little lemon zest to brighten it all up. Serve this at your next holiday get-together or, if you're like me, spoil yourself by making this for a quick lunch, topped with a fried egg and some sautéed chicken sausage. NOMS.

1. Preheat the oven to 400°F. Line a large baking sheet with parchment paper.

2. **Roast the squash:** Place the butternut squash on the prepared baking sheet, drizzle with the olive oil and maple syrup, then sprinkle with the chili powder, garlic powder, paprika, salt, cayenne, and a few grinds of pepper. Use your hands to toss to combine. Roast undisturbed until the squash is fork-tender and caramelized on the edges, about 30 minutes. Transfer to a platter or large shallow serving bowl.

3. **Make the crumble:** In a medium bowl, toss the arugula, pecans, dates, feta, olive oil, and lemon zest until combined. Sprinkle over the squash and serve immediately.

4. **To store:** Keep any leftovers in an airtight container in the fridge for up to 5 days. Rewarm the butternut squash in a skillet over medium heat until warmed through or microwave in 30-second intervals until warmed through. If making this dish ahead of time, wait to add the crumble until ready to serve, otherwise the arugula will wilt and break down.

SQUASH

4 cups cubed butternut squash (½-inch pieces; from a 3-pound butternut squash)

1 tablespoon extra-virgin olive oil

1 tablespoon pure maple syrup

½ teaspoon chili powder

½ teaspoon garlic powder

½ teaspoon sweet paprika

½ teaspoon kosher salt

⅛ teaspoon cayenne pepper

Freshly ground black pepper

CRUMBLE

1 to 2 cups arugula, finely chopped

½ cup toasted pecans, finely chopped

6 large pitted Medjool dates, finely chopped (about ½ cup)

2 ounces feta cheese (or gorgonzola), finely crumbled

1 tablespoon extra-virgin olive oil

Zest of 1 lemon

make it your way

TO MAKE DAIRY-FREE AND VEGAN: Leave out the feta or use dairy-free feta.

SPICED BUTTERNUT SQUASH WITH BACON: Add ¼ cup chopped cooked bacon to the crumble.

crispy, crunchy delicata squash with parm, panko & hot honey

SERVES 4 ■ PREP TIME: 20 MINUTES ■ COOK TIME: 20 MINUTES

If you haven't yet had delicata squash, it's time! You can actually eat the thin, tender, nutrient-packed skin, which means it's perfect as the base for a quick side dish that even my kids adore. The squash gets a coating of crunchy panko and flavorful Parmesan cheese, bakes until golden, then gets a drizzle of hot honey. I love this paired with Hot Honey Glazed Salmon That Goes with Everything (page 193) or as a beautiful holiday appetizer or side. My husband and kids love to dip the squash in ranch dressing—figures!

1. Preheat the oven to 400°F.

2. **Prep the squash:** Slice the squash in half lengthwise and scoop out the seeds with a spoon. Cut each half into ½-inch-thick half-moon slices. Set aside.

3. Place the panko on a large baking sheet, spread out in an even layer, and coat with cooking spray. Bake for 3 minutes, stir the panko (or just shake the pan), then bake until golden brown, 2 to 4 more minutes. (Keep the oven on—you'll need it later.) Transfer to a medium shallow bowl and cool for 5 minutes. Whisk in the Parmesan, garlic powder, Italian seasoning, paprika, salt, and lots of pepper. Set aside.

4. In another medium shallow bowl, whisk the eggs and milk until well combined. Set aside.

5. Line a large baking sheet with parchment paper or foil for easy clean up, then place an oven-safe wire metal rack on top. Coat the wire rack with cooking spray.

6. Dip each squash slice into the egg mixture, then use tongs or your hands to transfer to the bread crumbs and turn to completely coat. Transfer to the wire rack. Repeat with the remaining squash slices, placing them about ½-inch apart.

7. **Bake the squash:** Generously spray the tops of the squash slices with cooking spray. Bake until fork-tender, 20 to 25 minutes.

8. **Garnish and serve:** Transfer the squash to a platter or large plate and drizzle with hot honey, then sprinkle with fresh thyme and sea salt. (Alternatively, you can serve them with your favorite dipping sauce, such as ranch dressing, if you like.)

9. **To store:** Keep any leftovers in an airtight container in the fridge for up to 5 days. To reheat, place the squash on a parchment paper–lined baking sheet and bake at 350°F until heated through, about 10 minutes.

DELICATA SQUASH

2 delicata squash

1½ cups panko bread crumbs

Nonstick cooking spray

4 ounces grated Parmesan cheese (½ cup)

1 teaspoon garlic powder

1 teaspoon Italian seasoning

1 teaspoon sweet paprika

¾ teaspoon kosher salt

Freshly ground black pepper

2 large eggs

1 tablespoon whole milk or dairy-free milk of choice

GARNISH AND SERVING

2 tablespoons Quick Hot Honey (page 231) or plain honey

1 to 2 teaspoons fresh thyme leaves

Flaky sea salt (I like Maldon)

Ranch dressing or another dipping sauce (optional), for serving

make it your way

TO MAKE GLUTEN-FREE: Use gluten-free panko bread crumbs.

crispy roasted brussels with tahini gochujang sauce

SERVES 4 ■ PREP TIME: 10 MINUTES ■ COOK TIME: 30 MINUTES

BRUSSELS SPROUTS

1 pound Brussels sprouts, ends trimmed, outer leaves removed, and cut in half vertically

2 tablespoons extra-virgin olive oil (or sub avocado oil)

½ teaspoon kosher salt

SERVING

Tahini Gochujang Sauce (page 234)

1 teaspoon black sesame seeds

1 teaspoon white sesame seeds

make it your way

TO MAKE VEGAN: Be sure to use all vegan ingredients in the Tahini Gochujang Sauce.

The key to this crunchy, fiery, roasty-toasty side dish is to cook as much moisture as possible out of the Brussels sprouts. Be brave! They should be a deep, deep golden brown before you pull them out of the oven. This daring step is what will make them ultra-crispy and extra tasty. And you'll be amazed by how well the sprouts soak up the sauce but remain crisp on the outside: it will keep everyone coming back for more. And more . . . And more!

1. Preheat the oven to 450°F.

2. **Cook the Brussels sprouts:** Place the Brussels sprouts on a large baking sheet, drizzle with the olive oil, and sprinkle with salt. Use your hands to toss the Brussels in the oil, massaging them gently until each sprout is glossy. Spread them out on the pan, placing them cut-side down and ideally leaving at least an inch between each sprout. Roast until ultra-crispy and deep golden brown, flipping halfway through, 25 to 35 minutes. Cool the sprouts on the baking sheet for 5 minutes to crisp them up even more, then transfer to a serving bowl or platter.

3. **To serve:** Drizzle with 2 to 4 tablespoons of the Tahini Gochujang Sauce and sprinkle with the sesame seeds. Serve warm with the remaining sauce on the side for dipping, or drizzle additional sauce over the top.

4. **To store:** Keep any leftovers in an airtight container in the fridge for up to 5 days. To reheat, microwave in 30-second intervals until warm.

caramelized garlic carrots

SERVES 6 ■ PREP TIME: 10 MINUTES ■ COOK TIME: 25 MINUTES

CARROTS

2 tablespoons salted butter

1 pound medium or large carrots, cut diagonally into ½-inch slices

½ teaspoon kosher salt

Freshly ground black pepper

3 garlic cloves, thinly sliced

1 tablespoon honey

GARNISH AND SERVING

3 tablespoons Spicy Cilantro Yogurt Sauce (page 236)

A mix of torn fresh basil, cilantro, and mint

2 to 3 tablespoons chopped honey-roasted peanuts or cashews

make it your way

Add 3 to 4 cups of arugula to the platter before you top with the warm carrots.

I'm always looking for new ways to jazz up vegetables and make them unbelievably delish so that you'll want to keep making them again and again. Enter these beautiful, caramelized carrots that aren't your typical (ahem, boring) carrot side dish. The carrots cook with garlic in a little butter until tender and golden, then they're topped with creamy Spicy Cilantro Yogurt Sauce, tons of fresh herbs, and crunchy roasted nuts that keep you coming back for more. (Need convincing? The leftovers are great served warm or cold, mixed with arugula and cooked quinoa.) They may taste as if they were made by a fancy restaurant, but this one is all you, baby!

1. **Cook the carrots:** In a large skillet, melt the butter over medium heat. Add the carrots, salt, and pepper to taste, stirring well to coat.

2. Cover the skillet and cook until the carrots tenderize a bit, stirring occasionally to prevent the carrots from burning, 10 to 15 minutes. Remove the lid, add the garlic, and cook uncovered, stirring occasionally, until the carrots are fork-tender and caramelized on the edges, 8 to 10 minutes.

3. **Garnish and serve:** Add the honey and cook, stirring frequently, until the carrots are well coated, 1 to 2 minutes.

4. Transfer the carrots to a platter or a large, shallow bowl and drizzle with the Spicy Cilantro Yogurt Sauce. Garnish with the fresh herbs and peanuts. Serve warm.

5. **To store:** Keep any leftovers in an airtight container in the fridge for up to 4 days.

coconut rice (+ a few different ways to make it)

SERVES 4 TO 6 ■ PREP TIME: 10 MINUTES ■ COOK TIME: 15 MINUTES, PLUS 10 MINUTES STEAMING TIME

Not only do I adore the slightly sweet flavor of coconut rice, it's also super nutritious and so versatile. At one point I became so obsessed with coconut rice that I refused to make any other kind. It goes with just about everything and my kids love it, too! You can jazz the rice up with cilantro and lime, or give it a pop of brightness with turmeric and ginger. As always, you do you.

1. In a medium pot, stir together the rice, coconut milk, water, sugar, and salt and place over high heat. Bring to a boil, then cover, reduce the heat to low, and cook for 15 minutes. Remove from the heat and keep the lid on to allow rice to steam until tender, about 10 minutes. Fluff the rice with a fork and serve warm.

2. **To store:** Keep any leftovers in an airtight container in the fridge for up to 5 days. To reheat, microwave in 30-second intervals until warm.

1½ cups white jasmine rice, rinsed in a sieve until the water runs clear

1 (15-ounce) can light or full-fat coconut milk

1 cup water

1 teaspoon sugar

½ teaspoon kosher salt

make it your way

CILANTRO LIME COCONUT RICE: Stir in the zest and juice of 1 lime and ½ cup of chopped fresh cilantro before serving.

MANGO COCONUT RICE: Stir in 1 cup of diced mango before serving for a sweet rice snack. My kids love this!

ANTI-INFLAMMATORY COCONUT RICE: Add 1 teaspoon of ground turmeric (or sub 1 tablespoon of fresh grated turmeric), 1 tablespoon of fresh grated ginger, and 1 minced garlic clove to the pot before cooking.

arroz con gandules

SERVES 6 ■ PREP TIME: 5 MINUTES ■ COOK TIME: 40 MINUTES

2 teaspoons extra-virgin olive oil

⅓ cup finely diced yellow onion

⅓ cup finely diced green bell pepper

¼ cup finely chopped fresh cilantro

2 garlic cloves, minced

½ cup no-salt-added tomato sauce

1 tablespoon (2 packets) Goya Sazón con Culantro y Achiote (or Homemade Sazón, page 237)

⅛ teaspoon adobo seasoning (or just a pinch)

1 (15-ounce) can Goya green pigeon peas and their liquid

3 cups water

2 cups white basmati rice, rinsed in a sieve until the water runs clear

½ cup pimento-stuffed olives

It's not every day that I crave rice, but when I do it's always and forever Arroz con Gandules, the national dish of Puerto Rico! It's simple: a nutritious, flavorful, sofrito-infused rice with pigeon peas (gandules). This was a staple in my childhood, and once you taste it you'll understand why. Not only is this rice dish an important part of Mom's Puerto Rican Rice & Beans (page 130), I also like to serve it with other Puerto Rican favorites, such as Nana Aida's Crazy Good Chicken Stew (page 110) and Weeknight Chicken Picadillo (page 156).

1. In a medium pot, warm the olive oil over medium heat. Once the oil is hot, add the onion, bell pepper, cilantro, and garlic and sauté, stirring occasionally, until softened, about 5 minutes. Reduce the heat to medium-low and add the tomato sauce, sazón, and adobo seasoning. Simmer, stirring frequently, until the sauce comes together, about 2 minutes.

2. Add the pigeon peas and their liquid, plus the water, and bring to a boil. Once boiling, stir in the rice and olives, cover, reduce the heat to low, and cook until the rice is tender, about 20 minutes. Remove from the heat and allow the rice to steam for 10 minutes. Fluff with a fork and serve warm.

3. **To store:** Keep any leftovers in an airtight container in the fridge for up to 5 days. To reheat, warm rice in the microwave until heated through.

make it your way

Sub green peas for pigeon peas. Increase the water for the rice by ½ cup (for a total of 3½ cups). After you bring water to a boil, add 1½ cups of frozen peas (not thawed) with the rice.

crispy fried tostones

SERVES 4 ■ PREP TIME: 15 MINUTES ■ COOK TIME: 10 MINUTES

I grew up eating these with my mom's Puerto Rican dishes, or just on their own. If you're going to eat tostones, you should eat them the traditional way, and not resort to any kind of light version that just doesn't taste the same. You can, however, slice them more thinly to get more of a chip-like crunch, or choose to leave them a bit thicker for more chew. Cutting them 1 inch-thick is the traditional way, but hey, they're your tostones. Consider serving these alongside Mom's Puerto Rican Rice & Beans (page 130), Nana Aida's Crazy Good Chicken Stew (page 110) or Marry Me Ropa Vieja (page 203).

1. Use a sharp knife to cut off both ends from one of the plantains. Carefully cut a vertical slit through the peel along the length of the plantain, being sure not to cut into the flesh. Turn the plantain over and cut a slit through the peel on the other side. Use your fingers to remove the peel. Repeat with the remaining plantains.

2. Use a sharp knife to cut the plantains into ½-inch slices for plantain chips, or 1-inch slices for tostones.

3. **Cook the plantains:** Line a plate with paper towels. In a large, deep skillet, warm the avocado oil over medium heat until it shimmers. Once the oil is hot, add all the plantains and fry until golden brown, 3 to 4 minutes per side. Using a slotted spoon, transfer the plantains to the prepared plate to cool, then move to a cutting board. Turn the heat off to prevent the oil from smoking.

4. Use the bottom of a heavy mug or jar to smash the plantains to half of their original thickness. If your plantains stick to the object you smashed them with, use a butter knife to gently loosen.

5. Turn the heat to medium and warm the oil until it shimmers again. Working in batches and making sure not to crowd the pan, return the plantains to the hot oil and fry until medium golden brown, 1 to 2 minutes per side. Transfer to the paper towel-lined plate, season with the adobo and salt, and allow them to cool for 5 minutes. Repeat with the remaining plantains, adding more oil if necessary.

6. **To serve:** Dip in your favorite sauce or hot sauce, or serve as a part of a meal.

7. **To store:** Keep any leftover tostones in a reusable silicone bag or airtight container in the fridge for up to 2 days. Reheat them on a wire rack set over a baking sheet at 450°F until heated and crispy, 3 to 5 minutes.

4 green plantains

¾ cup avocado oil, plus more as needed

¼ teaspoon adobo seasoning

¼ teaspoon kosher salt

SERVING

Spicy Cilantro Yogurt Sauce (page 236) or Pickled Jalapeño Ranch Dressing (page 234)

dad's au gratin potatoes

SERVES 8 ■ PREP TIME: 30 MINUTES ■ COOK TIME: 1 HOUR 30 MINUTES

Nonstick cooking spray

POTATOES

2½ pounds Yukon Gold potatoes (6 to 7 medium potatoes), sliced into ⅛-inch-thick rounds

½ medium yellow onion, thinly sliced

SAUCE

3 tablespoons salted butter

¼ cup all-purpose flour

1½ cups whole milk or unsweetened almond milk

8 ounces shredded sharp Cheddar cheese (2 cups)

¾ teaspoon kosher salt, plus more to taste

½ teaspoon garlic powder

Freshly ground black pepper

TOPPINGS

2 ounces shredded Gruyère cheese (½ cup)

2 ounces grated Parmesan cheese (½ cup)

Chopped fresh chives or parsley

make it your way

TO MAKE GLUTEN-FREE: Use 1:1 gluten-free all-purpose flour.

DAD'S HAM & CHEESE AU GRATIN POTATOES: Add ½ cup of chopped cooked bacon or ham over the potatoes before adding the cheese sauce. Or stir the chopped bacon or ham into the cheese sauce.

My dad was a man who could bring the room to life with his tall stature, bright blue eyes, gigantic laugh, and his recipe for cheesy, creamy, bubbly au gratin potatoes. He served these during the holidays, often Easter and Christmas, but occasionally we'd have them for Sunday night dinner, paired with his crunchy fried chicken and gravy, which felt incredibly special. He passed these down to me, and now I'm passing them to you. Of course, what's not to love about potatoes, three types of cheeses, and sweet onions stuffed together in a pan and baked until they're a gorgeous golden brown?! Make these and you'll light up the room, just like Dad.

1. Preheat the oven to 375°F. Spray a 9-inch square baking dish with cooking spray.

2. **Make the potatoes:** Place the potatoes in the prepared dish in three or four rows, depending on how wide the potatoes are. You don't want them to be tight; make sure you leave enough space so the potato slices are slightly slanted. Add the onion slices in between and on top of potatoes (basically wherever you can fit them).

3. **Make the sauce:** In a medium pot, melt the butter over medium heat. Whisk in the flour and cook, whisking constantly, until a paste forms, about 30 seconds. Slowly stream in the milk, continuing to constantly whisk away any lumps, until smooth and combined. Raise the heat to medium-high, bring the mixture to a boil, then reduce the heat to medium-low and simmer, stirring occasionally, until the sauce thickens and resembles a creamy gravy, about 5 minutes. Reduce the heat to low and stir in the Cheddar, salt, garlic powder, and a few grinds of pepper. Taste and add more salt and pepper, if necessary.

4. **Bake the potatoes:** Pour the sauce evenly over the potatoes and onions and cover the pan with foil. Bake for 45 minutes.

5. **Top and serve:** Remove the foil and sprinkle the potatoes with the Gruyère and Parmesan. Return to the oven and bake, uncovered, until the potatoes can be easily pierced with a fork and the top is nice and golden brown, 30 to 45 minutes. (If you'd like an extra crispy, golden topping, switch the oven to the broiler setting on high and broil for 1 to 2 minutes, watching closely to prevent burning.) Allow to cool for 10 minutes, then top with chives and serve warm.

6. **To store:** Keep any leftovers in an airtight container in the fridge for up to 5 days. Reheat in the microwave in 30-second intervals until heated through.

7. **To make ahead:** Assemble the au gratin as directed, but before baking, cover the dish with foil, and place it in the fridge for up to 1 day before serving. When you're ready to serve, bake as directed, adding 10 to 15 minutes to the baking time if needed.

milk & honey oatmeal dinner rolls (or burger buns!) (PAGE 226)

milk & honey oatmeal dinner rolls (or burger buns!)

MAKES 15 DINNER ROLLS OR 9 BURGER BUNS ■ **PREP TIME: 25 MINUTES, PLUS 2 HOURS RISING TIME**
■ **COOK TIME: 20 MINUTES**

DRY INGREDIENTS

3 cups (360 grams) bread flour, plus more as needed

¾ cup (85 grams) white whole-wheat flour

2¼ teaspoons instant yeast (one ¼-ounce package)

2 teaspoons kosher salt

WET INGREDIENTS

1 cup (240 grams) whole milk

1 cup (95 grams) rolled oats

¼ cup (84 grams) honey

6 tablespoons (85 grams) salted butter, melted and cooled

2 large eggs, at room temperature

Nonstick cooking spray or extra-virgin olive oil

TOPPING AND SERVING

1 large egg

1 teaspoon water

2 to 3 tablespoons rolled oats

Salted Honey Butter (page 235), plus more for serving

Flaky sea salt (I like Maldon)

Bread is my love language. I love how it takes time and effort and patience to make, and how the beautiful result is always worth it and so satisfying. There's nothing better than showing love by taking your time to make something special for someone else, then watching them pull apart these fluffy, tender rolls and slather them with honey butter. These were inspired by the fluffiness of the Dave's Killer Bread burger buns. They're a wonderful homemade, wholesome, chewy alternative that can also be made into a dinner roll. Because making my own bread requires time and attention, I save these for holidays and special occasions or any time I'm in a labor-of-love kinda mood.

1. **Prepare the dry ingredients:** In a large bowl, whisk the bread flour, white whole-wheat flour, yeast, and salt.

2. **Prepare the wet ingredients:** In a large microwave-safe bowl, microwave the milk until slightly warmer than bath water, about 115°F, about 1 minute. In the bowl of a stand mixer fitted with the paddle attachment, add the warm milk, oats, honey, melted butter, and eggs and mix on medium speed until well combined, about 1 minute. (Alternatively, use a wooden spoon to mix until well combined.) Add the dry ingredients and mix with a wooden spoon until just incorporated. Fit the mixer with the dough hook attachment. Knead the dough on low speed until just slightly pulling away from the bowl, about 8 minutes (or about 10 minutes by hand). The dough will be very sticky, but that's how we want it.

3. Generously grease a large bowl with cooking spray. Transfer the dough to the prepared bowl, cover with plastic wrap and a towel, and let stand at room temperature until doubled in size, 1½ hours. The dough is done rising when you press a finger into it and the indentation stays or springs back very slowly.

4. Generously flour a surface. Punch down the dough and turn the dough out. Pat the dough into an approximately 8 × 8-inch square.

5. **Shape the dough:**

   ■ **TO MAKE ROLLS:** Grease a 9 × 13-inch baking dish with cooking spray. Cut the dough into 3 equal rectangles, then cut each of those rectangles into five equal pieces (about 66 grams each). Roll each piece into a smooth ball on an unfloured surface and place in the prepared dish, spacing evenly apart. Cover with a towel or plastic wrap and allow the dough to rise again until the rolls are touching, puffy, and doubled in size, about 1 to 1½ hours.

make it your way

TO MAKE DAIRY-FREE: Swap oat milk or almond milk for whole milk and melted vegan butter for regular butter.

make it nutrient-dense

Add healthy fats and fiber by topping the rolls with a variety of seeds mixed with the oats. I recommend mixing together 1 tablespoon of oats, 1 tablespoon of sunflower seeds, 1½ teaspoons of flaxseed, 1 teaspoon of black sesame seeds, and 1 teaspoon of poppy seeds. Sprinkle on top of the egg-washed rolls before baking.

▧ **TO MAKE BURGER BUNS:** Line a large baking sheet with parchment paper. Cut the dough into 3 equal rectangles, then cut each of those into three equal pieces (about 110 grams each). Roll each piece into a smooth ball on an unfloured surface, then flatten each piece with the palm of your hand so it is approximately 3 inches wide. Place each piece onto the prepared baking sheet, spacing at least 1 inch apart. Cover with a towel or plastic wrap and allow the dough to rise again until puffy, about 1 to 1½ hours.

6. **For either method:** You can cover and refrigerate the dish of rolls for up to 18 hours *before* the second rising. The next day, remove the rolls from the fridge and let them rise for 1½ to 2 hours, until puffy and doubled in size, before baking as directed.

7. **Bake and serve:** Once the rolls are nearly doubled in size, preheat the oven to 350°F. In a small bowl, whisk the egg and water until well combined. Brush the rolls with the egg wash and sprinkle evenly with the oats. Bake until golden brown, 20 to 25 minutes for dinner rolls or 15 to 20 minutes for burger buns. If you're not freezing them, after removing the rolls from the oven, immediately brush with a few tablespoons of Salted Honey Butter and top with flaky sea salt. Serve warm with extra honey butter, if desired.

8. **To store:** Place the rolls in a reusable silicone bag for up to 3 days. Reheat in the oven on a baking sheet at 350°F, until warmed through, 5 to 10 minutes, or in the microwave for 20 to 30 seconds. To freeze the baked rolls, allow them to cool to room temperature after baking (do not add the honey butter), then wrap them in plastic wrap and foil, or store in an airtight container or a reusable silicone bag in the freezer for up to 3 months. To reheat from frozen, thaw the rolls at room temperature, then reheat in the oven at 350°F for 5 to 10 minutes or in the microwave for 20 to 30 seconds. Immediately brush with Salted Honey Butter and top with flaky sea salt.

the flavor bible

There are so many little ways you can take a meal to the next level. Here are the sauces, dressings, and garnishes that I reference throughout this book that will instantly perk up sandwiches, salads, pastas, and proteins. If you have one (or more!) around at all times, you can always add a little "oomph" to your meals. Unless otherwise noted, my salad dressings and sauces can be stored in an airtight container in the fridge for up to 5 days. Make them in advance and they'll be ready to go when your next meal needs to be on the table ASAP.

CRUSHED PISTACHIO OLIVE DRESSING

Dress up any dish with fresh herbs, briny olives, and pistachios.

MAKES ABOUT 1 CUP

½ cup Castelvetrano olives, drained, pitted, and smashed or roughly chopped

⅓ cup roasted shelled pistachios, chopped

¼ cup extra-virgin olive oil

¼ cup chopped fresh leafy herbs (I like a mix of parsley, basil, and dill)

1 teaspoon lemon zest

3 tablespoons fresh lemon juice

1 garlic clove, grated

¼ teaspoon kosher salt

Freshly ground black pepper

In a medium bowl, stir together the olives, pistachios, olive oil, herbs, lemon zest and juice, garlic, salt, and pepper to taste until well combined.

more ways to use it Spoon it over grilled or roasted chicken or roasted potatoes. • Mix it into warm or cold pastas, lentils, white beans, chickpeas, or roasted vegetables. • Spoon it over Whipped Feta Yogurt Sauce (page 233) or baked feta for a yummy dip.

SUNSHINE DRESSING

This creamy, lemony dressing is truly sunshine in a bottle.

MAKES ½ CUP

3 tablespoons tahini

2 tablespoons fresh lemon juice (from about ½ lemon)

1 tablespoon pure maple syrup

2 teaspoons grated fresh ginger

½ teaspoon ground turmeric

¼ teaspoon garlic powder

¼ teaspoon kosher salt, plus more to taste

Freshly ground black pepper

1 to 2 tablespoons warm water, as needed

In a medium bowl, stir together the tahini, lemon juice, maple syrup, ginger, turmeric, garlic powder, salt, and pepper to taste until well combined. Add just enough warm water to thin out the dressing so that it's pourable.

more ways to use it Drizzle it on salads, lentils, and roasted vegetables and sweet potatoes. • Use it as a dip for fresh, crunchy veggies. • Toss it with smashed chickpeas and crunchy veggies in a wrap.

SESAME GINGER DRESSING

The ultimate marinade, dressing, or sauce.

MAKES ABOUT ⅔ CUP

3 tablespoons low-sodium soy sauce (or sub coconut aminos if gluten-free)

2 tablespoons toasted sesame oil

2 tablespoons extra-virgin olive oil

2 tablespoons rice vinegar

2 tablespoons tahini

1½ teaspoons pure maple syrup

1 tablespoon grated fresh ginger

2 garlic cloves, grated

In a medium bowl, whisk the soy sauce, sesame oil, olive oil, rice vinegar, tahini, maple syrup, ginger, and garlic until smooth and well combined.

more ways to use it Toss it with veggies before roasting. • Use it as a marinade for chicken or seafood. • Use it as a sauce in stir-fries.

CILANTRO LIME VINAIGRETTE

Say hello to summer in a jar with this beautiful herby vinaigrette.

MAKES ⅔ CUP

1 cup chopped fresh cilantro

⅓ cup extra-virgin olive oil

1 jalapeño, seeded and chopped

3 tablespoons fresh lime juice

1 tablespoon honey (or sub sugar if vegan)

1 garlic clove, roughly chopped

½ teaspoon kosher salt

Freshly ground black pepper

In a high powered blender, combine the cilantro, olive oil, jalapeño, lime juice, honey, garlic, salt, and pepper to taste. Blend until smooth.

more ways to use it Use it as a marinade for grilled chicken or seafood. • Enjoy it in taco, kale, or cabbage salads. • Toss it with quinoa, farro, or lentils.

MAPLE APPLE CIDER DRESSING

An easy fall or winter dressing with sweet and tangy flavor.

MAKES ABOUT ½ CUP

¼ cup extra-virgin olive oil

3 tablespoons apple cider vinegar

1 tablespoon pure maple syrup

1 teaspoon Dijon mustard

1 garlic clove, grated

½ teaspoon kosher salt

Freshly ground black pepper

In a medium bowl, whisk the olive oil, vinegar, maple syrup, mustard, garlic, salt, and pepper to taste until emulsified.

more ways to use it Use it as a marinade for chicken. • Toss it with roasted Brussels sprouts, butternut squash, or sweet potatoes. • Use it as a dressing over grain bowls.

QUICK HOT HONEY

Sweet honey with the perfect kick.

MAKES ½ CUP

½ cup honey

1 teaspoon red pepper flakes

½ teaspoon apple cider vinegar

¼ teaspoon kosher salt

In a small saucepan or pot, combine the honey, red pepper flakes, vinegar, and salt over medium-low heat. Bring to a simmer, stirring frequently, and cook for 1 minute. Transfer to an airtight jar and store at room temperature for up to 6 months.

more ways to use it
Enjoy it on top of crostini or pizza. • Drizzle it over grilled cheese, quesadillas, or breakfast sandwiches. • As a dip for chicken tenders or drizzled over fried chicken sandwiches.

BANGIN' SAUCE

Creamy, spicy, and perfect for dipping or topping just about anything.

MAKES ABOUT 1 CUP

⅓ cup plain whole-milk Greek yogurt (or sub vegan mayo)

⅓ cup mayonnaise (or sub vegan mayo)

2 tablespoons fresh lime juice

2 tablespoons sambal oelek

1 teaspoon honey (or sub pure maple syrup if vegan)

¼ teaspoon kosher salt

Freshly ground black pepper

In a medium bowl, whisk the Greek yogurt, mayonnaise, lime juice, sambal oelek, honey, salt, and pepper to taste until well combined.

more ways to use it Use it as a dip for chicken tenders, fries, or spring rolls. • Spread it on wraps, sandwiches, and burgers. • Enjoy it on top of tacos, grilled shrimp, or salmon.

JALAPEÑO LIME CASHEW SAUCE

Savory, garlicky, and dairy-free, too.

MAKES ABOUT 1 CUP

¾ cup raw cashews

2½ cups water, plus more as needed

1 jalapeño, halved and seeded

2 tablespoons fresh lime juice

1 garlic clove, roughly chopped

¾ teaspoon kosher salt

½ teaspoon onion powder

Freshly ground black pepper

In a large pot, combine the cashews with 2 cups of the water. Place over high heat and bring to a boil. Cook for 2 minutes, then remove from the heat and let the cashews soak for 30 minutes, then drain. In a high-powered blender, place the soaked cashews, remaining ½ cup of water, jalapeño, lime juice, garlic, salt, onion powder, and pepper to taste. Blend on high speed until the mixture is mostly smooth, about 1 minute. If it's too thick, add a few tablespoons of water and blend again.

more ways to use it Use it as a pasta salad dressing. • Enjoy it on tacos, burritos, enchiladas, and grain bowls. • Use it as a dip for veggies and crackers.

EASY BASIL PESTO

The best basil pesto ever!

MAKES ABOUT 1 CUP

2 cups fresh basil leaves

⅓ cup walnuts or pine nuts

2 garlic cloves, roughly chopped

⅓ cup extra-virgin olive oil, plus more as needed

¼ cup grated Parmesan cheese (leave out if dairy-free or vegan)

1 teaspoon lemon zest

Juice of ½ lemon

½ teaspoon kosher salt

Freshly ground black pepper

In a food processor, pulse the basil, walnuts, and garlic, stopping to scrape down the bowl as necessary, until well combined, about 1 minute. Add the olive oil, Parmesan, lemon zest and juice, salt, and pepper to taste and process until smooth and emulsified, streaming in an extra 1 to 2 tablespoons of olive oil, if necessary, 1 to 2 minutes.

more ways to use it Stir it into pasta salad or grain bowls. • Spread it on sandwiches, wraps, or chicken burgers. • Enjoy it on top of pizza or garlic bread.

MANGO JALAPEÑO SAUCE

Vibrant sauce with lovely heat.

MAKES ABOUT 1 CUP

1 large mango, diced

1 jalapeño, roughly chopped

¼ cup chopped fresh cilantro

2 tablespoons extra-virgin olive oil

1 tablespoon fresh lime juice

1 garlic clove, roughly chopped

½ teaspoon kosher salt

In a high-powered blender, blend the mango, jalapeño, cilantro, olive oil, lime juice, garlic, and salt until smooth, about 1 minute.

more ways to use it Use it as a sauce for stir-fries. • Use it as a marinade for grilled chicken or seafood. • Drizzle it over tacos, burritos, and grain bowls.

PEANUT-TAHINI DRESSING

Peanut sauce with a tangy kick.

MAKES ABOUT ½ CUP

2 tablespoons tahini

2 tablespoons natural creamy peanut butter

1 tablespoon fresh lime juice

2 teaspoons pure maple syrup

½ teaspoon Dijon mustard

½ teaspoon kosher salt

¼ teaspoon garlic powder

Freshly ground black pepper

2 to 3 tablespoons warm water

In a medium bowl, combine the tahini, peanut butter, lime juice, maple syrup, mustard, salt, garlic powder, and lots of pepper and whisk until well combined. Whisk in 2 tablespoons of warm water. If the dressing is still too thick to be poured, add more warm water, 1 teaspoon at a time.

more ways to use it Toss it with lo mein or rice noodles.

WHIPPED FETA YOGURT SAUCE (OR DIP!)

Tangy, savory, and salty—yes, please!

MAKES ABOUT 2 CUPS

1 cup plain whole-milk Greek yogurt

4 ounces feta cheese, crumbled

1 tablespoon extra-virgin olive oil

2 tablespoons chopped leafy fresh herbs, such as basil, parsley, and/or dill (optional)

1 teaspoon lemon zest

1 tablespoon fresh lemon juice

1 garlic clove, roughly chopped

Kosher salt and freshly ground black pepper

In a food processor or blender, process or blend the Greek yogurt, feta, olive oil, herbs (if using), lemon zest and juice, and garlic on high speed until smooth, scraping down the sides as necessary, about 1 minute. Add salt and pepper to taste.

more ways to use it Serve it with meatballs, chicken, or fish. • Use it as a dip for pita bread, crackers, or veggies. • Spread it on sandwiches, burgers, or wraps.

PICKLED JALAPEÑO RANCH DRESSING

You'll be amazed by how quickly this spicy and herby ranch disappears.

MAKES ABOUT 1 GENEROUS CUP

1 cup plain whole-milk Greek yogurt

¼ cup drained pickled jalapeño slices plus 2 tablespoons of their brine

⅓ cup chopped fresh cilantro

1 garlic clove, roughly chopped

½ teaspoon kosher salt

½ teaspoon onion powder

¼ teaspoon dried dill

¼ teaspoon dried parsley

Freshly ground black pepper

In a food processor or blender, process or blend the Greek yogurt, pickled jalapeños and brine, cilantro, garlic, salt, onion powder, dried dill, dried parsley, and pepper to taste on low speed until well combined and smooth, about 30 seconds.

more ways to use it Use it as a dip for pizza, quesadillas, or fries.

BASIC BUT WORTHY BALSAMIC DRESSING

The queen of versatility and the only balsamic dressing you'll ever need.

MAKES ABOUT ½ CUP

¼ cup extra-virgin olive oil

3 tablespoons balsamic vinegar

1 teaspoon pure maple syrup

½ teaspoon Dijon mustard

1 garlic clove, grated

In a medium bowl, whisk the olive oil, vinegar, maple syrup, mustard, and garlic until emulsified. If storing, mix well before using.

more ways to use it Drizzle it on your favorite salads or pizza. • Use it as a marinade for roasted or grilled chicken and vegetables. • Soak it with strawberries or peaches and spoon onto crostini spread with goat cheese.

TAHINI GOCHUJANG SAUCE

Spicy, bright, and nutty. Yum!

MAKES ABOUT ½ CUP

2 tablespoons tahini

2 tablespoons warm water, plus more as needed

2 tablespoons gochujang

1 tablespoon plain whole-milk Greek yogurt (or sub vegan mayo)

1 tablespoon pure maple syrup

1 tablespoon fresh lime juice

½ tablespoon grated fresh ginger

1 teaspoon toasted sesame oil

½ teaspoon garlic powder

Kosher salt and freshly ground black pepper

In a medium bowl, combine the tahini, warm water, 1 to 2 tablespoons of gochujang, the Greek yogurt, maple syrup, lime juice, ginger, sesame oil, garlic powder, and salt and pepper to taste. Whisk until well combined and pourable.

more ways to use it Drizzle it over stir-fries or rice bowls.

SALTED HONEY BUTTER

Butter upgraded with a sprinkle of salt and a drizzle of honey.

MAKES ABOUT ½ CUP

8 tablespoons (113 grams) salted butter, softened (or sub vegan butter)

3 tablespoons honey (or sub pure maple syrup if vegan)

½ teaspoon flaky sea salt (I like Maldon)

¼ teaspoon ground cinnamon (optional)

In the bowl of a stand mixer fitted with the whisk attachment, beat the butter, 2 tablespoons of honey, the salt, and cinnamon (if using) on medium-low speed until the butter is smooth and fluffy, about 2 minutes. Taste and add more honey if you want more sweetness. (Alternatively, whisk by hand until smooth and fluffy.) Store in an airtight container in the fridge for up to 1 week.

more ways to use it Use it on French toast, pancakes, and waffles. • Slather it over cornbread, scones, or muffins. • Spread it over your morning toast.

CILANTRO PISTACHIO PESTO

An unexpected, ultra flavorful pesto.

MAKES ABOUT ⅓ CUP

1 cup packed fresh cilantro

½ cup roasted shelled pistachios (or sub cashews)

3 tablespoons extra-virgin olive oil

2 tablespoons water

1 jalapeño, roughly chopped

2 garlic cloves, roughly chopped

Juice of ½ lime

½ teaspoon kosher salt

Freshly ground black pepper

In the bowl of a food processor, combine the cilantro, pistachios, olive oil, water, jalapeño, garlic, lime juice, salt, and pepper to taste. Pulse until well combined, stopping to scrape down the bowl as necessary, about 1 minute. Add another 1 to 2 tablespoons of water if it seems too thick and process again.

LEMON VINAIGRETTE

A lemon vinaigrette with options.

MAKES ABOUT ½ CUP

¼ cup extra-virgin olive oil

3 tablespoons fresh lemon juice

1 tablespoon sugar, pure maple syrup, or honey (if not vegan)

½ teaspoon Dijon mustard

1 garlic clove, grated

½ teaspoon kosher salt

In a medium bowl, whisk the olive oil, lemon juice, sugar, mustard, garlic, and salt until emulsified.

GREEK-INSPIRED LEMON VINAIGRETTE: Add 1 teaspoon of dried oregano and another ½ teaspoon of Dijon mustard.

LEMON BASIL VINAIGRETTE: Add ½ cup of loosely packed fresh basil leaves. Put all the ingredients in a blender and blend until smooth.

FETA BASIL VINAIGRETTE: Add ½ cup of loosely packed fresh basil leaves and 2 ounces (heaping ⅓ cup) of crumbled feta cheese. Put all the ingredients in a blender and blend until smooth.

HONEY MUSTARD SAUCE

The most incredible sweet and tangy marinade or dressing.

MAKES ABOUT ½ CUP

3 tablespoons Dijon mustard

2 to 3 tablespoons honey, to taste

2 tablespoons extra-virgin olive oil

1 tablespoon apple cider vinegar

1 tablespoon fresh lemon juice

1 garlic clove, grated

¼ teaspoon kosher salt

Freshly ground black pepper

In a medium bowl, whisk the mustard, honey, olive oil, vinegar, lemon juice, garlic, salt, and pepper to taste until smooth and well combined.

more ways to use it Use it as a marinade for chicken or seafood. • Enjoy it as a dip for fries or chicken nuggets or tenders. • Use it as a salad dressing.

SPICY CILANTRO YOGURT SAUCE

A wonderful herby yogurt sauce that pairs oh-so-well with proteins and veggies.

MAKES ABOUT ½ CUP

½ cup roughly chopped fresh cilantro

¼ cup plain whole-milk Greek yogurt

1 small jalapeño, roughly chopped

1 tablespoon fresh lime juice

1 teaspoon extra-virgin olive oil

1 teaspoon sugar or honey

1 garlic clove, roughly chopped

¼ teaspoon kosher salt, plus more to taste

Freshly ground black pepper

In a high-powered blender, blend or process the cilantro, Greek yogurt, jalapeño, lime juice, olive oil, sugar, garlic, salt, and pepper to taste until well combined.

more ways to use it Serve it over grilled or roasted chicken, steak, or seafood. • Drizzle it over tacos, quesadillas, or enchiladas. • Spread it on sandwiches and wraps.

HERBY GOLDEN BREAD CRUMBS

An herby, crunchy topping that you'll want to keep on hand.

MAKES 1 CUP

2 tablespoons salted butter (or sub vegan butter)

2 fresh sage leaves, chopped

1 sprig of fresh rosemary, leaves removed and chopped

1 cup panko bread crumbs (gluten-free, if desired)

1 teaspoon fresh thyme leaves

¼ teaspoon garlic powder

¼ teaspoon kosher salt

1. In a medium skillet, melt the butter over medium heat. Add the sage and rosemary and fry, stirring occasionally, until the sage is crispy, 2 to 4 minutes. Add the panko to the pan and cook, stirring occasionally, until the panko is toasted and turns golden brown, 2 to 4 minutes.

2. Transfer to a small bowl and mix in the thyme, garlic powder, and salt. Use immediately or keep in an airtight container at room temperature for up to 1 week.

more ways to use it
Sprinkle them on top of your favorite pasta recipes. • Mix them into meatballs and meatloaves.

PICKLED RED ONIONS

Red onions made slightly sweet.

MAKES ABOUT 2 CUPS

1 medium red onion, very thinly sliced

½ cup distilled white vinegar

½ cup water

1 tablespoon sugar

1 teaspoon kosher salt

1. Pack the onion slices into a 16-ounce mason jar or another heat-safe container.

2. In a small saucepan, whisk the vinegar, water, sugar, and salt over medium heat. Bring the mixture to a simmer and cook, whisking until the sugar and salt dissolve, about 1 minute.

3. Pour the vinegar mixture into the jar and use a spoon to press the onion slices down so that they're fully submerged. Let the onions cool to room temperature, then cover the jar and place in the fridge. The pickled onions are ready to use once they turn a vibrant pink color, 1 to 2 hours. Store in an airtight container in the fridge for up to 2 weeks.

HOMEMADE SAZÓN SEASONING

A DIY version of the famous Latin seasoning powder.

MAKES ABOUT ⅓ CUP

1 tablespoon ground coriander

1 tablespoon ground cumin

1 tablespoon ground annatto seeds (or sub ground turmeric)

1 tablespoon garlic powder

1 tablespoon kosher salt

2 teaspoons dried oregano

In a small bowl, stir together the coriander, cumin, annatto, garlic powder, salt, and dried oregano until well combined. Store in an airtight container or jar at room temperature for up to 6 months.

more ways to use it Toss it with potatoes before roasting. • Use it to season ground beef, chicken, or turkey. • Add it to soups and stews for a flavor boost.

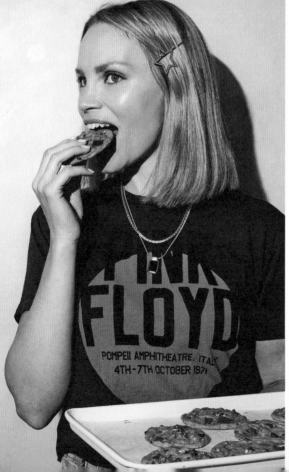

your girl never forgets dessert

I firmly believe that dessert should not only be reserved for special occasions. I grew up baking with my dad. For so many years after his death, I deprived myself of sweets before realizing that baking and sharing my creations with others is incredibly therapeutic and brings back the best memories of my father. Since then, baking has become my love language. These recipes are for all types of occasions, from "lunch dessert" (yup, you read that right), to a quick cookie after dinner, to a party-worthy showstopper that will leave you feeling proud of your efforts.

energy bites

that taste
like dessert

TART CHERRY BOMBS

Cherry lovers, meet your dream snack.

Energy bites are one of my favorite snacks to keep on hand when I need a little boost during the day. They are especially delicious as a lunch dessert—which should be a regular thing, right? They're great for adults to enjoy post-workout or as a quick grab-and-go snack, and are awesome for kids because they're packed with nutrition. Well guess what, ya girl made you four energy bite recipes that taste positively indulgent.

1. **Make the dough:** In a food processor, process the dough ingredients until well combined and sticky, about 1 minute. You may need to scrape down the sides a few times with a spatula, then process again. The mixture may seem crumbly at first, especially if the recipe calls for dates. Squeeze a little bit between your fingers and if it is nice and sticky and easily forms together, you should be able to shape it into balls (see the tips below for more).

2. **Add the mix-ins:** If the recipe calls for any mix-ins, stir those in with a wooden spoon or use your hands to work into the dough.

3. Use your hands to roll 1 tablespoon of dough into a ball. Set it aside and repeat with the remaining dough.

4. **Coat the bites:** If the recipe calls for a coating, put it on a shallow plate. Roll each ball in the coating.

5. **To store:** Keep the bites in a reusable silicone bag, plastic freezer storage bag, or an airtight container in the fridge for up to 1 week, or in the freezer for up to 3 months (let the energy bites soften in the fridge or at room temperature before enjoying from the freezer).

DOUGH

1 cup pitted soft Medjool dates (10 to 12 large dates)

1 cup dried tart cherries

1 cup raw cashews

½ cup rolled oats (gluten-free, if desired)

1 tablespoon chia seeds

½ teaspoon kosher salt

½ teaspoon vanilla extract

½ teaspoon almond extract

tips

Nice plump dates are a must! If your dates are on the drier side or are slightly hard, soak them in a medium bowl of warm water for 10 minutes, then drain and pat dry before using.

If your balls don't stick together, add 1 tablespoon of water at a time, pulsing again until the mixture comes together.

OMEGA-3 COSMIC BROWNIE

This one tastes like your favorite childhood brownie!

DOUGH

1 cup pitted soft Medjool dates (10 to 12 large dates)

1 cup walnuts

3 tablespoons cacao powder or unsweetened cocoa powder

1 teaspoon vanilla extract

¼ teaspoon kosher salt

COATING

⅓ cup artificial dye-free rainbow sprinkles

When forming the dough, you may need to add 1 to 2 tablespoons of water, if necessary, to bind everything together.

MRS. NAUGHTY GRAHAM

Taste so much like Teddy Grahams, they feel a little naughty.

DOUGH

½ cup almond butter (or sub cashew butter)

⅓ cup flaxseed meal

⅓ cup unflavored protein powder of choice (plant-based, if desired)

¼ cup honey (or pure maple syrup if vegan)

1 tablespoon hemp hearts

2 teaspoons chia seeds

1 teaspoon ground cinnamon

1 teaspoon vanilla extract

MIX-INS

3 tablespoons mini chocolate chips (dairy-free, if desired)

TOASTED COCONUT CARAMEL DELIGHTS

Your beloved Girl Scout Samoa cookies in healthy-bite form.

DOUGH

1 cup pitted soft Medjool dates (10 to 12 large dates)

¾ cup raw cashews

½ cup toasted unsweetened shredded coconut

2 teaspoons vanilla extract

½ teaspoon kosher salt

MIX-INS

2 tablespoons mini chocolate chips (dairy-free, if desired)

COATING

½ cup toasted unsweetened shredded coconut

To toast the coconut: In a small skillet over medium-low heat, toast the coconut, stirring frequently, until golden brown, about 5 minutes.

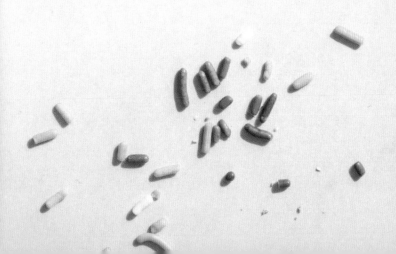

change your life brown butter chocolate chip cookies (PAGE 246)

change your life brown butter chocolate chip cookies

**MAKES 2 DOZEN ▓ PREP TIME: 30 MINUTES, PLUS 2 HOURS CHILLING TIME
▓ COOK TIME: 5 MINUTES, PLUS 10 MINUTES PER BATCH**

WET INGREDIENTS

1 cup (226 grams) unsalted butter, sliced

1½ cups (320 grams) packed dark brown sugar

¼ cup (50 grams) granulated sugar

1 large egg plus 1 large egg yolk, at room temperature

1 tablespoon vanilla extract

1 tablespoon plain whole-milk Greek yogurt

DRY INGREDIENTS

2¼ cups (270 grams) all-purpose flour

1 teaspoon baking soda

½ teaspoon kosher salt

¾ cup (135 grams) semisweet chocolate chips

¾ cup (135 grams) milk or dark chocolate chips or chunks

Flaky sea salt (I like Maldon)

I first embarked on creating the world's best chocolate chip cookie back in 2012 while I was still going through the grief and heartbreak of my father's death. He was a man who loved his sweets, and I found myself baking often to remember him and to soothe and comfort my soul. It took a year to perfect this recipe—a year full of spoonfuls of cookie dough, trial and error, and plenty of chocolate-stained scribbled notes. The resulting chocolate chip cookie is both sweet and salty and draws you in from the first bite thanks to the warm, nutty, caramel flavor of salted brown butter, two types of chocolate chips, and a crackly top with sea salt. What's more: This cookie somehow stays soft and chewy in the middle for days. They went viral right away, and so many readers declared that they would never make another chocolate chip cookie recipe again. I know my dad would feel the same way.

1. Line a large plate or baking sheet with parchment paper.

2. **Brown the butter:** Melt the butter in a small saucepan over medium heat. Once melted, whisk constantly; the butter will begin to crackle, then foam. After a few minutes, the butter will begin to turn a golden amber color. As soon as the butter turns brown and gives off a nutty aroma, 5 to 8 minutes, remove from the heat and immediately transfer it to a medium bowl, scraping all the butter and brown bits from the pan. Set aside until cool enough to touch, about 15 minutes.

3. **Mix the wet ingredients:** In the bowl of a stand mixer fitted with the paddle attachment, mix the brown butter, brown sugar, and granulated sugar until well combined, about 1 minute. Beat in the egg, egg yolk, vanilla, and yogurt until the mixture is smooth and creamy and similar in appearance to a caramel sauce, about 1 minute. (Alternatively, you can do this with a whisk; it will take roughly the same amount of time.)

4. **Prepare the dry ingredients:** In another large bowl, whisk the flour, baking soda, and salt until well combined. With the mixer running on low speed, slowly add the dry ingredients to the wet ingredients and mix just until combined, about 1 minute. Add both types of chocolate chips and mix on low speed until just incorporated into the dough (don't overmix!). Cover the bowl with plastic wrap and place in the fridge for 10 minutes.

CHANGE YOUR LIFE STUFFED COOKIES: These are SO good when the cookie dough balls are stuffed with a dollop of Nutella. Chill 1 small jar of Nutella in the fridge to solidify ahead of time. Flatten each dough ball and place 1 teaspoon of chilled Nutella in the middle and fold the dough around it; gently roll into a ball, making sure that the Nutella is not seeping out of the dough. Add more dough, if necessary. Chill dough as directed in step 5 and bake as directed.

5. **Chill the dough:** Use a medium cookie scoop or spoon to measure 2 heaping tablespoons of the dough, roll the dough into balls with your hands, and place onto the prepared plate or baking sheet. Repeat with all of the dough. Cover the balls with plastic wrap and refrigerate for a minimum of 2 hours and a maximum of 24 hours. (Chilling the dough will allow the flavors to come together, the butter to solidify so that the cookies do not spread too much, and the sugar to concentrate into a deeper butterscotch flavor. Please note that the dough needs to chill to be perfect. Have patience, because the results are worth it!)

6. When you are ready to bake, place a rack in the middle of the oven and preheat to 350°F. Line a large baking sheet with parchment paper. Remove the dough from the fridge to allow them to soften for 15 minutes.

7. **Bake the cookies:** Transfer the dough balls to the prepared baking sheet, placing them 2 inches apart. (Not all cookies will fit on the sheet for one batch.) Bake until the edges of the cookies just begin to turn golden brown, 9 to 11 minutes. (They will look a bit underdone in the middle but will continue to cook once out of the oven.)

8. Cool the cookies on the sheet for 5 minutes to allow them to set, then sprinkle each cookie with flasky sea salt. Transfer to a wire rack to cool completely. Once the baking sheet has cooled, repeat with the remaining dough balls.

9. **To store:** Keep cookies in an airtight container or reusable silicone bag at room temperature for up to 1 week, then transfer to the freezer for up to 3 months. For freezing instructions, see page 22.

everything-but-the-kitchen-sink cookies

MAKES 16 TO 18 ■ PREP TIME: 15 MINUTES ■ COOK TIME: 10 MINUTES PER BATCH

WET INGREDIENTS

1 cup (213 grams) packed dark brown sugar

1 large egg, at room temperature

1 teaspoon vanilla extract

½ cup (112 grams) virgin coconut oil, melted and cooled

DRY INGREDIENTS

1 cup (112 grams) fine blanched almond flour

¾ cup (69 grams) oat flour (gluten-free, if desired)

½ cup (48 grams) rolled oats (gluten-free, if desired)

½ teaspoon baking soda

¼ teaspoon kosher salt

MIX-INS AND TOPPINGS

¾ cup (90 grams) roughly chopped mini peanut butter cups

¾ cup (50 grams) roughly chopped pretzel twists (gluten-free, if desired)

¼ cup (50 grams) chocolate-coated candies (I like Unreal brand)

¼ cup (45 grams) dark or semisweet chocolate chips

Flaky sea salt (I like Maldon)

Save this recipe for when it's eight p.m. and you are desperately craving a homemade cookie. These bakery-style cookies have crispy edges and chewy middles, *and* they go from a mishmash of pantry ingredients to your lips in less than 30 minutes. Sold! Butterscotch chips? Leftover chocolate bars? Potato chips? Need them to be dairy-free or vegan? Feel free to experiment; you can't go wrong.

1. Preheat the oven to 350°F. Line a large baking sheet with parchment paper.

2. **Combine the wet ingredients:** In a large bowl, whisk the brown sugar, egg, and vanilla until well combined. Next, whisk in the coconut oil until completely smooth and well-incorporated and the mixture resembles caramel, about 30 seconds.

3. **Add the dry ingredients:** Add the almond flour, oat flour, oats, baking soda, and salt and mix with a wooden spoon until well combined.

4. **Add the mix-ins and toppings:** Add ½ cup of the peanut butter cups and ½ cup of the pretzels (reserving the other ¼ cup of each for pressing into the dough balls), the chocolate candies, and chocolate chips to the dough; mix with a wooden spoon until evenly distributed.

5. Use a large cookie scoop or your hands to roll ¼ cup of the dough into a ball. Place the dough balls 4 inches apart on the prepared baking sheet as you finish, working until you fill up the baking sheet. Top each dough ball with a few of the reserved chopped peanut butter cups and pretzels.

6. Bake until the edges are just turning golden brown, 10 to 12 minutes. Sprinkle the hot cookies with flaky sea salt and cool on the baking sheet for 10 minutes. Transfer to a wire rack to cool completely. Once the baking sheet has cooled, repeat with the remaining dough.

7. **To store:** Keep cookies in an airtight container or reusable silicone bag at room temperature for up to 1 week, then transfer to the freezer for up to 3 months. For freezing instructions, see page 22.

make it your way

TO MAKE DAIRY-FREE: Use all dairy-free mix-ins.

TO MAKE VEGAN: Use 1 Flax Egg (page 16) and all vegan mix-ins.

TO MAKE GLUTEN-FREE: Use gluten-free pretzels and make sure your oat flour and oats are gluten-free.

KITCHEN SINK SCOTCHEROO COOKIES: Replace the chocolate candies with peanut butter chips and replace the chocolate chips with butterscotch chips.

tip

Before baking your cookies, I recommend doing a test bake. Drop one cookie dough ball onto your baking sheet and bake it per the instructions. After baking, you can see if you need to make any adjustments to the dough. For example, if the test cookie spread too much, I suggest adding 2 to 4 tablespoons of flour. If the test cookie doesn't spread at all, you may want to carefully flatten the dough balls with the palm of your hand.

the queen bee's old-fashioned iced lemon oatmeal cookies

MAKES 24 TO 30 ▪ PREP TIME: 20 MINUTES ▪ COOK TIME: 10 MINUTES PER BATCH

You know those classic iced oatmeal cookies that everyone loves? This is a more fun, brighter, spring-ier version, for those who truly love lemon—which is pretty much all of my website readers *and* my dad's mom. She was fondly called The Queen Bee and could be found with a lemon treat and a steaming cup of hot coffee at any time of day. That was just her vibe. These started off as an experiment, but after I ate three in a row and watched Tony do the same, I knew they were something special. Try the baked cookies straight out of the freezer for an irresistible treat.

1. Preheat the oven to 350°F. Line a large baking sheet with parchment paper.

2. **Mix the wet ingredients:** In a small bowl, mix the granulated sugar and lemon zest. Use your fingers to rub the lemon zest into the sugar for about 30 seconds to infuse the lemon flavor into the sugar.

3. Transfer the lemon sugar to the bowl of a stand mixer fitted with the paddle attachment and cream with the butter and brown sugar until light and fluffy, about 2 minutes. Beat in the eggs, vanilla, and almond extract until smooth and creamy, about 1 minute. (Alternatively, use a whisk to beat by hand.)

4. **Add the dry ingredients:** Add the flour, oats, baking soda, and salt and beat on medium-low speed until just combined, about 1 minute. (Alternatively, use a wooden spoon to mix by hand.)

5. Use a medium cookie scoop or your hands to roll 2 heaping tablespoons of dough into a ball. Place the dough balls 2 inches apart on the prepared baking sheet as you finish, working until you fill up the baking sheet.

6. **Bake the cookies:** Bake until just set in the middle and golden brown on the edges, 9 to 11 minutes. Allow the cookies to cool on the baking sheet for 5 minutes before transferring to a wire rack to cool completely. Once the pan is cool, repeat with the remaining dough.

7. **Make the lemon icing:** In a small bowl, combine the powdered sugar, lemon zest and juice and use a fork to mix until completely smooth. Stir in the milk, 1 teaspoon at a time, until a thick icing forms.

8. Spoon 2 teaspoons of icing on top of each cookie and spread out as best as you can with a spoon, then return to the wire rack to let the icing harden, about 5 minutes.

9. **To store:** Keep cookies in an airtight container or reusable silicone bag at room temperature for up to 1 week, then transfer to the freezer for up to 3 months. For freezing instructions, see page 22.

WET INGREDIENTS

½ cup (100 grams) granulated sugar

Zest of 2 lemons

1 cup (226 grams) salted butter, softened

1 cup (213 grams) packed dark brown sugar

2 large eggs, at room temperature

1 teaspoon vanilla extract

½ teaspoon almond extract

DRY INGREDIENTS

2 cups (240 grams) all-purpose flour (or sub white whole-wheat flour)

2 cups (190 grams) rolled oats

1 teaspoon baking soda

¼ teaspoon kosher salt

LEMON ICING

1½ cups (170 grams) powdered sugar

1 teaspoon lemon zest

1 tablespoon fresh lemon juice

1 to 3 teaspoons milk of choice, as needed

make it your way

BLUEBERRY LEMON OATMEAL COOKIES: In a medium bowl, toss 1 heaping cup of frozen blueberries with 2 tablespoons flour. Gently fold the blueberries into the dough after step 5; try your best not to break the blueberries.

double strawberry oatmeal cream pies (little debras)

**MAKES 20 SANDWICH COOKIES ■ PREP TIME: 40 MINUTES
■ COOK TIME: 5 MINUTES, PLUS 10 MINUTES PER BATCH**

WET INGREDIENTS

1 cup (226 grams) salted butter, cut into 8 pieces

1 cup (213 grams) packed dark brown sugar

½ cup (100 grams) granulated sugar

2 large eggs, at room temperature

1 teaspoon vanilla extract

½ teaspoon almond extract

DRY INGREDIENTS

2 cups (240 grams) all-purpose flour

1¾ cups (166 grams) rolled oats (gluten-free, if desired)

1 teaspoon baking soda

½ teaspoon kosher salt

1½ cups (34 grams) freeze-dried strawberries (from one 1.2-ounce bag)

FILLING

¾ cup (17 grams) freeze-dried strawberries

¾ cup (170 grams) salted butter, softened

1¾ cups (198 grams) powdered sugar

1 teaspoon vanilla extract

1 to 2 tablespoons milk of choice, as needed

Little Debbie is all grown up! Those sweet oatmeal pies—Tony's favorite childhood dessert—are now dressed for a grown-up party with my beloved brown butter and so much strawberry flavor (thanks to freeze-dried strawberries) in the cookies AND the fluffy frosting sandwiched in the middle. These Little Debras can do no wrong: They're fun to make with kids (who can munch on the leftover freeze-dried strawberries), perfect for Valentine's Day, and even delectable cold straight from the fridge. Plus, you can make endless variations!

1. Preheat the oven to 350°F. Line a large baking sheet with parchment paper.

2. **Prepare the wet ingredients:** Melt the butter in a small saucepan over medium heat. Once melted, whisk constantly; the butter will begin to crackle, then foam. After a few minutes, the butter will begin to turn a golden amber color. As soon as the butter turns brown and gives off a nutty aroma, 5 to 8 minutes, remove from the heat and immediately transfer to the bowl of a stand mixer to prevent burning. Make sure you scrape all the yummy brown bits from the pan; this is where the flavor is! Set aside to cool for 10 minutes.

3. Add the brown sugar and granulated sugar to the bowl, then place the bowl in a stand mixer fitted with the paddle attachment and mix on medium speed until well combined, about 1 minute. Add the eggs, vanilla, and almond extract and mix on medium speed until smooth and creamy, about 1 minute. (Alternatively, beat the ingredients by hand until smooth and creamy.)

4. **Add the dry ingredients:** Add the flour, oats, baking soda, and salt; beat on low speed until just combined, 1 to 2 minutes. Add the freeze-dried strawberries and mix again on low speed (or with a wooden spoon) until incorporated into the dough, about 1 minute. Allow the dough to rest for 5 minutes to firm up a bit (do not skip this step!).

5. Roll 1 heaping tablespoon of dough into a ball and place on the prepared baking sheet. Repeat with more dough, placing the balls 2 inches apart, until you've filled up the baking sheet. (Not all cookies will fit on the sheet in one batch.)

6. **Bake the cookies:** Bake until the cookies are just golden brown on the edges, 8 to 10 minutes. Cool the cookies on the sheet for 5 minutes, then transfer to a wire rack to finish cooling. Once the baking sheet has cooled, repeat with the remaining dough.

TO MAKE DAIRY-FREE: Use melted vegan butter (do not attempt to brown) and dairy-free milk.

TO MAKE GLUTEN-FREE: Use gluten-free 1:1 all-purpose flour and gluten-free oats.

DOUBLE STRAWBERRY OATMEAL COOKIES: Skip the filling and you'll get 36 to 40 chewy oatmeal cookies.

STRAWBERRIES AND CREAM OATMEAL PIES: Add 1 cup of white chocolate chips to the batter with the dried strawberries.

CHOCOLATE CHIP STRAWBERRY OATMEAL PIES: Add 1 cup of dark chocolate chips to the batter with the freeze-dried strawberries.

LITTLE DEBRA ICE CREAM SANDWICHES: Swap the filling with a small scoop of strawberry ice cream.

7. **While the cookies cool, make the filling:** Place the freeze-dried strawberries in a high powered blender and blend into a fine powder, about 1 minute. In the bowl of a stand mixer fitted with the whisk attachment, beat the softened butter on high speed until light and fluffy, about 1 minute. Add the freeze-dried strawberry powder, powdered sugar, and vanilla and beat, starting on low speed and slowly increasing to high, until creamy and uniformly pink, 2 to 3 minutes. Scrape down the sides of the bowl with a spatula. Add 1 tablespoon of milk and beat again until smooth and spreadable, about 1 minute. If necessary, add another 1 tablespoon of milk to achieve the desired consistency. (Alternatively, whisk the ingredients by hand.)

8. Spread the flat bottom side of a cookie with about 1 tablespoon of filling, leaving a small uncovered border around the edge of the cookie. Place another cookie on top, flat-side down, then very gently press down to create a cookie sandwich. Repeat with the remaining cookies. Let the sandwiches sit at room temperature for at least 1 hour to firm up the frosting.

9. **To store:** Keep the cookies in an airtight container or reusable silicone bag at room temperature for 1 day, then transfer them to the fridge for up to 1 week or the freezer for up to 3 months. For freezing instructions, see page 22.

chocolate chunk espresso coconut oatmeal cookies

MAKES 20 TO 24 COOKIES ▩ **PREP TIME: 20 MINUTES** ▩ **COOK TIME: 10 MINUTES PER BATCH**

This cookie started because I love coconut and oatmeal, and I wanted to create a cookie that had both. The result: This chocolatey, chewy, crisp-edged stunner that tastes similar to Girl Scouts' Samoas or Caramel DeLites, but reimagined for grown-up tastes with a hint of espresso and toasted pecans. Sweetened coconut is essential to their nostalgic taste. Best afternoon pick-me-up ever!

1. Preheat the oven to 350°F. Line a large baking sheet with parchment paper.

2. **Mix the dry ingredients:** In a large bowl, whisk the flour, oats, espresso powder, baking soda, and salt until well combined.

3. **Mix the wet ingredients:** In another large bowl, whisk the brown sugar and coconut oil until smooth, about 30 seconds. Add the egg, egg yolk, and vanilla, and mix until the batter is smooth and the consistency of caramel. Add the dry ingredients to the wet ingredients and mix with a wooden spoon until well combined.

4. **Add the mix-ins:** Fold in the shredded coconut, pecans, and chocolate chunks so that they're evenly distributed. Let the dough sit at room temperature for 10 to 15 minutes to allow the flour and oats to absorb the wet ingredients and create a better consistency.

5. Use a medium cookie scoop or your hands to roll 2 heaping tablespoons of dough into a ball. Place the dough balls 2 inches apart on the prepared baking sheet as you finish, working until you fill up the baking sheet.

6. **Bake the cookies:** Bake until the edges begin to turn golden brown, 10 to 12 minutes. Do not overbake; you want the cookies to stay fudgy in the middle! Remove from the oven and sprinkle with flaky sea salt. Let cool for 10 minutes on the baking sheet, then transfer to a wire rack to finish cooling. Once the baking sheet has cooled, repeat with the remaining dough.

7. **To store:** Keep cookies in an airtight container or reusable silicone bag at room temperature for up to 1 week, then transfer to the freezer for up to 3 months. For freezing instructions, see page 22.

DRY INGREDIENTS

1 cup plus 2 tablespoons (135 grams) all-purpose flour

1 cup (95 grams) rolled oats

2 tablespoons espresso powder

1 teaspoon baking soda

½ teaspoon kosher salt

WET INGREDIENTS

1 cup (213 grams) packed dark brown sugar

¾ cup (168 grams) virgin coconut oil, melted and cooled

1 large egg plus 1 egg yolk, at room temperature

1 teaspoon vanilla extract

MIX-INS AND TOPPING

1 cup (85 grams) sweetened shredded coconut

1 cup (112 grams) toasted pecans, roughly chopped

1 (3.5-ounce/100-gram) 70% dark chocolate bar, roughly chopped

Flaky sea salt (I like Maldon)

make it your way

TO MAKE DAIRY-FREE: Use a dairy-free chocolate bar.

M&M ESPRESSO OATMEAL COWBOY COOKIES: Add a heaping ⅓ cup chocolate-covered candies (I like Unreal brand) to the dough with the chocolate chunks, then place a few more on top of each dough ball before baking.

salted scotcheroos

MAKES 16 ■ PREP TIME: 15 MINUTES ■ COOK TIME: 5 MINUTES, PLUS 1 HOUR CHILLING TIME

BASE

¾ cup (192 grams) natural creamy peanut butter (or sub almond butter or cashew butter)

⅓ cup (104 grams) pure maple syrup (or sub honey)

2 tablespoons virgin coconut oil

¼ teaspoon kosher salt

1 teaspoon vanilla extract

3 cups (112 grams) crispy brown rice cereal or Special K cereal

TOPPING

½ cup (90 grams) dark or semisweet chocolate chips

½ cup (90 grams) butterscotch chips

1 tablespoon virgin coconut oil

DRIZZLE AND SPRINKLE

2 tablespoons butterscotch chips

½ teaspoon virgin coconut oil

Flaky sea salt (I like Maldon)

When I was growing up in Minnesota, Special K bars and scotcheroos were just as popular as Rice Krispie treats. The blend of peanut butter, butterscotch, and chocolate all in one bite was a nostalgic special treat that always appeared at any family gathering. In this lighter, less-sweet version, you can either use brown rice crispies or Special K cereal, and you may find yourself so obsessed with its crunchy, salty, butterscotch-y flavor that you sneak into the kitchen and saw off random corners when your family isn't looking. Not that I would ever do this myself, of course.

1. Line an 8-inch square pan with parchment paper. Set aside.

2. **Make the base:** In a medium pot, combine the peanut butter, maple syrup, coconut oil, and salt over medium-low heat. Cook, stirring frequently with a wooden spoon, until the mixture is smooth, warm, and well combined, 1 to 2 minutes. Remove from the heat and stir in the vanilla. Transfer the mixture to a large bowl and stir in the crispy brown rice cereal; stir until the cereal is completely coated. Pour into the prepared pan and use a rubber spatula to press the cereal down and flatten the top.

3. **Make the topping:** In a medium microwave-safe bowl, combine the chocolate chips, butterscotch chips, and coconut oil. Microwave on high in 30-second intervals, stirring in between, until melted and smooth. Pour the mixture over the bars and tilt the pan to spread evenly.

4. **Make the drizzle:** In a small microwave-safe ramekin, combine the butterscotch chips and coconut oil and microwave in 30-second intervals, stirring in between, until melted. Drizzle the butterscotch mixture back and forth over the bars, then use a toothpick or a butter knife to drag the butterscotch through the chocolate to create a wavy design or swirls.

5. **Chill and sprinkle:** Place the pan in the fridge until the bars are completely cool and the chocolate is hardened, at least 1 hour. Sprinkle with sea salt, then cut into 16 bars. Store in an airtight container in the fridge for up to 1 week. Let sit at room temperature for 5 minutes before serving.

make it your way

TO MAKE GLUTEN-FREE: Be sure to use crispy brown rice cereal.

make it your way

TO MAKE DAIRY-FREE: Use dairy-free chocolate chips.

TO MAKE VEGAN: Use 2 Flax Eggs (page 16) instead of regular eggs. Be sure to also use dairy-free chocolate chips.

ALMOND BUTTER BROWNIES: Instead of tahini, use natural creamy almond butter.

tip

Try these brownies straight out of the fridge for the ultimate fudgy texture! They are also great topped with ice cream.

the famous tahini brownies

MAKES 16 ▪ PREP TIME: 10 MINUTES ▪ COOK TIME: 20 MINUTES

While visiting the Middle East on a work trip, I found myself devouring everything made with tahini. It was whipped into the creamiest hummus, drizzled on roasted vegetables, and even taken to the next level in gorgeous baked goods. I came home inspired to create recipes with all things tahini. Next thing I knew, these internet-famous brownies were born. They just so happen to be gluten-free and can easily be made dairy-free, yet I still prefer them to any other brownie because of the fudgy texture and nutty flavor.

1. Preheat the oven to 350°F. Grease an 8-inch or 9-inch square baking dish with cooking spray and line with parchment paper. Set aside.

2. **Make the brownie batter:** In a large bowl, whisk the tahini, coconut sugar, maple syrup, eggs, and vanilla until smooth and well combined. Gently stir in the cocoa powder, coconut flour, baking soda, and salt until the batter is smooth and thick. Fold the chocolate chips into the batter; it will be very thick.

3. Spray a rubber spatula with cooking spray and use it to help spread the batter into an even layer in the prepared baking dish.

4. **Bake the brownies:** Bake for 16 to 22 minutes, until a knife inserted into the middle comes out with just a few moist crumbs attached. Cool for 15 minutes before adding the chocolate drizzle.

5. **Make the chocolate drizzle:** Place the chocolate chips and coconut oil in a small microwave-safe bowl. Microwave in 30-second intervals, stirring in between, until melted and smooth. Generously drizzle over the brownies.

6. Cool the brownies for 10 to 15 minutes before slicing so they hold up well.

7. **To store:** Keep brownies in an airtight container or reusable silicone bag at room temperature for up to 2 days, then transfer to the fridge for up to 1 week. Enjoy straight from the fridge or let the bars come to room temperature before eating. For freezing instructions, see page 22.

Nonstick cooking spray

BROWNIES

1 cup (230 grams) tahini

½ cup (77 grams) coconut sugar (or sub packed dark brown sugar)

¼ cup (78 grams) pure maple syrup

2 large eggs, at room temperature

1 teaspoon vanilla extract

⅓ cup (27 grams) unsweetened cocoa powder (or sub cacao powder)

1 tablespoon coconut flour

½ teaspoon baking soda

¼ teaspoon kosher salt

⅓ cup (60 grams) chocolate chips

CHOCOLATE DRIZZLE

2 tablespoons chocolate chips

½ teaspoon virgin coconut oil

DAIRY-FREE (IF MODIFIED), **GLUTEN-FREE (IF MODIFIED)**, **VEGAN (IF MODIFIED)**, **VEGETARIAN**

make-it-your-way crumble bars

MAKES 12 TO 16 BARS ■ **PREP TIME: 20 MINUTES** ■ **COOK TIME: 40 MINUTES**

BASE AND TOPPING

1½ cups (138 grams) oat flour (gluten-free, if desired) or 1½ cups (180 grams) all-purpose flour

1 cup (95 grams) rolled oats (gluten-free, if desired)

½ cup (107 grams) packed dark brown sugar (or sub coconut sugar)

¼ teaspoon baking soda

¼ teaspoon kosher salt

8 tablespoons (113 grams) salted butter, melted

1 teaspoon vanilla extract

¼ teaspoon almond extract

FILLING

1 pound (heaping 3 cups) fresh or frozen raspberries, blueberries, cherries, or blackberries or 3 cups diced fresh strawberries or peaches (or use a mix!)

3 tablespoons pure maple syrup

1 tablespoon tapioca flour (or sub arrowroot or cornstarch)

Zest of 1 lemon

1 tablespoon fresh lemon juice

1 teaspoon vanilla extract

¼ teaspoon kosher salt

Bookmark this recipe and make it whenever you find beautiful fruit. Strawberries, raspberries, even peaches in summer? The frozen blueberries that caught your eye in wintertime? All of them will sing in these pie bars with a crumble topping that are easy to throw together and extra-impressive when served with ice cream. So many ways to make them your own!

1. Preheat the oven to 350°F. Line an 8-inch square pan with parchment paper. Set aside.

2. **Make the base and topping:** In a large bowl, use a fork to mix together the oat flour, oats, brown sugar, baking soda, and salt. Add the melted butter, vanilla, and almond extract and stir until the dough begins to clump together and forms a nice crumble.

3. Place 1¾ cups of the mixture into the prepared pan and use your hands to press into an even layer on the bottom of the pan. Place the remaining mixture in the fridge (it will become your topping).

4. **Make the filling:** In a medium pot, heat the berries, maple syrup, tapioca flour, lemon zest and juice, vanilla, and salt over medium heat. Use a wooden spoon to press down and break down the berries just a bit. Bring to a boil, then reduce the heat to medium-low and simmer, stirring occasionally, until the mixture is thickened and coats the back of a wooden spoon, about 5 minutes. Pour the mixture over the crust and use a spoon to spread evenly over the base.

5. **Bake the bars:** Take the remaining crumble out of the fridge and sprinkle it over the filling. Bake until the filling is bubbly and the topping is golden, about 30 minutes. Cool the bars in the pan on a wire rack completely before cutting into 12 or 16 bars or storing.

6. **To store:** Wrap the pan in foil or store individual bars in an airtight container in the fridge for up to 5 days. Serve straight out of the fridge or bring to room temperature before slicing. For freezing instructions, see page 22.

make it your way

TO MAKE DAIRY-FREE AND VEGAN: Use vegan butter.

a buttery pie crust worth talking about

MAKES 1 SINGLE-LAYER PIE CRUST ▪ PREP TIME: 20 MINUTES ▪ CHILLING TIME: 30 MINUTES

This might seem to be just another pie crust, but let me assure you, it is most definitely *not*. Its shocking flakiness comes from the addition of a little vodka! Surprisingly, it creates the most tender pie crust you'll ever bake, according to so many of my readers who swear they will never go back to another recipe. Note that if you're making a double crust pie, the recipe should be doubled. Or tripled or quadrupled; I keep extras stashed in my freezer for whenever I have the urge to bake a pie!

1. **Combine the ingredients:** Cut the butter into small cubes and set on a plate. Place in the freezer for 15 to 30 minutes so it gets VERY COLD.

2. In a food processor, pulse the flour, sugar, and salt a few times to combine. Add the cold butter cubes and pulse until the mixture starts to get a little clumpy, 20 to 30 seconds.

3. **Process the dough:** Add the vodka, then add 2 tablespoons of the ice water. Pulse until the dough starts to come together and resembles small beads. Squeeze a small amount of dough between your fingers; it should stick together well. If it crumbles apart, add more ice water, 1½ teaspoons at a time, just until it comes together. If your dough is too wet, add 1½ teaspoons flour until it comes together. Do not overwork the dough; it should not form into one dough ball yet, and should be rather clumpy.

4. **Chill the dough:** Generously flour a surface. Turn out the dough and press it into a disk, then wrap with plastic wrap or place in a reusable silicone bag. Chill in the fridge for at least 30 minutes and up to 2 days. (The dough can also be well wrapped in plastic and foil and frozen for up to 3 months. Thaw the frozen pie crust in the fridge overnight, then proceed.)

5. **Roll out the dough:** When you're ready to bake, remove the dough from the fridge and allow it to sit at room temperature for 10 to 15 minutes. Generously flour a clean surface and a rolling pin. Roll the dough out into an 11-inch round. If the dough sticks to the surface, form it back into a ball, re-flour the surface, and roll it out again. Pie dough is very forgiving.

6. **Transfer to the pan:** Fold the dough in half to transfer it to a 9-inch pie pan, then unfold the dough and gently press it into the pan. (If you mess up and the dough cracks, that's completely okay—just reshape the dough into a disk and roll it out again.) Trim the extra crust around the edges of the pie plate and discard the excess dough. Flute the edges of the crust however you'd like (I normally use my finger and thumb to pinch the dough, or you can use a fork).

7. Cover tightly with plastic wrap and place the pie pan in the fridge for at least 30 minutes and up to 2 days before baking. For freezing instructions, see page 22.

8 tablespoons (113 grams) salted butter

1¼ cups (150 grams) all-purpose flour, plus more as needed

1 teaspoon sugar

½ teaspoon kosher salt

1 tablespoon vodka

2 to 3 tablespoons ice water, as needed

giant blueberry pie poppin' tart

SERVES 12 ■ PREP TIME: 2 HOURS ■ COOK TIME: 45 MINUTES

FILLING

2 cups (300 grams) fresh or frozen blueberries

¼ cup (50 grams) granulated sugar

1 teaspoon lemon zest

1 tablespoon fresh lemon juice

1 tablespoon cornstarch

1 tablespoon all-purpose flour

1 tablespoon salted butter

1 teaspoon vanilla extract

DOUGH AND EGG WASH

All-purpose flour, for dusting and rolling

2 batches of A Buttery Pie Crust Worth Talking About (page 265; unrolled), or 2 store-bought pie crusts, chilled

1 large egg

1 tablespoon water

ICING AND TOPPING

1½ cups (170 grams) powdered sugar

2 to 3 tablespoons whole milk, as needed

½ teaspoon almond extract

2 to 3 tablespoons artificial-dye-free rainbow sprinkles

Many of us grew up eating Pop-Tarts for breakfast and now realize they are really dessert. So I figured we should indulge our Pop-Tart nostalgia with this special creation, which my husband promptly deemed the most exciting thing he's ever eaten in his life. Watch all of your friends turn into squealing children as they bite into their slices.

1. Line a large baking sheet with parchment paper.

2. **Make the filling:** In a large pot, combine the blueberries, sugar, lemon zest and juice, cornstarch, and flour and place over medium heat. Cook, stirring frequently, until the blueberries begin to break down and release their juices, about 5 minutes. Add the butter and vanilla and continue to cook, stirring frequently, until the mixture thickens and coats the back of a spoon, 5 to 7 minutes. Remove the pot from the heat and set aside to cool for 10 minutes.

3. Place a small sieve over a medium bowl. Add ¼ cup of the blueberry filling to the sieve and use a spoon to mash down the filling. This will strain out any large pieces of blueberries. You should have about 1 tablespoon of blueberry liquid for the frosting. Set aside.

4. **Roll out the dough:** Generously flour a surface and a rolling pin. Working one at a time, roll out a disk of pie dough into a 12 × 9-inch rectangle, as close in size as possible. Use the rolling pin to roll the rectangle back around the rolling pin to help easily transfer it, then lay it out onto the prepared baking sheet. Roll out the other disk, leaving it on the surface for now.

5. Spread the filling onto the pie dough on the baking sheet, leaving a 1-inch border around the edge. Roll the remaining dough back around the rolling pin and gently place it over the filling. Seal the dough by using the back of a fork to crimp the edges together. (If needed, dip the fork in flour to prevent sticking.) Use the same fork to poke a few holes in the center of the pop tart. Cover the baking sheet with plastic wrap and place it in the fridge for 30 minutes to 1 hour to chill the dough and create a flaky pastry.

6. Meanwhile, preheat the oven to 375°F.

7. **Egg wash and bake:** In a medium bowl, whisk the egg and water until well-beaten and brush all over the top of the dough. Bake until the pie is golden brown on top, 25 to 30 minutes. Cool for 30 minutes on the baking sheet before icing.

8. **Make the icing:** In the medium bowl containing the reserved blueberry liquid, add the powdered sugar, 2 tablespoons of milk, and the almond extract. Whisk until smooth and spreadable. If the icing is too thick to spread, whisk in additional milk, 1 teaspoon at a time. Spread over the pop tart, leaving a ½ inch border on the edges. Immediately top with sprinkles. Cut the pie into 12 slices and serve.

the best cherry pie you'll ever eat

SERVES 9 ■ **PREP TIME: 1 HOUR 30 MINUTES** ■ **COOK TIME: 1 HOUR 20 MINUTES**

I spent years trying to make the perfect Thanksgiving cherry pie that would please my cherry-loving mother and husband. After tons of experiments, I came up with this version using frozen tart cherries, which give the pie a vibrant flavor that balances with the sweet crumb topping, not to mention the beautiful, next-level addition of almond extract and amaretto. Tart cherries, bright in color and packed with antioxidants, are very different from the dark sweet cherries that you'll find fresh in the produce section of the grocery store. If you haven't tried tart cherries, now's the time! I was thrilled that The Kitchn called this pie "an absolute all-star" after it triumphed in their taste test of cherry pie recipes. It's great with vanilla bean ice cream.

1. Preheat the oven to 350°F.

2. **Prepare the crust:** Shape the pie dough in a pie pan (see the directions on page 265), cover with plastic wrap or foil, and place in the fridge.

3. **Make the filling:** In a large pot, heat the cherries, sugar, cornstarch, flour, and almond extract over medium heat, stirring occasionally, until the cherries break down and the sugar melts, about 5 minutes. Add the butter and amaretto and cook, stirring constantly while the mixture thickens and bubbles around the edges, until it is thick enough to coat the back of a spoon, 5 to 10 minutes. Remove from the heat and set aside to cool for 15 minutes.

4. **Make the crumble topping:** In a medium bowl, mix the flour, brown sugar, and oats. Add the melted butter and stir with a fork until the mixture resembles clumpy wet sand. (You may need to use your fingers to squeeze together the large clumps.) Cover the bowl with plastic wrap and refrigerate for at least 10 minutes so that the butter hardens.

5. Remove the prepared pie pan from the fridge and place onto a large baking sheet to avoid any spillage. Pour the cooled filling into the crust, then top with an even layer of the crumble.

6. **Bake the pie:** Bake, checking the crust after 30 minutes and covering it with foil or a pie shield if it is browning too quickly, until the filling is very bubbly and the crumble is slightly golden brown, 60 to 70 minutes.

7. Place the pie on a wire rack and cool completely, at least 4 hours. (Be patient; this is necessary to set the pie filling!) Serve at room temperature or just slightly warmed with vanilla ice cream.

8. **To store:** Let the pie completely cool and then wrap the full pie in foil and store in the fridge for up to 5 days. Enjoy pie slices straight from the fridge or microwave in 30-second intervals until warm.

PIE

A Buttery Pie Crust Worth Talking About (page 265), or 1 store-bought pie crust

6 cups (840 grams) frozen tart cherries

1 cup (200 grams) granulated sugar

2 tablespoons cornstarch

2 tablespoons all-purpose flour

½ teaspoon almond extract

1 tablespoon salted butter

1 tablespoon amaretto

CRUMBLE TOPPING

1 cup (120 grams) all-purpose flour

½ cup (107 grams) packed dark brown sugar

⅓ cup (32 grams) rolled oats

6 tablespoons (85 grams) salted butter, melted

Vanilla ice cream, for serving (optional)

one-bowl lemon poppy seed yogurt snacking cake

SERVES 9 ■ PREP TIME: 20 MINUTES ■ COOK TIME: 30 MINUTES, PLUS COOLING TIME

Nonstick cooking spray

WET INGREDIENTS

½ cup (113 grams) plain whole-milk Greek yogurt

½ cup (168 grams) honey

⅓ cup (67 grams) extra-virgin olive oil or avocado oil

2 large eggs

Zest of 2 lemons

¼ cup (50 grams) fresh lemon juice

½ teaspoon almond extract

DRY INGREDIENTS

1½ cups (168 grams) fine blanched almond flour

1 cup (92 grams) oat flour (gluten-free, if desired)

1½ tablespoons poppy seeds

2 teaspoons baking powder

¼ teaspoon kosher salt

FROSTING

1½ cups (170 grams) powdered sugar

8 tablespoons (113 grams) salted butter, softened

Zest of 1 lemon

1 tablespoon fresh lemon juice

GARNISH

Fresh raspberries, blueberries, or sliced strawberries

Lemon zest

What's a snacking cake, you ask? It's a lightly sweetened, easy-to-make cake that's perfectly acceptable for every meal, or in between them, no matter the time of day. Breakfast cake? Why not. Lunch dessert? Absolutely. Late night treat straight out of the fridge with a fork? Yep! This vibrant, bright lemon cake is sweetened with honey and reminds me of a lemon poppy seed muffin that's dense but fluffy at the same time. I adore this with a cup of coffee and have a feeling you will, too. Be warned: The frosting is so delightfully good, I guarantee you'll find yourself seeking out ways to use it again and again. Slather it on your next carrot cake and prepare to fall in love.

1. Preheat the oven to 350°F. Line an 8-inch square pan with parchment paper and spray with cooking spray. Set aside.

2. **Mix the wet ingredients:** In a large bowl, whisk the Greek yogurt, honey, olive oil, eggs, lemon zest and juice, and almond extract until smooth and well combined.

3. **Add the dry ingredients:** To the same bowl, add the almond flour, oat flour, poppy seeds, baking powder, and salt and mix with a wooden spoon until well combined. Pour the batter into the prepared pan and smooth the top.

4. **Bake the cake:** Bake until a tester inserted into the center comes out clean, 25 to 30 minutes. Allow the cake to cool completely in the pan.

5. **Make the frosting:** In the bowl of a stand mixer fitted with the whisk attachment or in a large mixing bowl (if using a hand mixer), beat the powdered sugar, butter, and lemon zest and juice on high speed until smooth, about 1 minute. Spread the frosting over the cooled cake.

6. **Garnish:** Once ready to serve, top with a few fresh berries and grate over extra lemon zest, then cut the cake into 9 slices. Enjoy immediately or store the cake in the fridge for up to 5 days, covered to ensure freshness.

make it your way

TO MAKE DAIRY-FREE: Use dairy-free yogurt. Swap vegan butter for regular butter in the frosting.

Feel free to swap the oat flour for 1:1 gluten-free all-purpose flour or regular all-purpose flour.

my favorite cake ever: tahini pumpkin cake with
brown butter cream cheese frosting (PAGE 274)

my favorite cake ever: tahini pumpkin cake with brown butter cream cheese frosting

SERVES 12 ▪ **PREP TIME: 30 MINUTES** ▪ **COOK TIME: 25 TO 40 MINUTES, PLUS COOLING TIME**

Nonstick cooking spray

WET INGREDIENTS

1 (15-ounce, 425 grams) can pumpkin puree

1 cup (154 grams) coconut sugar

4 large eggs, at room temperature

½ cup (156 grams) pure maple syrup

½ cup (113 grams) plain whole-milk Greek yogurt

⅓ cup (77 grams) tahini (or sub almond butter)

⅓ cup (75 grams) virgin coconut oil, melted and cooled (or sub melted salted butter or vegan butter)

2 teaspoons vanilla extract

DRY INGREDIENTS

2 cups (224 grams) fine blanched almond flour

1½ cups (138 grams) oat flour (gluten-free, if desired)

2 tablespoons pumpkin pie spice

2 teaspoons baking soda

¼ teaspoon kosher salt

make it your way

TO MAKE DAIRY-FREE: Use dairy-free yogurt. Do not use brown butter in the frosting; instead use softened vegan butter and vegan cream cheese.

No joke. This is literally the best cake I've ever had in my life. And that includes classic cakes from bakeries. No offense to my other cake recipes that I also love so dearly—but *this* cake! *This* is the recipe that I crave the very most. It is SUPREMELY moist, perfectly spiced, and just so happens to be gluten-free, naturally sweetened, and loaded with a whole can of pumpkin. Did I mention that it's topped with a silky frosting that tastes like caramel? OBSESSED is an understatement. Bottom line: I will be upset if you don't make this cake.

1. Preheat the oven to 350°F. Line the bottom of three 6-inch round cake pans or two 8-inch round cake pans with parchment paper rounds. Spray the parchment paper and sides of the pans with cooking spray. (All of this is essential to prevent the cake from sticking!)

2. **Mix the wet ingredients:** In a large bowl, whisk the pumpkin puree, coconut sugar, eggs, maple syrup, Greek yogurt, tahini, coconut oil, and vanilla until smooth and well combined, about 1 minute.

3. **Mix the dry ingredients:** In another large bowl, whisk the almond flour, oat flour, pumpkin pie spice, salt, and baking soda until evenly combined. Add the dry ingredients to the wet ingredients and mix with a wooden spoon until smooth and well combined.

4. **Bake the cake:** Divide the batter evenly between the prepared pans and smooth the tops. Bake until a tester inserted into the center comes out mostly clean with just a few crumbs attached, 25 to 35 minutes in the 8-inch pans or 30 to 40 minutes in the 6-inch pans. Cool the cakes completely (you can make them up to a day ahead, then wrap tightly with plastic wrap and store at room temperature or in the fridge).

5. **Make the frosting:** Melt the butter in a small saucepan over medium heat. Once melted, whisk constantly: The butter will begin to crackle, then foam. After a few minutes, the butter will begin to turn a golden amber color. As soon as the butter turns brown and gives off a nutty aroma, 5 to 8 minutes total, remove from the heat, place in a small bowl, and transfer to the fridge for 45 to 60 minutes to allow the butter to resolidify so that it's similar to room temperature butter but not completely hardened (poking it should leave an indent). If it hardens too much, allow it to soften up at room temperature.

6. In the bowl of a stand mixer fitted with the whisk attachment or in a large mixing bowl (if using a hand mixer), beat the brown butter on high speed until light and fluffy, about 1 minute. Add the cream cheese and beat again until creamy, about 1 minute. Add the powdered sugar, vanilla, and salt and beat until light and fluffy, 2 to 3 minutes.

FROSTING

8 tablespoons (113 grams) salted butter, sliced

8 ounces (224 grams) cream cheese, softened

3 cups (339 grams) powdered sugar

1 teaspoon vanilla extract

¼ teaspoon kosher salt

7. **Frost the cake:** Spread about 2 tablespoons of the frosting in the middle of a cake stand or platter (this will help anchor the cake). Invert the first layer of the cake onto the stand so the flat side of the cake is up. Top with about ½ cup of frosting. Using an offset spatula, spread the frosting to the edge of the cake in an even layer. Place the next layer of cake, flat-side up, on top of the first layer, and repeat, topping with an additional ½ cup of frosting and spreading it to the edge. Place the third layer (if using) flat-side up on top, then frost the top and sides of the cake with ½ to ¾ cup of frosting, using a bench scraper to create a uniform, very thin layer of frosting around the cake. It helps to do this while slowly spinning the cake stand and gently pressing the scraper against the side of the cake. (This step is called a crumb coat, which will allow for a beautiful, seamless look once complete.)

8. Transfer the cake to the fridge for at least 20 minutes, until the crumb coat layer of frosting has firmed up to the touch. Once the cake is chilled, repeat the process of frosting the top and sides of the cake with the remaining frosting, using an offset spatula. Since the cake has been chilled, the crumb coat should allow for a smoother finish.

9. **To store:** Keep slices in an airtight container in the fridge for up to 5 days. For freezing instructions, see page 22.

if i'm eating chocolate cake, i'm eating one with cookies and cream espresso cream cheese frosting

SERVES 16 ■ **PREP TIME: 30 MINUTES** ■ **COOK TIME: 20 TO 35 MINUTES, PLUS COOLING TIME**

Nonstick cooking spray

WET INGREDIENTS

1 cup (213 grams) packed dark brown sugar

½ cup (156 grams) pure maple syrup

½ cup (113 grams) vanilla whole-milk Greek yogurt

4 large eggs, at room temperature

¼ cup (57 grams) warm brewed coffee or warm cold brew

¼ cup (56 grams) virgin coconut oil, melted and cooled

1 tablespoon espresso powder

1 tablespoon vanilla extract

DRY INGREDIENTS

2¼ cups (252 grams) fine blanched almond flour

¾ cup (60 grams) cacao powder (or sub unsweetened cocoa powder)

¾ cup (69 grams) oat flour (gluten-free, if desired)

1 teaspoon baking powder

¾ teaspoon kosher salt

½ teaspoon baking soda

I will not apologize for the many requirements a chocolate cake needs to have to satisfy me. I demand a slightly fudgy texture, a rich chocolate flavor, and a unique frosting—none of that too-sweet, chocolate-on-chocolate, just-for-chocolate's-sake stuff. Well, I finally crafted a dense, brownie-like cake that checks all of these boxes, and you will never ever believe that it's easily gluten-free and dairy-free! The highlight: a fluffy-as-hell cookies-and-cream frosting spiked with espresso and topped with a gorgeous chocolate drip. I may never make another chocolate cake again.

1. Preheat the oven to 350°F. Line the bottom of three 6-inch round cake pans or two 8-inch round cake pans with parchment paper rounds. Spray the parchment paper and the sides of the pan with cooking spray. (All of this is essential to prevent the cake from sticking!)

2. **Mix the wet ingredients:** In a large bowl, whisk the brown sugar, maple syrup, Greek yogurt, eggs, coffee, coconut oil, espresso powder, and vanilla until smooth and well combined, about 1 minute.

3. **Mix the dry ingredients:** In another large bowl, whisk the almond flour, cacao powder, oat flour, baking powder, salt, and baking soda until evenly combined. Add the dry ingredients to the wet ingredients and mix with a wooden spoon until well combined and smooth.

4. **Bake the cake:** Divide the batter evenly between the prepared pans and smooth the tops. Bake until a tester inserted into the center comes out mostly clean with just a few crumbs attached, 20 to 30 minutes in the 8-inch pans or 25 to 35 minutes in the 6-inch pans. Cool the cakes completely (you can make them up to a day ahead, then wrap tightly with plastic wrap and store at room temperature or in the fridge).

5. **Make the frosting:** In a food processor or blender, pulse the cookies until they are fine and resemble crumbs, about 1 minute. Set aside. In the bowl of a stand mixer fitted with the whisk attachment or in a large mixing bowl (if using a hand mixer), beat the cream cheese and butter on high speed until light and fluffy, about 2 minutes. Add the powdered sugar, espresso powder, milk, and vanilla and beat until light and fluffy, about 2 minutes. Add the crushed cookies and mix on low speed until incorporated into the frosting, about 1 minute.

(recipe continues)

FROSTING

10 Oreo cookies or similar cookie (gluten-free, if desired)

8 ounces (224 grams) cream cheese, softened

8 tablespoons (113 grams) salted butter, softened

3 cups (339 grams) powdered sugar

1 tablespoon espresso powder

1 tablespoon milk of choice

1 teaspoon vanilla extract

CHOCOLATE DRIP

¾ cup (135 grams) semisweet chocolate chips

1 to 2 teaspoons virgin coconut oil

make it your way

To make dairy-free: Use dairy-free yogurt. Use softened vegan butter, vegan cream cheese, and dairy-free milk in the frosting. Use dairy-free chocolate chips in the chocolate drip.

TO MAKE GLUTEN-FREE: Use gluten-free Oreos and make sure your oat flour is gluten-free.

KID-FRIENDLY CHOCOLATE CAKE: Not into coffee, or making this for kids? Use warm water in the batter instead of coffee and leave the espresso powder out of both the cake and frosting.

6. **Frost the cake:** Spread about 2 tablespoons of the frosting in the middle of a cake stand or platter (this will help anchor the cake). Invert the first layer of cake onto the stand so the flat side of the cake is up. Top with about ½ cup of frosting. Using an offset spatula, spread the frosting to the edge of the cake in an even layer. Place the next layer of cake, flat-side up, on top of the first layer, and repeat, topping with an additional ½ cup of frosting and spreading it to the edge. Place the third layer (if using) flat-side up on top, then frost the top and sides of the cake with ½ to ¾ cup of frosting, using a bench scraper to create a uniform, very thin layer of frosting around the cake. It helps to do this while slowly spinning the cake stand and gently pressing the scraper against the side of the cake. (This step is called a crumb coat, which will allow for a beautiful, seamless look once complete.)

7. Transfer the cake to the fridge for at least 20 minutes, until the crumb coat layer of frosting has set. Once the cake is chilled, repeat the process of frosting the cake with the remaining icing, using an offset spatula. Since the cake has been chilled, the crumb coat should allow for a smoother finish. Chill in the fridge for another 10 minutes.

8. **Make the chocolate drip:** In a medium microwave-safe bowl, combine the chocolate chips and 1 teaspoon coconut oil. Microwave in 30-second intervals, stirring in between, until the chocolate is smooth, completely melted, and pourable. If it's too thick, stir in another teaspoon of coconut oil. Remove the cake from fridge and pour the mixture over the top of the cake. It should naturally start to drip down the sides, but if it doesn't, use a spoon to spread the chocolate toward the edges to help the process. Immediately place the cake back in the fridge for 5 to 10 minutes to harden the chocolate.

9. **To store:** Keep slices in an airtight container in the fridge for up to 5 days. For freezing instructions, see page 22.

acknowledgments

To my absolutely incredible AK Community: Thank you for all of your love and support throughout the years. I wouldn't be here without you making my recipes and cheering me on through all the ups and downs. I appreciate all of you more than words can say. After years of making recipes on the internet and them finding their way into your homes (and hearts!), this book is officially my love letter to you. I hope you love it as much as I have loved creating it for you.

To my husband, Tony: You are my rock and I am so unbelievably grateful for your forever unwavering love and support, especially as I wrote this cookbook while we had a newborn and were living in our basement during our renovation. We have been through an incredible amount together and you have always believed in me and encouraged me to go after my dreams, and I'll always be so thankful for that. Thank you for always being willing to jump in and help me, from testing recipes with me to trying out my latest creation. I love you so very much.

To my hunny bunnies, Sidney, Viggo, and Lachlan: It is the greatest joy and honor of my life to be your mother. I love you more than words can describe. I hope one day you will read this book and know how much joy you brought me while I wrote this. Sidney, you loved to bake with me and were always willing to lend a helping hand, especially with anything involving chocolate chips!

Viggo, you would often sit on my lap and try to edit my manuscript with me and look at all of the beautiful pictures. Lachlan, I often carried newborn you on my hip while cooking. That time will always be so special to me.

To my dad: I miss you each and every day. I hope this cookbook makes you smile. Writing about you and honoring your journey in life was beautiful and forgiving for my spirit. I love you so very much, Daddy. I will see you again soon.

To my mother: Thank you for being the most supportive, loving, and kind mom that a girl could ask for. You inspired many of the recipes in this cookbook and I loved all of our time in your little galley kitchen testing and brainstorming in between Lachlan's short naps—ha! Thank you for always helping and encouraging me to be exactly who I was meant to be. From the moment I started Ambitious Kitchen, you have had my back. I love you so very much, Mom!

To my grandmother Gloria, aka G: Your passion for food and energy for life encourages me each and every day. Thank you for passing your love of food on to me.

To Judy Linden: We have been on such a journey together, and I'm so grateful for your support and hand-holding. You are my favorite, and I'm so grateful to work with you.

To Elisa Ung: Where would I be without you? You helped me pull together this book in no time at all, and I'm so incredibly grateful you were able to pull out exactly what needed to be said. The voice of this book is absolutely a dream, and I couldn't have done it without you by my side! Thank you for working with me and being such a gem.

To Abra Owens: I love you more than words can describe and I want to thank you for being so critical to everything I do. Ambitious Kitchen wouldn't be what it is without you, period. You have been by my side for more than seven years now, and somehow it still feels like we just met at Beatrix for coffee. Thank you for always being willing to jump into whatever I throw at you, for always being excited to learn new things, for making me laugh, and for just being YOU. My wing woman, always and forever!

To Rebecca Fennel: You bring the most incredibly thoughtful ideas to the table, and I'll always be grateful you said YES to coming to work for me. Thank you for jumping in whenever I needed you during this process and for supporting my business when I couldn't. I'm so very grateful for you.

To Kristin Williams: Thank you for jumping in and putting in the work when it came to this cookbook. I love seeing your passions come to life, and I feel so very grateful to call you a friend.

To McKenzie Mitchell and Haley Scarpino: Thank you for being my lovely testers. Your feedback was critical to pulling this book together and making it extra delicious!

To Kristin Teig, Marian Cooper Cairns, and team: Thank you so much for bringing this book to life through beautiful imagery and styling. What a dream team we had! This book wouldn't be as beautiful as it is without you, and I hope we can do it all again one day soon!

To Melissa Elias: You are such a gem, and I'm so glad we got to work together on this book. Every dish, linen, glass, and bowl brought my vision to life even more. Thank you for putting so much effort into sourcing pieces that felt like me. I adore you.

To my editor, Jenn Sit: Thank you for holding my hand through this process and making everything come to life so effortlessly. I appreciate your hard work, guidance, and patience! You always cheered me on, and I can't thank you enough.

To Stephanie Huntwork: I will never forget your incredible work designing this cookbook. Thank you for bringing my specific visions to life and making this book really feel like me. I am so very grateful for your talent.

To Callie and Meagan: Thank you for your love and support over the years, no matter where I was at in my life. I love you both so very much.

To my Smith and Saint team: Thank you for hard work and dedication to my brand. Your support, advice, and encouragement (okay, and sometimes a gentle push) has been exactly what I needed over the years we have been together. I love and appreciate you!

To everyone who has supported my dreams over the years, made a recipe from my site or even just shared one with a friend, I cannot thank you enough. You are the reason this book exists.

index

Note: page references in italics indicate photographs.

Copyright © 2024 by Monique Volz
Photographs copyright © 2024 by Kristin Teig

Published in the United States by Clarkson
Potter/Publishers, an imprint of the Crown
Publishing Group, a division of Penguin
Random House LLC, New York.
ClarksonPotter.com

CLARKSON POTTER is a trademark and
POTTER with colophon is a registered
trademark of Penguin Random House LLC.

Library of Congress Cataloging-in-Publication
    Data
Names: Volz, Monique, author. | Teig, Kristin,
    photographer.
Title: The Ambitious Kitchen cookbook :
    125 ridiculously good for you, sometimes
    indulgent, and absolutely never boring
    recipes for every meal of the day / Monique
    Volz ; photographs by Kristin Teig.

Identifiers: LCCN 2023047316 (print)
    | LCCN 2023047317 (ebook) | ISBN
    9780593581650 (hardcover) | ISBN
    9780593581667 (ebook)
Subjects: LCSH: Cooking. | LCGFT: Cookbooks.
Classification: LCC TX714 .V656 2024 (print)
    | LCC TX714 (ebook) | DDC 641.5—dc23/
    eng/20240314
LC record available at https://lccn.loc.
    gov/2023047316
LC ebook record available at https://lccn.loc
    .gov/2023047317

ISBN 978-0-593-58165-0
Ebook ISBN 978-0-593-58166-7

Printed in China

Editor: Jennifer Sit
Editorial assistant: Elaine Hennig
Designer: Stephanie Huntwork
Production editor: Terry Deal
Production manager: Kim Tyner
Compositors: Merri Ann Morrell and
Hannah Hunt
Food stylist: Marian Cooper Cairns
and Beth Somers
Food stylist assistants: Sammy Carman, Lisa
Rothkopf, and Jane Katte
Prop stylist: Melissa Elias
Photo assistant: Naomi Chu
Copyeditor: Sasha Tropp | Proofreaders: Lydia
O'Brien and Elizabeth Briskin
Indexer: Therese Shere
Publicist: Kristin Casemore
Marketer: Andrea Portanova

10 9 8 7 6 5 4 3 2 1

First Edition